Sonoma, Ca 95476

DISCARD

Sonoma Valley High School Library
20000 Broadway St.
Sonoma, CA 95476

ATLANTIS DESTROYED

By the same author:

Classic Landforms of the Sussex Coast
(1982; second edition 1996)

The Wilmington Giant: The Quest for a Lost Myth (1983)

The Stonehenge People: An Exploration of Life in Neolithic Britain,
4700–2000 BC (1987)

The Knossos Labyrinth: A New View of the 'Palace of Minos' at
Knossos (1989)

Minoans: Life in Bronze Age Crete (1990)

Book of British Dates: A Comprehensive Dictionary of British Dates
from Prehistoric Times to the Present Day (1991)

Neolithic Britain: New Stone Age Sites of England, Scotland and Wales
(1992)

The Making of Stonehenge (1993)

World History: A Chronological Dictionary of Dates
(1994; second edition 1995)

The Cerne Giant (1996)

Knossos, Temple of the Goddess (1997)

ATLANTIS DESTROYED

Rodney Castleden

London and New York

First published 1998
by Routledge
11 New Fetter Lane, London EC4P 4EE

Simultaneously published in the USA and Canada
by Routledge
29 West 35th Street, New York, NY 10001

© 1998 Rodney Castleden

Typeset in Goudy by
Keystroke, Jacaranda Lodge, Wolverhampton
Printed and bound in Great Britain by
Biddles Ltd, Guildford and King's Lynn

All rights reserved. No part of this book may be reprinted or reproduced
or utilised in any form or by any electronic, mechanical, or other means,
now known or hereafter invented, including photocopying and
recording, or in any information storage or retrieval system, without
permission in writing from the publishers.

The right of Rodney Castleden to be identified as author of this work
has been asserted by him in accordance with the Copyright, Designs and
Patents Act 1988.

British Library Cataloguing in Publication Data
A catalogue record for this book is available from the British Library

Library of Congress Cataloguing in Publication Data
A catalogue record for this book has been requested

ISBN 0–415–16539–3

FOR LAURENCE NOWRY

Listen, Socrates, to the story; extraordinary as it is, it is absolutely true.

Plato: Timaeus (c. 355 BC)

It is as certain as such a thing can be that the whole story of Atlantis, including the statement that Solon had met with tales about the island in Egypt, is one of Plato's imaginative fictions.

A. E. Taylor: Plato: Timaeus and Critias (1929)

CONTENTS

List of illustrations   ix
Acknowledgements and preface   xiii

1 **'All the island and many other islands also'**   1
   The Atlantis legend 1
   Thera: a window onto Atlantis 8
   Eruption after eruption 10

2 **Preludes to discovery**   14
   The folklore tradition 14
   Nineteenth-century glimpses of a Minoan past 15
   The backdrop of the Cyclades 17
   Bronze age Knossos 23
   Bronze age Athens 28

3 **Thera: the second rediscovery**   32
   The discovery of Ayia Irini 32
   Mavor and Marinatos 34
   The dig at Akrotiri begins 38

4 **The bronze age city of Thera emerges**   43
   'I see with the eyes of my soul . . .' 43
   Architecture of a Late Cycladic city 46
   The island: bronze age Thera 55

5 **Atlantean arts and crafts**   58
   Pottery 58
   Stone 59
   Metal-working 60

CONTENTS

Textiles 60
Furniture 64

6 **Theran food and trade**   66
   Agriculture and pastoralism 66
   Trade 67
   Ships 75

7 **Writing and wall-painting**   80
   Writing 80
   Wall-paintings 82
   Frescoes of Building 6 (the House of the Ladies) 84
   Frescoes of Building 11 (Block Beta) 86
   Frescoes of Building 12 (Block Delta) 89

8 **Art, religion and society**   90
   A panorama of Atlantis 90
   Growing up 99

9 **The last days of Akrotiri**   114
   After the eruption 126

10 **Atlantis destroyed**   134
   The Minoan trading empire as Atlantis 134
   The Knossos Labyrinth as the Atlantean Temple of Poseidon 137
   Plato and truth 147
   Plato and Sicily 154
   Plato and Sparta 160
   The source of the Atlantis story 164

11 **Deconstruction of Atlantis**   172
   The Old Atlantis 172
   The New Atlantis 182

   Appendix Dating the Thera eruption: a major controversy   191
   Notes   193
   Bibliography   205
   Index   219

ILLUSTRATIONS

FIGURES

1.1	A conventional 'Atlantic' Atlantis: Bory de St Vincent's map (1803)	4
1.2	The Aegean Sea	6
1.3	Santorini or Thera, showing the location of the bronze age city at Akrotiri	9
1.4	Reconstruction of bronze age Thera	11
1.5	Bronze age Thera seen from the west	12
2.1	The bronze age town of Phylakopi	18
2.2	The Knossos Labyrinth: shrines and sanctuaries	24
2.3	The Athenian Acropolis in the bronze age, view from the west	29
2.4	Ayia Irini, the bronze age town	30
3.1	The temple at Ayia Irini	33
3.2	Terracotta goddess from the Ayia Irini temple	34
3.3	Exchanges of ideas among Kea, Melos, Thera and Crete	35
4.1	Plan of the excavated area at Akrotiri	44
4.2	The bronze age town at Akrotiri	47
4.3	Fresco Town 5 on the South Frieze; this is almost certainly Akrotiri	47
4.4	Town 5, ships and skyline from the South Frieze; field sketch of the western skyline and coastline as seen by the author from the Akrotiri excavation	48
4.5	The streets of Akrotiri	50
5.1	Courting swallows from the Spring Fresco	59
5.2	Agia Triadha sarcophagus, Crete	62
5.3	Reconstructed stool	65
6.1	Minoan trade routes in the Aegean	68
6.2	The Tomb of Rekhmire wall-painting (detail)	70
6.3	Reconstruction of the east gate of Akrotiri, based on fresco evidence	72
6.4	Reconstruction of a Theran ship, based on fresco evidence	76

7.1	A female 'presentation' scene, based on fragments of wall-painting found in the Pillar Crypt, Melos	85
7.2	The Boxing Boys fresco	87
7.3	Two fresco antelopes challenge one another	88
7.4	One of the Boxing Boys (fresco detail)	88
7.5	The Spring Fresco	89
8.1	Building 4: plan of the first floor	91
8.2	Room 5: the decorative scheme at eye level and its relationship with the room's function	91
8.3	Room 5: the decorative scheme at frieze level	93
8.4	North Frieze detail: shipsheds, women collecting water, herdsmen, soldiers	93
8.5	Shipshed at Kommos, reconstructed from excavation	94
8.6	Town 4 (Departure Town) on the South Frieze	96
8.7	Building 1 (Xeste 3) at Akrotiri	100
8.8	Bloodstained sacral horns: wall-painting in the Building 1 adyton	102
8.9	Agia Triadha sarcophagus: animal sacrifice	104
8.10	Boy carrying bowl	105
8.11	Boy carrying robe	105
8.12	Boys' initiation ceremony: the surviving figures	106
8.13	Procession on the Grand Staircase at Knossos	107
8.14	Room 3, Building 1: ground floor; the decorative scheme and its relationship with the room's function	107
8.15	Room 3, Building 1: first floor; one of the mature women in the procession	108
8.16	The Minoan Heaven: the goddess enthroned, with attendant monkey and griffin, and girl offering crocuses	110
8.17	The face of the goddess	111
9.1	Stages in Thera's development	117
9.2	Progress of a tsunami from Thera to Crete	122
9.3	A nineteenth-century reconstruction of the 1755 Lisbon earthquake	123
9.4	Thickness of surviving ash layer on seabed; reconstructed ash footprint, with inferred wind direction	124
9.5	Sites showing evidence of destruction in 1520 BC (Late Minoan IA)	127
9.6	Early fifteenth-century Anatolian colonies may have been founded in Crete	129
9.7	The spread of Mycenean control during the fifteenth century	130
10.1	The Plain of Mesara (shaded)	135
10.2	The Minoan trading empire	136
10.3	The Knossos Labyrinth: a reconstructed view from the south-east	139

10.4	Bull-Leaping Fresco from Knossos	140
10.5	The Knossos Labyrinth as a temple	142
10.6	Plato's world	151
10.7	Syracuse	156
10.8	The states of the Peloponnese in the fifth and fourth centuries BC	161
10.9	Salamis	166
11.1	Plato's Atlantis story applied to the Aegean	174
11.2	Evolution of the Atlantis story in antiquity	177
11.3	The first known map of Atlantis, published by Athanasius Kircher in 1665	183
11.4	Profile of the Mid-Atlantic Ridge, as portrayed by Donnelly (1882)	185
11.5	Ignatius Donnelly's map of Atlantis (1882)	186
11.6	The empire of Atlantis	188
11.7	The Azores	190

PLATES

1.1	Knossos destroyed	5
1.2	The temple of Zakro in Crete	7
1.3	Fresh black lava on the active volcanic cone of Nea Kameini	10
1.4	Nea Kameini: the two active craters	11
2.1	Phaistos, a Minoan temple in southern Crete	26
2.2	Zakro, a Minoan temple on the east coast of Crete	27
3.1	Stone mortars eroded from the ash by stream and wave erosion	36
3.2	Minoan masonry techniques in use in Thera	39
3.3	The bronze age city at Akrotiri, general view	41
4.1	The remains of the Minoan building on Mavros Rachidhi	49
4.2	View east from Mavros Rachidhi	49
4.3	Telchines Street, Akrotiri. A street in Minoan Gournia, Crete	52
4.5	North wall of Building 17	53
4.6	Door of Building 4	53
4.7	Triangle Square with Building 4	55
4.8	A fallen staircase	56
8.1	Building 1 at Akrotiri	100
9.1	Staircase in Building 13 crushed during an earthquake: view from North Square	115
9.2	The interior of Building 17	116
9.3	Minoan ash lining a ravine eroded west–east across the Phira Quarry	118
9.4	Cliffs south-east of Akrotiri, showing chaotic ash with black fragments of the bronze age crater walls	118

9.5	The caldera wall	121
9.6	Agia Triadha	131
9.7	Leaving Thera for the north	132
10.1	Mochlos, a Minoan port on the north coast of Crete	137
10.2	The trident of Poseidon, used as a mason's mark at Knossos	140
10.3	The Knossos Labyrinth as restored by Evans	143
10.4	The pillar in the East Pillar Crypt at Knossos	146
10.5	Plato. A first-century AD Roman copy in marble of the bronze portrait by Silanion	149

TABLE

8.1	Size of 'Minoan' settlements	97

ACKNOWLEDGEMENTS AND PREFACE

I would like to thank Laurence Nowry, the Canadian journalist and broadcaster, for taking an interest in my research when we met by chance on Thera; a stimulating discussion at the excavation continued with greater animation in tavernas, and subsequently by letter. Thanks are due to the guards at Akrotiri, who allowed me into areas closed to tourists. I must thank Brian McGregor and his staff at the Ashmolean Library in Oxford, and John and Celia Clarke, who generously offered hospitality during my Oxford reading weeks. I am grateful to the many correspondents who have given me unsolicited encouragement. I am especially grateful to Sinclair Hood, one of our senior Aegean scholars, who has tolerantly discussed Knossos and the Minoans with me, and patiently gritted his teeth at what must have seemed pure heresy. I should also mention Peter James's book about Atlantis, which opportunely came out just as I finished my first draft, and which stimulated some challenging new lines of thought.

I am grateful to my editors at Routledge, Andrew Wheatcroft and Vicky Peters, for overcoming my doubts and steering me past several other projects towards the treacherous, shoal-ridden waters surrounding Atlantis. It was while working on *The Knossos Labyrinth* that I made my own personal discovery of Atlantis. I was reinterpreting the Labyrinth as a temple when I realized I was describing something startlingly like the Temple of Poseidon and Cleito in the metropolis of Atlantis as described by Plato. I had read the ideas of Marinatos and Luce linking the bronze age eruption of Thera with the destruction of Atlantis; I was aware of the repeatedly floated theory that Atlantis was a memory of the lost Minoan civilization; I was also aware that for a variety of reasons the theory had not found universal acceptance.

I decided to take Plato's story apart and examine all its elements against currently available archaeological evidence to see whether a southern Aegean Atlantis was a valid proposition. I wanted to determine once and for all – if such a thing is ever possible – whether the lost land existed, and if so where it was, what its inhabitants were like, how and when they and Atlantis came to be destroyed. If the story is a fiction from start to finish, then we need no longer hunt for vestiges of historical memory. The matter needed resolving, though I was daunted by the scale of the problems involved. Plutarch (in his *Life of Solon*) sensed that the matter of Atlantis was too much for Plato, just as it had been for Solon: 'Plato was particularly ambitious to create an elaborate masterpiece out of the subject of Atlantis . . . He was late in beginning and the task proved too long for his lifetime, so the more we enjoy what he actually wrote, the more we must regret what he left undone.' With Plato's and Solon's example before me, I set sail for Atlantis with trepidation.

1

'ALL THE ISLAND AND MANY OTHER ISLANDS ALSO'

THE ATLANTIS LEGEND

Plato's story of Atlantis has the unenviable reputation of being the absurdest lie in all literature. One major problem has been the long eclipse which Plato's reputation as a philosopher and political thinker suffered during the twentieth century. Some scholars have written about Plato in such vitriolic terms as to test the boundaries of the term 'scholarship'. He has been damned for his assumed moral decadence, on the strength of what he wrote in the *Symposium*, even though he argued for legislation against homosexuality in the *Laws*; he has been condemned for the obscurity of his cosmology and for his totalitarian politics, his approach to state education sounding uncomfortably like the strategy behind the Hitler Youth.[1] The adoption of the Atlantis allegory by the Nazis seriously damaged Plato's reputation. Hitler admired Plato's cyclical view of history involving periodic catastrophes and the return of the demi-gods, discussing it frequently with Hermann Rauschning, who observed, 'Every German has one foot in Atlantis, where he seeks a better fatherland and a better patrimony. This double nature of the Germans [to live in both real and imaginary worlds] is especially noticeable in Hitler and provides the key to his magic socialism.'[2] There is also a parallel, 'alternative' twentieth-century literature which has sometimes sought to establish the truth of Plato's story by refuting what has been learnt through the natural sciences, and that too has alienated academics. Few scholars have been prepared to expose themselves to ridicule from their colleagues by discussing the matter, and it is symptomatic of the climate of opinion in the twentieth century that a young academic who saw a link between the Minoan civilization and Atlantis at the time of Evans's Knossos excavation felt that he had to publish his ideas anonymously.[3]

The story which has produced such extremes of credulity and incredulity was written down for the first time that we can be certain of between 359 BC, when Plato returned to Athens from Sicily, and 351 BC, when he died at the age of 81. In a preamble he claimed the story had been handed down to his narrator, Critias, from a distinguished ancestor of Critias, the statesman Solon, who heard it in Egypt in about 590 BC. The *Timaeus* was written as a sequel to the *Republic*, and its opening pages show Socrates asking for a narrative to illustrate the ideal state in action.

Critias' story about the war between Atlantis and the prehistoric Athenians is by no means the main part of the *Timaeus*, a seventy-five-page discourse on cosmology by the astronomer Timaeus. The discourse throws no light on Atlantis. At first sight it looks as if Plato realized the usefulness of the story only after completing the *Republic*, and slipped it into his next dialogue as an after-thought. It nevertheless reappears in the *Critias* (113C–121C), and the short account in the *Timaeus* (23D–25D) is really a trailer for that.[4] The *Timaeus* version has one of the priests of Sais in Egypt lecturing Solon on the absence of any truly ancient traditions among the Greeks: 'You remember but *one* deluge . . . '

> **23C** 'At one time, Solon, before the greatest destruction by water, what is now the Athenian state was the bravest in war and also supremely well organized in other respects. It is said that it possessed the finest works of art and the noblest polity of any nation under heaven of which we have heard tell.'
>
> **D** On hearing this, Solon said that he marvelled, and with the utmost eagerness requested the priest to tell him in order and exactly all the facts about those citizens of old. The priest then said, 'I will tell it, both for your sake and that of your city, and most of all for the sake of the Goddess who is both your patron and foster-mother and ours. Receiving the seed of you from Ge and Hephaestus, she founded your city first, a thousand years before ours,
>
> **E** 'of which the constitution is recorded in our sacred writings to be 8,000 years old. I will tell you in outline the laws of your citizens, who lived 9,000 years ago, and the noblest of their exploits: the full account we shall go through some other time, with the actual writings before us.
>
> **24A** 'To get a view of their laws, look at the laws here; for you will still find here many examples of those you had then. You see, first, how the priesthood is sharply separated off from the rest; next, the class of craftsmen, of which each sort works by itself without mixing with any other; then the class of shepherds, hunters and farmers.
>
> **B** 'The militia in particular, as no doubt you have noticed, is a class apart from all the others, compelled by law to devote itself exclusively to the work of training for war. A further feature is the character of their equipment with shields and spears; we were the first of the peoples of Asia to bear these weapons; it was the goddess who instructed us, just as she instructed you first of all the dwellers in your part of the world. Next, with regard to wisdom;
>
> **C** 'you see how much care our law has devoted from the very beginning to cosmology, by discovering all the effects which the divine causes produce upon human life, down to divination and the art of

medicine which aims at health, and by its mastery also of all the subsidiary sciences. So when, at that time, the Goddess had furnished you, before all others, with this orderly and regular system, she established your city, choosing the spot where you were born since she perceived that its well-tempered climate would bring forth a harvest of men of supreme wisdom.

D 'So it was that the Goddess, being herself both a lover of war and a lover of wisdom, chose the spot which was likely to bring forth men most like herself, and made this her first settlement. That is why you lived under the rule of such laws as these – yes, and laws still better – and you surpassed all men in every virtue, as became those who were the offspring and nurslings of gods. Truly, many and great are the achievements of your city, which are a marvel to men as they are here recorded; but there is one which stands out above all in heroic valour.

E 'Our records relate how once your city stopped a mighty army as it insolently advanced to attack the whole of Europe, and Asia as well, from a distant base in the Atlantic Ocean. In those far-off days the ocean was navigable; for in front of the mouth which your countrymen tell me you call "the pillars of Heracles" there was an island larger than Libya and Asia together; and it was possible for the travellers of that time to cross from it to the other islands, and from the islands to the whole of the opposite continent which encircles the outer ocean.

25A 'The sea that we have here, lying within the mouth just mentioned, is evidently a basin with a narrow entrance; what lies beyond is a real ocean, and the land surrounding it may rightly be called, in the fullest and truest sense, a continent. In this island of Atlantis there existed a confederation of kings, of great and marvellous power, which held sway over all the island, and over many other islands also and parts of the continent; and, moreover, of the lands here within the Straits they ruled over Libya as far as Egypt, and over Europe as far as Tuscany.

B 'So this host, being all gathered together, made an attempt on one occasion to enslave by a single onslaught both your country and ours and the whole of the territory within the straits. It was then, Solon, that the manhood of your city showed itself conspicuous for valour and energy in the sight of all the world.

C 'She took the lead in daring and military skill. Acting partly as leader of the Greeks, and partly standing alone by herself when deserted by all others, after encountering the deadliest perils, she defeated the invaders and set up her trophy. Those who were not as yet enslaved she saved from slavery; all the rest of us who dwell within the limits set up by Heracles she ungrudgingly set free.

D 'But afterwards there occurred portentous earthquakes and floods, and in one terrible day and night of storm the whole body of your

3

warriors was swallowed up by the earth, and Atlantis likewise was swallowed up by the sea and vanished; the ocean at that spot to this day cannot be navigated or explored, owing to the great depth of shoal mud which the island created as it subsided.'

The more detailed *Critias* breaks off at the moment where Zeus is about to pass judgement on the mortals. Since that moment in the 350s BC, the story of Atlantis has hovered between fable and folk tale, taken as history by some, acknowledged as allegory by others. Today some take it literally, others see it as didactic novella; in the ancient world too opinion was divided. Is the story true? If so, where was Atlantis? The longer version mentions 'the extremity of the island near the Pillars of Heracles' (*Crit.* 114B) and 'the war between the dwellers beyond the pillars of Heracles [Atlanteans] and all that dwelt

Figure 1.1 A conventional 'Atlantic' Atlantis: Bory de St Vincent's map (1803)

4

within them' (*Crit.* 108E). The shorter version is clearer still: 'in front of the mouth which [Greeks] call the pillars of Heracles, there was an island larger than Libya and Asia together' (*Tim.* 24E). Plato is evidently describing an island-continent out in the Atlantic Ocean, just west of the Straits of Gibraltar. There are nevertheless possibilities other than the obvious one. Although Plato may have placed Atlantis far to the west in an ocean whose immensity was in his time only just being recognized, the original of his story, the Atlantis described by Egyptian priests 250 years earlier, was smaller and nearer to home. The term 'Atlantic' is misleading; as late as the first century BC, Diodorus (3. 38) was using it for the *Indian* Ocean, so it may be wiser to translate it less precisely as 'outer' or 'distant' ocean. We cannot assume ancient authors meant the same as us by either 'pillars of Heracles' or 'Atlantic'.

Both place names and geographical perceptions shift with time, and the world of fourth-century Athens was already larger than the world of the Egyptian priests of 600 BC. To the Egyptians, a huge island in the ocean to the west could have been Sicily or even Crete. To the early Greeks the pillars support-ing the corners of the vault of heaven might be anywhere remote. Even as late as Strabo's time (3. 5. 5) opinions differed about the location of the pillars of Heracles; some thought it was the mountains on each side of the Straits of Gibraltar, others argued it was even further west. There was even disagree-ment about whether the pillars were real pillars, perhaps made of bronze,

Plate 1.1 Knossos destroyed: tumbled wall stones at the south-west corner of the temple; Silver Vessels Sanctuary (restored by Evans and again in 1990s) behind the trees

or mountains. Before the sixth century BC several mountains on the edges of mainland Greece were seen as supports for the sky. Amongst others, the two southward-pointing headlands on each side of the Gulf of Laconia were pillars of Heracles. Then, to the Greeks, a large island with one end just outside the pillars of Heracles could only have meant Crete. The exotic civilization of Atlantis could then have been the Minoan civilization, which threatened the mainland Greek and Anatolian cultures not 9,000 but 900 years before Solon. Support for a Peloponnesian location for the pillars comes, unexpectedly, from Egypt. The Medinet Habu texts, dating from 1200 BC, describe the Sea Peoples invading from islands to the north (possibly the Aegean) 'from the pillars of heaven', by which the Egyptians probably meant that the invaders came from the end of the world as *they* knew it.

The power that held sway over all the island and over many other islands also was the economic and possibly political power of the Minoan civilization, which was centred in Crete but enmeshed most of the Aegean region and reached out to trade, among other places, with North Africa ('Libya') and Italy ('Tuscany'). The island of Crete was not swallowed up by the sea, but perhaps the tradition was a misremembering of what happened to the Minoan trading empire, which

Figure 1.2 The Aegean Sea

Plate 1.2 The temple of Zakro in Crete is partly drowned by subsidence: the open space
of the Bull Court can be seen in the middle distance, the Minoan town top
right

contracted during the fifteenth century culminating in the fall of the Knossos
Labyrinth in 1380 BC. It was as if the invisible network of trading routes and
political controls had sunk to the bottom of the Aegean, perhaps in the face of
competition from Mycenae, metaphorically 'swallowed up by the sea'.

The thesis of this book is that the story is not one piece of identifiable
proto-history but several, and that Plato drew them together because he
wanted to weave them into a parable that commented on the state of the world
in his own times. It is clear from Plato's other writings that he had mixed
motives: he wanted to entertain, improve and exalt his readers. A distant
memory of the Minoan civilization was available, preserved for his use, as he
said, by the seventh-century priests in the Nile delta. The wealth, orderliness
and strangeness of the Minoans are sketched in for us. Atlantis has often been

referred to as a Utopia, a fantastic extension of the ideal state Plato alluded to in the *Republic*, but it is really not that. It is the Athenians who are described in utopian terms. It is they who have relinquished private property (*Crit.* 110D), and have prolific fields and boundless pastures. It is Athens that is the excellent land with well-tempered seasons (*Crit.* 110E, 111B–C, 111E, 112A). Attica is the Utopia, not Atlantis, for all its marvels.

The second strand in Plato's proto-history is hinted at in the words 'all the island and over many other islands also' (*Tim.* 25E). Atlantis is an archipelago consisting of one large island and a group of smaller islands: the Aegean islands controlled by the Cretans in the sixteenth century BC. Such details of the destruction of Atlantis that Plato gives us speak of a geological cataclysm: earthquakes and subsidence taking significant parts of Atlantis below the waves. Small-scale gradual subsidences (and emergences) are common on all the Aegean islands – they tilt as a result of the ongoing collision between African and European plates – but something large-scale and sudden is meant. Red, white and black rocks are mentioned as building materials on Atlantis. Volcanic rocks like these exist on Santorini, an island that was the scene of a massive, destructive eruption in the bronze age, about a century before the Minoan civilization collapsed.

THERA:
A WINDOW ONTO ATLANTIS

On the southernmost edge of Thera, the main island of Santorini, the principal town of this civilization outside Crete was entombed and preserved by ashfall from the eruption. Was this the metropolis of Atlantis? It has been suggested that along the way, perhaps in transposing the story from Egyptian to Greek for Solon, there was a translation error, that Plato was really describing locations on two different islands, that the plain round the royal city was the Plain of Mesara on Crete, while the metropolis was on Thera.[5]

Thera's location, central in the Aegean and southernmost of the Cyclades, goes far towards explaining why it became prosperous in the bronze age. Within the small ring of islands – Thera, Therasia and Aspronisi – is a huge oval bay 10 kilometres across, the focus of the eruption that destroyed the bronze age civilization on Santorini. Where once hill country rose to volcanic peaks, the sea is now 400 metres deep. The steep walls of this caldera showing the layers of ash and lava of ancient volcanic eruptions give the bay a hostile coastline. Santorini's main town, Phira, perches on the caldera rim, overlooking the bay. Today there are thirteen villages on Santorini and 6,000 people. Thirteen rural settlements are known from the bronze age too, but given the processes of destruction and burial it is unlikely that that we will ever see the complete pattern.[6] Ancient Santorini was probably more populous than today, with over 6,000 people in the city of Akrotiri alone.

Figure 1.3 Santorini or Thera, showing the location of the bronze age city at Akrotiri

Santorini suffers serious climatic problems, including perennial drought. Add earthquakes and volcanic eruptions, and Santorini becomes a very hostile place. The Aegean has always been dangerously earthquake-prone; here the African plate, invisible beneath the Mediterranean floor, drives slowly but inexorably under Europe. All Aegean islands are prone to earthquakes. The effect of the 1956 earthquake is still felt in Santorini. Forty-eight were killed and hundreds injured.[7] The ensuing panic and disruption of everyday life caused many to leave, reinforcing a century-long trend to move to an easier life on the Greek mainland. Since 1956 hot gases and sulphurous emissions have steamed continuously from the craters and fissures in the middle of the bay. The forces that ravaged Santorini in 1956 will do so again as they did in antiquity, when they emptied it of its bronze age Atlanteans.

In the centre of the caldera are the two newest islands in the Santorini group, Palea and Nea Kameini, the Santorini volcano rebuilding on its old foundations. Though no more than a few tens of metres high out of the water, they have been built to that height from the seabed, so they are already substantial volcanic peaks. The first documented eruption was in 197 BC, when people from Rhodes saw an eruption that resulted in the creation of a small island: they called it Iera, 'holy', and dedicated an altar to Poseidon, the god of the Atlanteans.[8] For the volcano to have broken the sea surface in 197 BC it must have been building up to that level during a series of earlier eruptions that went unreported. Wave action later eroded the top of this volcano off, creating the Bankos Reef.[9]

Plate 1.3 Fresh black lava on the active volcanic cone of Nea Kameini, with the caldera wall in the background

ERUPTION AFTER ERUPTION

It was the eruptions of AD 19, 46–47 and 60 that created the island of Theia, 'Divine', now called Palea Kameini. The eruption of AD 60 was reported by Philostratus, together with the peculiar detail that the sea receded about one kilometre from the south coast of the island. This may have been associated with a tsunami, commonly produced by earthquakes focused on the seabed, and likely to occur during a submarine eruption.[10] In AD 726, Santorini experienced another major eruption. This was adjacent to Theia (Palea Kameini), produced a third island and threw ash as far as Macedonia and Anatolia.

In 1573 an eruption created the islet of Mikra Kameini to the east of Palea Kameini. In 1650 a series of earthquakes led up to a major submarine eruption off the north-east coast of Thera, forming a temporary island called Kouloumbos. Poisonous gases released during the eruption blinded or killed many Therans and their livestock. In the eighteenth century, Leychester reported that the new island had disappeared (eroded by wave action), forming a reef. According to other sources, the flames of the 1650 eruption were visible from Heraklion, and tsunamis swept among the Turkish ships beached on the island of Dia, close to the north coast of Crete. For four years beginning in 1707 there were explosive eruptions of lava back in the caldera between Theia, now called Palea Kameini, and Mikra Kameini. The build-up of lava created a new island called Nea

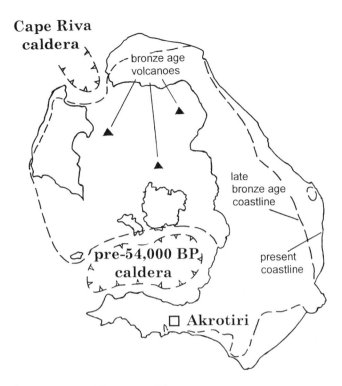

Figure 1.4 Reconstruction of bronze age Thera

Plate 1.4 Nea Kameini: the two active craters, one in the centre, the other bottom left

11

Kameini: the eruptions of 1866–70 trebled its size. The King George I crater, formed at this time, is now 131 metres high. But for our story the main importance of this eruption sequence is that it attracted geologists and archaeologists to Santorini, where for the first time they recognized traces of a forgotten bronze age civilization.

There was a major explosion on Nea Kameini in August 1925 and the eruption that followed lasted nine months. 100 million cubic metres of lava poured out, joining Nea Kameini and Mikra Kameini and producing a lava dome. A further eruption in 1928 formed the Tholos and Nautilus craters. In 1939–41, the Nea Kameini craters were active again. In 1950 another explosion on the top of Nea Kameini led to the formation of the newest dome, Liatsikas, beside the King George I crater.

Figure 1.5 Bronze age Thera seen from the west.
Note the volcanic peaks on the site of the North Bay

For the last two millennia a long series of volcanic eruptions in the Santorini island group is well documented. Cone after cone has been added to the centre of the bay, the rim of which is the outer edge of a much bigger crater than any that has been active in the last 2,000 years. Unless the process is interrupted by another caldera eruption, the bay will eventually be refilled with lava and Santorini will be one island.[11]

The geology shows that before the caldera eruption of 1520 BC Thera had already been disembowelled by more than one earlier eruption and the bronze age island had a substantial South Bay occupying the southernmost third of the modern caldera. This south-west basin may have been formed during a caldera eruption before 54,000 BC. Another caldera eruption near Cape Riva in 18,300 BC created the north-west basin, so there may have been a bay, or at least low ground, between northern Therasia and Thera during the Minoan period.[12] The volcanic peaks visible on Santorini in the Minoan period had developed over a million years, from several vents within a pre-existing island group of non-volcanic origin. Mesa Vouno and Profitis Elias, for instance, stood above the waves of the ancient Mediterranean much as they do now, long before the volcanic cone complex was built. Monolithos and Platinamos too stood up from this ancient sea, as peaked islets of schist and marble. In the bronze age, Monolithos was still a separate islet, but Mesa

12

Vouno and Profitis Elias were already engulfed in the volcano which made a single 'Greater Thera', an island shaped like a huge fish-head with its mouth gaping towards the south-west.

2

PRELUDES TO DISCOVERY

THE FOLKLORE TRADITION

The Golden Age beauty of pre-destruction Thera was often recalled in later Greek legends. Herodotus gave it the name Kallisti, 'Fairest One.' Writing in 440 BC, Herodotus was passing on a tradition that may have been transmitted orally for a thousand years.[1] Herodotus indicates that in his time the island was remembered as having once been fertile and beautiful, unlike the ravaged crater we now see.

In the ninth century BC a fortified Dorian colony existed up on windy Mesa Vouno, an important stepping-stone for east–west trade: Cyprus, Crete, Melos and the south-eastern shore of Greece were other halts on this route. Herodotus attributed the introduction of writing into Greece to 'Phoenician colonists' arriving by way of Kallisti, perhaps a folk memory of the Minoan culture that had come by way of Thera.[2] Herodotus also tells us that before Kallisti, in the earliest times of which he knows, the island was called Strongyle, 'the Round One'. This could refer to the near-circular interior of the caldera, and so date from the post-1520 era, or from an earlier time when the outer coastline was more exactly circular. Circularity is a major feature of the Metropolis of Atlantis. Plato describes circles of sea surrounding the Metropolis (*Crit.* 113D, 115E) and three circular walls of stone sheathed in brass, tin and orichalcum (*Crit.* 116B). By the Minoan period at least part of the central bay, the area called the South Bay, had already been blasted out, but it would be stretching the idea of oral tradition to absurdity to suggest that Strongyle was a name remembered from 23,000 or 54,000 BC. The Minoan island of Thera was almost circular with a single major bay like a bite taken out of its south-western edge: the bay too may have been almost circular. Against the antiquity of the name Strongyle is the evidence that in the Minoan period the island was actually known as Thera.[3]

The Parian Marble dates the voyage of the hero Danaus and his daughters from Egypt to Greece via Rhodes and Crete to 1511 BC, and Kadmos' arrival in Greece from Thera shortly before, in 1519 BC. This is very close to the likeliest date for the great bronze age eruption of Thera, 1520 BC: maybe the Kadmians landing on the beaches of Greece were refugees from the Theran disaster.[4]

14

NINETEENTH-CENTURY GLIMPSES OF A MINOAN PAST

Towards the end of the nineteenth century, the realization gradually dawned that a bronze age civilization had flourished in the Aegean before Mycenae. It was the building of the Suez Canal beginning in 1859 that drew attention to Santorini. Its ash made an ideal cement for harbour works at Port Said. The areas quarried for ash by the Suez Canal Company were the south coast of Therasia and Balos Bay on Thera. On the south coast of Therasia, blocks of stone which the workmen knew at once were man-made walls began to get in the way of the quarrying. From 1866 the site was archaeologically excavated, first by the owner, M. Alaphouzos, and later by the French vulcanologist Ferdinand Fouqué, who had come to Santorini to observe the volcanic eruption of 1866–70 and was diverted to the island's equally exciting archaeology. Fouqué's first objective was to discover whether the walls had been built before the pumice fell or raised on a cleared terrace after the prehistoric eruption.[5]

At this stage neither Minoan nor Mycenean civilizations had been recognized, so it was difficult for Fouqué to interpret what he found, though he knew it was pre-Greek. There were six rooms of a 'large farmhouse' and the remains of an old man caught by the eruption. The ruins were impressive. One room was 8.5 metres long, two others 6 metres long. The boundary wall of the paddock had a stone cylinder a metre high at one corner: no-one knows what this was for.[6] Fouqué noted five more free-standing buildings spread along 125 metres of the Alaphouzos quarry, which implies at least a village. The pottery he found was very similar to that found later at the key site of Akrotiri.[7]

Fouqué abandoned Therasia without completing his dig, finding the site too difficult, and turned his attention to Akrotiri, near the south-western tip of Thera. He found a site where the ash had been eroded away at the bottom of a ravine and prehistoric artefacts were exposed, but the landowner refused to let him excavate.

Fouqué's negotiations led to two other Frenchmen, Mamet and Gorceix, being granted funds by the French government and permission to dig by the Greeks. In 1870, Mamet and Gorceix started excavating on the east side of the Akrotiri ravine and were immediately rewarded as walls preserved to a height of 2 metres came into view, then a store room filled with painted vases, many containing remains of carbonized food. One piece of pottery was found to carry a painted linear script. More significantly still, in view of what was to come later, wall-paintings were discovered, just before the excavators were forced to stop for fear of the trench walls collapsing. The wall-paintings were beautiful and still intact on the walls. Nothing like these paintings at Akrotiri would ever be found at the Minoan sites waiting to be discovered on Crete: even the Great Temple at Knossos would not yield anything as complete or as well preserved. They proved beyond doubt that the French archaeologists had discovered the homes of wealthy, civilized people.

Gorceix and Mamet found a second house nearby, then a third near Balos on the caldera rim. Here ash quarrying had again been checked by a layer of stone blocks, the remains of ancient dwellings, this time superior to those on Therasia. The interiors were plastered and painted yellow. The lack of windows, large earthenware jars and earth floors showed these were service or store rooms. The complete skeleton of a goat suggested that livestock had been abandoned when disaster struck. Another room yielded a copper saw and an olive trunk with its branches still unsawn. Beyond the excavation area a whole stratum of similar dwellings ran along the cliff face.[8]

Fouqué now recognized that Mamet, Gorceix and himself were unearthing something more than a bronze age village, but he was not sure what. He noticed that the pottery was similar to that found in Rhodes, Melos and Cyprus. He also noted 'in the Louvre an Egyptian painting depicting an Egyptian king receiving Greek envoys. The presents they bring are similar to the ones in Thera.' This is the first reference to trade between Minoans and Egyptians. In due course, after the Minoan remains at Knossos were unearthed, the linear script, architecture, pottery and wall-painting styles, indeed the lifestyle itself of Late Cycladic Thera would all come to be recognized as Minoan. What Fouqué, Mamet and Gorceix were looking at were the remains of a hitherto-unsuspected civilization, which was seized on with amazing insight by Louis Figuier, who, in 1872, was the first to identify Santorini as Atlantis.

The sites of those initial discoveries have been destroyed by continued quarrying.[9] After the Fouqué, Mamet and Gorceix digs the remains on Santorini were virtually abandoned for a hundred years, with the exception of the Zahn dig of 1899. The long neglect after such a promising beginning can be explained by a variety of factors: the intervention of political instability and war, the indifference of professional archaeologists, a lack of funds for exploration, and also the lack of a conceptual framework for the finds. Ironically, the small-scale Zahn dig of 1899 came to an unobtrusive close just as the great Evans dig at Knossos started, shelved just as Evans was bringing to light the metropolis of the civilization that would make sense of the finds on Thera.

Robert Zahn excavated to the east of the Akrotiri site, though the exact location of his dig cannot be traced with certainty. Mamet and Gorceix dug in the same area as the celebrated Marinatos excavations of the 1960s and 1970s. Zahn dug in the next ravine to the east, the Potamos valley. It was a logical choice; if stream erosion in the western ravine had exposed bronze age houses it was quite likely that the settlement continued through the interfluve to reappear in the floor of the next ravine. Zahn found a bronze age house, a circular gold trinket, traces of fishing nets, bones of dog, pig and donkey. There was evidence to suggest pressing olives and grinding grain. Zahn also found the remains of coriander, anise, barley, chick peas and pottery including a jar rim with an inscription in an unrecognized script: it would turn out years later to be Linear A.[10]

Although the excavators were unaware of the significance of their finds, by 1900 the bronze age city at Akrotiri had in effect been discovered, sampled, sounded with test pits, proved to extend across a large area and shown to be bursting with a wide range of artefacts. A prosperous, civilized community of prehistoric farmers, foresters, weavers, potters and fishermen had lived in the south-west corner of Thera and it had been obliterated under a deep fall of pumice and ash. It seems extraordinary that the site should then have been virtually forgotten, but it was, just as the Greeks forgot the destruction of Atlantis until Egyptian priests reminded them 900 years later.

Melos is the south-westernmost of the Cyclades, a stark volcanic island with a fine central harbour that is a volcanic crater of the same type as Thera's. A team of British archaeologists arrived on Melos in the 1890s, intending to excavate the island's classical city. The classical site proved disappointing, so the excavators turned in 1896 to the bronze age site of Phylakopi, which was already known from surface finds. The site was revisited in 1911 and 1974–7, but its character was already established in the 1890s. Phylakopi was a prehistoric port established initially to control the trade in obsidian quarried on the island. The massive town wall defending the port from the southern, landward, side dates from the Mycenean period, but there are traces of an earlier (Late Cycladic) wall of the same period as Akrotiri;[11] the shrine complex discovered by Colin Renfrew in 1974–7 is also Mycenean.[12]

The town plan is more orderly than either Ayia Irini or Akrotiri have proved to be, with near-straight roads intersecting at right angles and houses grouped in sub-rectangular blocks; the layout is strongly reminiscent of Palaikastro, implying a Cretan connection. A few fragments of fresco were found in the nineteenth-century dig, in a style similar to that of the wall-paintings later found at Akrotiri. The Flying Fish Fresco has fish swimming among rockwork, reminiscent of the Spring Fresco at Akrotiri.[13] The significance of the site nevertheless remained unrecognized until a more complete picture of the evolution of Aegean civilization emerged. It was as if archaeologists were waiting for the excavation and interpretation of the key sites of Knossos and Akrotiri to supply them with a context. Significantly, the archaeologist in day-to-day control at Phylakopi in the 1890s was Duncan Mackenzie, who became Evans's lieutenant at Knossos.

THE BACKDROP OF THE CYCLADES

It is appropriate to break off the unfolding narrative in 1900, at the point where the Phylakopi and Thera digs ceased and the Knossos dig started, in order to evaluate the cultural setting out of which the Minoan civilization developed. The Minoan civilization evolved gradually on Crete, but its exportation to Thera during the sixteenth century BC may have been felt as abrupt and intrusive by Therans, especially since there was a conspicuous expansionist phase when Cretans went out and founded trading posts and colonies on the Aegean islands.

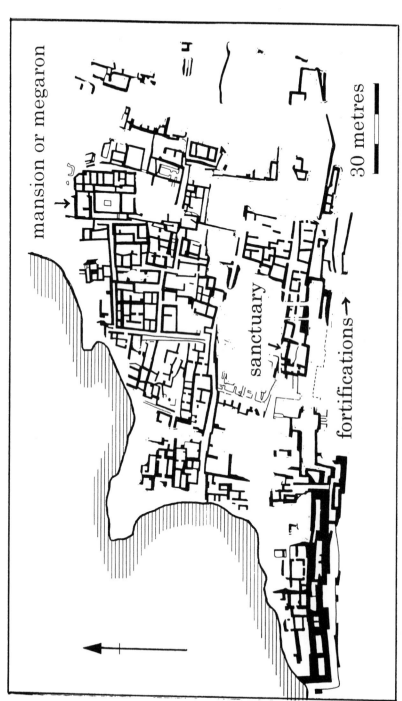

Figure 2.1 The bronze age town of Phylakopi

The Minoan influence from Crete was not the only cultural influence on sixteenth-century Therans. The Cyclades had then been settled for 3,000 years and formed a culture area experiencing complex interactions of people, ideas, raw materials and trade goods both island to island and between islands and mainlands to east and west. The Cyclades were first inhabited around 5000 BC and, even before this time, in about 7000 BC, obsidian from quarries on Melos had found its way to the north-east Peloponnese: this useful tool-stone was probably collected by sailors picking up useful raw materials wherever they found them on uninhabited Aegean islands.[14]

The earliest known settlements in the Cyclades were the late neolithic villages on Antiparos, Thera and Kea, probably founded by settlers from the Greek mainland. The Kephala site on Kea has been dated to 3900 BC. On Thera traces of a substantial neolithic village dating from 4500 BC have been found directly beneath the ruins of the bronze age city of Akrotiri. Unfortunately, repeated digging down to bedrock to build foundations for successive houses over the next 3,000 years all but annihilated evidence of the earliest phase. Pieces of neolithic pottery were found under the bronze age house known as Xeste 3 (here called Building 1: see Figure 4.1), fragments of Early Cycladic pottery dating to around 2700 BC and Middle Cycladic pottery from around 1700–1600 BC were found under Building 1.[15]

Thera was in a key position, the link between the Cyclades and Crete. As such it was a natural conduit for Cretan influence, a stepping-stone between Crete, Melos and Kea, Paros and Naxos, and mainland Greece. One passage in the *Timaeus* (24E) is very close to this idea: 'It was possible for the travellers of that time to cross from [the main island of Atlantis] to the other islands [in the Atlantis group], and from the islands to the whole of the opposite continent [Anatolia].'

The traits of a distinctive Cycladic culture developed early on: building stone-built graves, making terracotta heads and stone vases.[16] An Early Cycladic I phase beginning in about 2800 BC and lasting 200 years was marked by the use of cist (stone-box) graves and the manufacture of marble luxury objects. This development was stimulated by the presence of marble on many of the islands; emery (Naxos), obsidian (Melos) and pumice (Thera) were all useful materials for cutting and polishing the marble.[17] The marble objects used as grave goods are the earliest true luxury goods to be made in the Aegean and represent the beginning of a long and significant European tradition; the manufacture and exchange of high-status goods are hallmarks of the European bronze age. Some stylized figurines display the characteristics of individual craftsmen. Though not much is known about the organization of this important industry, it seems likely that the prosperity of Paros and Naxos, the islands with the best-quality marble, was partly due to the industry. The distinctive pale figurines are instantly recognizable – the violin- or cello-shaped figures made in the two centuries before 2600 BC and the more naturalistic 'folded arms' female figurines of the following 300 years. Perhaps the most memorable are the figures of musicians found in a tomb on Keros.

The early bronze age in the Cyclades lasted 1,200 years, a long period which saw slow but considerable increases in total population and numbers of settlements and the emergence of an increasingly rich and characteristic Cycladic culture. Regular contacts with people outside the islands developed, as did a gradually more sophisticated and complex social organization. Some elements in all this are well known, such as the trade patterns in obsidian, but not all; it may be that if we knew more about the Cycladic people's wooden artefacts we might view the culture differently. Nevertheless, in the earliest phase, until 2600 BC, exchanges of ideas, raw materials and manufactured goods were limited island to island within the Cyclades.

By 2600–2300 BC (Early Cycladic II) there was expansion in every sphere of activity. Painted decoration was added to pottery: there were new pottery shapes, including an elegant sauceboat and a saucer-shaped bowl, both of which have been found on the Greek mainland, showing that trade was under way. Cycladic pottery was included in a grave in eastern Crete. There was also a marked increase in the number of settlements, especially on Naxos and Amorgos. The important town of Ayia Irini was founded on the island of Kea. More evidence of important trading contacts comes from an Early Minoan tomb near Arkhanes in central Crete: there were fifty-five obsidian blades, probably traded from Melos via Thera, together with thirteen Cycladic marble figurines. This collection of Cycladic material may mean that the tomb was that of an ex-patriot Theran merchant.

By this time a village stood on the Akrotiri site on Thera. Two rock-cut chambers north-east of Building 12 were found to contain raw, unused potter's clay of a type not native to Thera. These hollows are Early Cycladic rock-cut tombs whose roofs collapsed: they were emptied of human remains when the Middle Cycladic settlement spread over the site, and converted into cellarage. It was common for cemeteries to be a little apart from the settlements, and the Early Cycladic settlement may have occupied a small area on the harbour waterfront 100 metres to the south-west.

In 2300–2100 BC (Early Cycladic IIIA) new pottery shapes were appearing, such as the tankard and a tall tubular vessel introduced from Anatolia. Sailing ships seem to have been in use in the Aegean from this time on, leading to the development of harbour settlements in eastern Crete at Mokhlos, Palaikastro and Zakro, and free-lance trading was probably under way.[18]

Within the Cyclades, this opening-up to external influences was accompanied by the abandonment of some settlements, the rebuilding of others and the addition of fortifications, e.g. at Panormos on Naxos. Burial in cist tombs went out of fashion and the making of marble figurines went into a sharp decline. There were also new metal types and a new apsidal house plan, both coming from Anatolia. The sum of all these changes points to the unwelcome arrival of immigrants or invaders from Anatolia, a change precipitating a range of social and cultural disturbances.[19] There seems to have been a sharp decline in the number of people living in the Cyclades at this time and in their standard of living, as well as a major break in contact with the outside world.

By 2100 BC, the beginning of Early Cycladic IIIB, the power struggle, whether political, cultural or both, had been resolved. The Cycladic culture re-emerged and redefined itself. In pottery this was expressed in geometric designs painted dark on white slip; there were also remarkable beaked jugs that seem to hold their heads up like marching guardsmen. Towns emerged as major centres, with Phylakopi and Paroikia as important sites: Ayia Irini was refounded at this time. As the townships became more substantial they absorbed people from the small scattered villages of the earlier periods. Possibly after the unsettled and threatening conditions of the previous phase people sought the safety of towns; it may also be that after this brought the populations of whole islands together the administrative, economic and social advantages of urban living became more evident.[20] The town at Akrotiri may have developed as an agglomeration of Early Cycladic villages. It is known that there was an early settlement there because a wide range of Early Cycladic pottery was found, including imports from Melos, Naxos and Amorgos.[21] Relations with Crete were still at a very low level. Virtually no Middle Minoan IA pottery found its way to the Cyclades, although a little Cycladic pottery reached Crete. This phase ended in 1950 BC with an earthquake powerful enough to destroy Phylakopi.

In the middle bronze age following this destruction (Middle Cycladic, early phase, 1950–1700 BC), the Second City of Phylakopi was built on the ruins of the First with a carefully gridded plan and well-built houses: virtually all the people on Melos lived there. There were increasing numbers of settlements but still usually only one per island, like Paroikia on Paros. Naxos, a richer island, had four. As a small and relatively infertile island, Thera may have had just one major township, and that stimulated as much by developing trade with Melos and Crete as by any wealth generated from the island's resources; there may, however, have been a second town in the South Bay.[22]

The relationship with the Crete of the temples developed apace and the Cyclades were increasingly drawn into Crete's orbit. The development of the temples and the powerful centralized administration they imply would have affected the Aegean economy generally. Possibly the new style of Cretan organization was associated with the organization of the metal industry; the growth of bronze production may have led to a drop in Cretan demand for Melian obsidian, and a shift in the centre of economic power from Melos to Crete. The political, possibly military, expansion of Crete was not yet under way, but its economic power was in the ascendant. Thera, on the Cretan edge of the Cycladic world, felt these shifts acutely. The Theran city at Akrotiri disengaged itself from the islands of the northern Aegean at this time in order to develop a closer relationship with Crete. In 1700 BC the city was substantially the same as the late bronze age city wrecked by the caldera eruption in 1520 BC. Houses fell and were rebuilt in between, but the town plan remained substantially the same. By the late phase of the Middle Cycladic, 1700–1550 BC, new fortifications were built at Ayia Irini, suggesting that prosperous trading was attracting piracy. Pottery patterns from this time onwards increasingly derived from Crete. It was Crete that set the trends, sending economic and cultural shock waves through the Aegean.

The Cretan temples were rebuilt in virtually their final form and an expansion of overseas trade followed. In the Cyclades, contacts with Crete almost entirely replaced those with the Greek mainland. Oddly, Cycladic exports to Crete ceased at the very time when Cretan influence on the Cyclades was increasing very fast. Perhaps the Cretans were more interested in selling and in creating markets for their manufactured goods, perhaps the goods were paid for in archaeologically invisible ways: food, timber, slaves. Some exchanges did go on. Pottery found its way from Melos to Naxos, Ayia Irini, Crete and the Greek mainland, and from Naxos and Thera to Knossos.

The Cycladic towns expanded and became more sophisticated in their architecture, and this may have been encouraged by the splendid examples of fine masonry to be seen at the Cretan temples. The Crete-driven, temple-driven Minoan culture began to swamp the Aegean. The Middle Cycladic ended with what seems to have been a massive earthquake, destroying the Second City of Phylakopi and probably badly damaging other towns round the Cyclades: certainly Ayia Irini on Kea was extensively rebuilt at the start of the following period. Many houses at Akrotiri on Thera were destroyed by an earthquake at this time; enormous quantities of debris from the ruined houses were spread out in the streets and squares.

The design of the Theran city changed slightly. In rebuilt dwellings the old ground floors had in several instances to be turned into semi-basements owing to an accumulation of up to 2 metres of demolition debris in the streets. It was within this debris that the drainage conduits of the late bronze age city were laid.[23] In the West House (Building 4) basement are the remains of an earlier house built on a different orientation.[24] There was massive destruction at Knossos at the same time that the Cycladic towns were damaged, and all this evidence points to a great earthquake affecting the whole Aegean.[25] For Thera and Crete to be affected by the same earthquake it would have to be deep-seated, with a focus perhaps 100 kilometres below the earth's surface; the earthquake of 1956 BC, by contrast, was shallow-seated and therefore affected Thera but not Crete.[26]

The late bronze age, beginning with Late Cycladic I in 1550 BC, opened with a flurry of rebuilding in the earthquake-damaged towns. A Third City was built at Phylakopi and provided with new fortifications; Ayia Irini was rebuilt. At Akrotiri, the most spectacular of all the Cycladic settlements – in terms of what has survived – there was also rebuilding. Many of the new buildings at Akrotiri stood on the ruins of older ones and the old street plan was preserved. In this last phase, the run-up to the final catastrophe at Akrotiri in 1520 BC,[27] a powerful Cretan influence was felt in Cycladic culture. The architecture and in particular the wall-paintings of Thera are often cited as evidence of this strong influence from the south, but the indigenous threads of Cycladic culture wove a complex web amongst Helladic and Anatolian as well as Cretan influences. Significantly, at this final stage in Thera's bronze age story, its destiny differed very markedly from that of other Cycladic towns: Thera had a particularly close relationship with Minoan Crete, an intimacy that ended with the volcanic eruption that destroyed Thera though neither Ayia Irini nor Phylakopi: they were to be destroyed later by some other agency, between 1520 and 1450 BC.

BRONZE AGE KNOSSOS

During the nineteenth century, while fragments of the bronze age civilization came to light in Phylakopi and Santorini, another major component in the Atlantis story was also re-emerging from obscurity: the bronze age site of Knossos. In the 1830s Robert Pashley described the site he correctly identified as Knossos, though the bronze age ruins were obscured by Roman brickwork.[28] In 1878 Minos Kalokairinos, guided by the surface scatter of bronze age pottery and limestone blocks, initiated the first dig at Knossos. Before he was stopped by the authorities, Kalokairinos opened part of the West Wing, the store rooms containing rows of colossal jars. An American journalist, W. J. Stillman, had the idea that the building was the Labyrinth of Greek mythology and reported news of the discovery to the Archaeological Institute of America, alerting the international community to the possibilities that a full-scale excavation might offer.

Schliemann showed interest in the site, but it was left to Arthur Evans to continue Kalokairinos' work, resuming in 1900. Evans saw evidence of a labyrinthine building with fragments of frescoes on walls blackened by the smoke of a great conflagration. By the fifth day the truth dawned on Evans: that he had found a pre-Greek, pre-Mycenean civilization with its own writing. In 1900, the building was still believed to measure 55 metres from north to south, 43 metres from east to west. It was only as the excavation progressed that it proved to be the West Wing of a much larger structure. Evans opened up more completely the West Wing cellarage. It was in the Throne Sanctuary that the sheer exoticism of Knossos struck Evans for the first time. On the walls, he found paintings of griffins relaxing proudly in a mountain landscape, floors paved with gypsum slabs and panels of red-painted plaster, strange alabaster vases shaped like gigantic inkwells, an enclosed sunken area of unknown purpose approached down steps, and a beautifully carved gypsum throne with a high back facing the sunken area. Scattered across the floor of the throne room were the remains of a large jar that had fallen over. There were streaks of soot everywhere. The scene spoke vividly of some desperate ritual: perhaps the last king of Knossos had presided here over the last rites before his palace was engulfed in flames. It may be possible to interpret the finds in the Throne Sanctuary differently from Evans, but however interpreted they were sensational, showing that there had been another great Aegean civilization before the Mycenean civilization.[29]

By 1905 it was clear from its size and wealth that the great building at Knossos must have been the focus of the new civilization. The top 12 metres of the low hill on which the temple ruins stood were made of the debris of earlier phases of settlement on the spot. There had been a neolithic village on the site in 6100 BC, rebuilt ten times over, each time a little larger. By 3000 BC when the village had become a town of 2,000 people and covered about the same area as the later temple, major trade commodities were appearing: grapes, olives and metals. These created new webs of economic and political relationships among Crete and the other islands. From this time there was an onrush of developing trade, exchanges of ideas and increasing wealth. Societies in the Aegean region became more elaborate, stratified and organized, and it was within this context that the Cycladic culture seen in Thera and islands to the north evolved, and out of this that the Minoan culture developed in Crete.

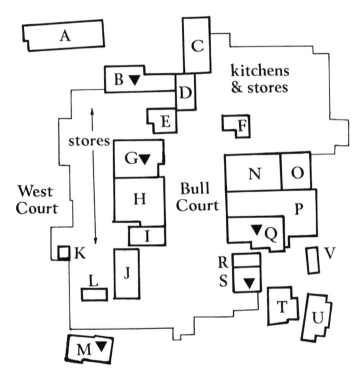

Figure 2.2 The Knossos Labyrinth: shrines and sanctuaries
Note: A: Theatral Area, B: Initiation Area, C: Pillar Hall, D: Bull Chamber, E: Lotus Lamp Sanctuary, F: North-East Sanctuary, G: Throne Sanctuary, H: Snake Goddess Sanctuary, I: Destroyed sanctuary, J: Cupbearer Sanctuary, K: West Porch Shrine, L: South-West Pillar Crypts, M: Silver Vessels Sanctuary, N: Great Goddess Sanctuary, O: Temple Workshops, P: Double-Axe Sanctuary, Q: Dolphin Sanctuary, R: Triton Shell Sanctuary, S: Late Dove Goddess Sanctuary, T: Chancel Screen Sanctuary, U: South-East Sanctuary, V: Monolithic Pillar Crypt. Black triangle = adyton

The spectacular temple culture which emerged in Crete in about 2000 BC was not a sudden explosion. It is possible to see forerunners of the temples in multi-room buildings raised between 2600 and 2000 BC, some on the sites of the later temples. The murals at Knossos and other artefacts found at contemporary sites on Crete show a rich and exotic world revolving round elaborate religious ceremonies including bull sacrifices and the spectacularly dangerous bull-leaping ritual. Religious practices absorbed huge quantities of time, labour and wealth.

Women were dominant in that world. The Grandstand Fresco shows a huge but orderly crowd, of both men and women, watching a formal spectacle from an architectural facade remarkably like the east front of the West Wing, the wall facing into the Central Court. A group of high-status women, shown larger and in greater detail, sits in a place of honour, watching a spectacle in the Central Court, possibly the bull dance.

The temple was the focus of city life at Knossos: it stood at the centre of a city extending over 500 metres in all directions. The road system converged on the West Court, a concourse within the temple precinct yet outside the Labyrinth itself. The West Court was probably the public meeting place, where ordinary citizens might come to see a priestess 'appearing' at an upper storey window in the guise of a goddess, bedecked in a multi-layered overskirt, patterned apron, elaborate headdress, and with a sleeved bodice that left her breasts exposed. This priestess-goddess is shown in numerous artworks, such as the statuette found in the Temple Treasury and dating from about 1600 BC. The men in the murals were proud of bearing, yet subservient to the high-status women. Whether this was true throughout Cretan society or prevailed only in the temples is hard to tell, as nearly all the scenes are religious in nature. We cannot see the whole panorama of Minoan life in the finds from Knossos.

Nevertheless, the artwork was so distinctive that Arthur Evans knew he had unearthed the power centre of a previously unsuspected *pre*-Mycenean civilization. He also knew it had evolved independently of the Greek mainland, out in the islands, which were open to contacts with Anatolia, Libya and Egypt. This in turn led to a re-evaluation of the finds on Santorini. The houses excavated by Fouqué from 1866 onwards, Mamet and Gorceix in 1870, and Zahn in 1899 – all were recognized to be bronze age in date. But were they Mycenean, or did they belong to the newly discovered civilization, named 'Minoan' by Evans? It now seemed likely that they represented a colonial offshoot of the Minoan civilization. Evans developed the idea of a Minoan sea-empire, with Cretan rulers in political and economic control of the Aegean Sea. Greek legends about King Minos and the Tribute-Children suggested an oral tradition of a bronze age Cretan dynasty menacing and dominating the coastal cities of the Greek mainland.

An entirely new scenario for the Aegean bronze age emerged. Before the ascendancy of the Mycenean civilization, which had flourished on the mainland for three or four centuries from about 1500 BC, there had been an earlier civilization, more spectacular and more ambitious than the Mycenean, with a focus out

Plate 2.1 Phaistos, a Minoan temple in southern Crete: view towards Bull Court along the North Wing Corridor (with central drain)

in the south Aegean. Its capital city, a thriving metropolis of 80,000 people according to Evans's estimate, was Knossos, where a great dynasty ruled in barbaric splendour from a sprawling palace, first over a small region of central Crete, then over the whole of Crete and over colonies set up on the other Aegean islands. This outline is remarkably close to Plato's description of Atlantis. Indeed, the Egyptologist James Baikie was pointing out parallels between Plato's Atlantis and the picture emerging from Evans's excavations in the early 1900s, supported in 1909 and 1913 by K. T. Frost.[30] There was little interest in Baikie's and Frost's proposal, but their idea opened a door into a corridor many others would walk down during the twentieth century: an interpretation of bronze age Crete as Atlantis.

After Evans's work at Knossos, the connection between Knossos and Thera looked obvious. There had been Cretan colonies or trading stations on many islands in the Aegean, and Thera was an obvious location for one. Then, as Evans's work at Knossos came to an end, another great figure in Aegean archaeology, Spyridon Marinatos, began to make his own discoveries and find another link connecting the ancient destinies of Crete and Thera.

In 1932 Marinatos excavated a Minoan villa on the beach at Amnisos. According to his own account, Marinatos was prompted to go to Amnisos because of a reference in Strabo, a traditiony mention that a harbour town and arsenal once existed at Amnisos. Amnisos is more famously mentioned in Homer as the harbour town of late bronze age Knossos,[31] but perhaps Marinatos did not want to call on Homer as evidence and rouse suspicion that he saw himself as Schliemann's heir. His hunch was in any case justified. He found a villa with frescoes and another filled with pumice. Publishing his finds in 1939, Marinatos proposed a new and important link between the islands – that the bronze age eruption of Thera had brought to an end the Minoan civilization on Crete.[32]

Marinatos found pumice and beach sand among Minoan ruins. He found large stone blocks dislocated as if by the powerful dragging action of a large mass of water. Pumice pointed to a major volcanic eruption. The beach sand on this subsiding north coast of Crete must have been sent inland by powerful waves from a shoreline perhaps 50 metres to the north. The great mass of water could have been a tsunami caused by the eruption on Thera. Marinatos mulled over these ideas for some years before offering them in print, and the editor of *Antiquity* published a disclaimer saying that more evidence was needed.[33] Nicolas Platon, excavating a seashore temple at Zakro in eastern Crete, was convinced by the presence of pumice and thick layers of volcanic ash that he had found evidence to support Marinatos's theory.[34]

We arrive at a situation where remains of an exotic bronze age civilization are found on two adjacent Aegean islands, in each case associated with and apparently engulfed by pumice and ash and other traces of a great volcanic eruption. In the 1950s Marinatos was still developing the idea that the Minoan civilization was wiped out by the Thera eruption, but he had done no further

Plate 2.2 Zakro, a Minoan temple on the east coast of Crete: the rectangular space in the centre is the Bull Court

work to test it. The 'additional support from excavations on selected sites' recommended by Glyn Daniel in 1939 was only to come in 1967, at Akrotiri, but it was to come from Marinatos.

BRONZE AGE ATHENS

Atlantologists have been obsessed with finding Atlantis to the extent that they have often forgotten that there is another country, another city, in Plato's story. The story is as much about Athens as about Atlantis. This section of the *Critias* is glossed over because everyone knows where Athens is, and there is a natural assumption that Plato must be rehearsing a well-worn traditionary account of his city's history. Nevertheless, for the story to have any internal consistency, the Athens he describes needs to be the Athens of the bronze age, contemporary with the Atlantean cities of Knossos and Therassos, the bronze age name of Akrotiri.

Ideas about Athens' prehistory were still in a formative stage when Plato lived, but there was at least one history of Attica from the earliest times (a work by Hellanicus written in around 400 BC), a survey of Athenian prehistory in the history of the Peloponnesian War by Thucydides, and allusions to it in the plays of Euripides, Sophocles and Aeschylus. Whether Plato got his material from Athenian or, as he said, Egyptian historians, he used it more than once – it crops up again in the *Menexenus* – but this in no way helps to trace its origin; it would be possible for the account of Athens to have been drawn from Solon's notes twice over. Interestingly, Plato does not say who was king of Athens at the time of the destruction of Atlantis. He might have put in Cranaus, who according to one tradition was king at the time of Deucalion's flood; but he deliberately put the story earlier still because he knew it was a piece of very ancient history. To emphasize this, he said it was the third flood before Deucalion's.

Several points in Plato's description of proto-Athens match the late bronze age Acropolis very closely. There was no-one there in 9600 BC, but a settlement was founded around 3500 BC, and a city stood there in the Mycenean period. The use of the plural form 'Athenai' reflects the union of several city-states and this parallels the tradition that Theseus achieved the federation of Attica, centred on Athens, after which time the lesser cities were emptied and their citizens made to resettle in Athens. Excavation at Brauron, one of the twelve cities of Attica, shows that it was abandoned in about 1300 BC without any trace of destruction, suggesting that its citizens simply packed and left.[35]

There was a decline in literacy when proto-Athens was destroyed in around 1200 BC. Plato mentions that only the unlettered survived, and it does seem that in the cities that have been excavated Linear B then went out of use. The tightly disciplined and highly stratified society Plato describes (*Tim.* 24A–B, *Crit.* 117B–C, *Crit.* 119A–C) is exemplified by the Linear B tablet archives found in several Mycenean cities. None have been found on the Athenian Acropolis,

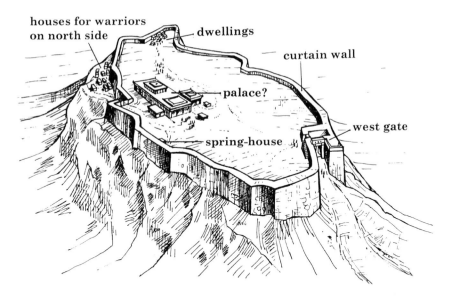

Figure 2.3 The Athenian Acropolis in the bronze age, view from the west
Source: developed from an air photograph of the Acropolis today and the plan published by Broneer (1956)

because most of the earlier remains on the site were destroyed by later temple-building. The tradition available to Plato, from Homer, was that the Myceneans were wild, swashbuckling warrior-heroes. The more disciplined side of this society lay hidden until the discovery and decipherment of Linear B tablets in the twentieth century, and therefore should not have been known to Plato.

Plato tells us that 'warriors lived on the Acropolis surrounded by a single wall like the garden of a single house' (*Crit.* 112B). The Mycenean citadels at Mycenae and Tiryns are exactly like this, and the remains of a thirteenth-century curtain wall can still be seen surrounding the Athenian Acropolis. He goes on to describe warriors living on the north side of the Acropolis, and archaeology shows that the settlement was indeed concentrated on the north side. This is not in Thucydides.

Plato also mentions 'a single spring within the area of the present Acropolis, subsequently choked by the earthquake' (*Crit.* 112D). This spring remained hidden and entirely unsuspected until the 1930s, when a spring-house was found just inside the north wall, where Mycenean Athenians had sunk a shaft to reach groundwater 35 metres below. The excavators inferred that the well had indeed been damaged in an earthquake near the end of the thirteenth century, after which it had not been reopened.[36] Plato did not have access to this archaeological information, so the only explanation is that some record or description of the Acropolis as it was before 1230 BC was somehow preserved, in spite of the literacy failure in around 1200 BC.

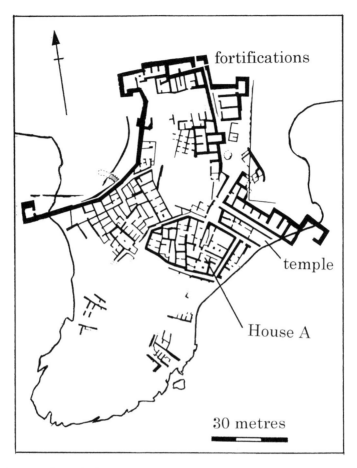

Figure 2.4 Ayia Irini, the bronze age town

Recent archaeological evidence suggests that Mycenae and the other towns of the Argolid were destroyed in the decades around 1200 BC by a major earth-quake and the ensuing fires, landslides and floods. It may have been the same earthquake that choked the well on the Athenian Acropolis, but Athens and the other towns of Attica survived; possibly they were swamped by the influx of refugees from the Peloponnese, and this led to a disintegration of the Mycenean way of life.[37] It begins to look as if the Mycenean civilization was crippled by a major natural disaster in a similar way to that proposed for the Minoan, and perhaps we need to reconsider the role of physical geography in the ebb and flow of civilizations. Certainly Plato was right to say that proto-Athens came to an end at a time of natural disaster.

The proto-Athenian element may have been preserved in Athens until the time of Solon but, if so, why do the details listed by Plato not appear in the accounts of other Greek authors? An alternative must remain that all the genuinely bronze age elements (Cretan, Cycladic and Athenian elements alike) were transmitted to Egypt and conserved there.

Information was certainly transported in antiquity; the wooden covers of a book survived in a bronze age shipwreck off the south coast of Turkey.[38] Possibly the transmission did not occur until after the earthquake that sealed the well on the Acropolis, that is, in about 1225 BC, though that would mean that some centre of literacy in the Mycenean world kept documents about Minoan Crete and the destruction of Thera for 300 years. Possibly the account of Athens was preserved in Egypt, but arrived separately, after the other bronze age material, and it was Solon who collated all three elements in Egypt. Certainly it is easier to understand the sheer exoticism of the Atlantis story if it is seen as a bronze age story conserved in Egypt rather than as a classical Greek tradition. The very fact that later Greek and Roman historians were unable to reconcile Atlantis with the conventional mythology suggests the story came into the classical Greek world from outside.

Sonoma Valley High School Library

3

THERA: THE SECOND
REDISCOVERY

In Marinatos' mind, Atlantis was self-evidently Minoan Crete, its coastlands swamped by tsunamis sent out by the Thera eruption. If the Aegean location appeared strange when the classical Greek version of the story held that Atlantis was far to the west, then that would be explained by the story originating in Egypt, as Plato said. To the ancient Egyptians, Crete and the other Aegean islands were far to the west. In 1950, Marinatos wrote:

> The Egyptians heard about the sinking of an island, which was Thera, but this island, small and insignificant, was unknown to them. This event they transferred to the neighbouring Crete, an island which was dreadfully struck and with which they had lost contact suddenly.

In other words, the Platonic story, filtered through the perception of Egyptian priests, compressed and combined two separate but related events, the explosion and large-scale subsidence of Thera and the (possibly consequent) implosion and collapse of the Cretan economy. That the great Atlantean civilization had flourished on Thera too had not yet occurred to Marinatos.

THE DISCOVERY OF AYIA IRINI

The discovery of a bronze age town at Ayia Irini on Kea in the north-west Cyclades was another stepping-stone towards Atlantis. Kea is small, 22 kilometres long, with a cliffed coastline and three harbours offering shelter from the strong north winds. The bronze age town straddled a small peninsula running out into the northern end of the largest harbour, Koressia Bay. The sea has risen 2 metres since the bronze age, encroaching 10 metres all round the peninsula and leaving the ruins of the massive town wall stranded out in shallow water to east and west. The fortifications were first built in about 1750 BC, rebuilt about 1550 BC, and replaced under Mycenean domination in the fourteenth century BC.[1] The sixteenth-century wall-ends sticking up out of the sea are very conspicuous and many archaeologists had already noticed them when, in 1960, John Caskey began his excavations.[2]

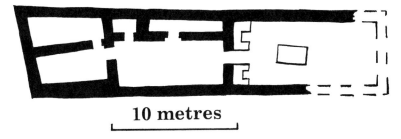

10 metres

Figure 3.1 The temple at Ayia Irini

What Caskey found was a small bronze age port consisting of a scrum of Cycladic houses, home to perhaps a thousand people. A great deal of pottery from Crete was found, implying that it was a Cretan colony during part of its long history. In view of what was shortly to emerge on Thera, the finds of fragments of miniature fresco were highly significant. They may be reconstructed as scenes of hunting, food preparation, offerings and general celebration, and possibly illustrate a festival of some kind.[3]

The discovery of a temple at Ayia Irini was even more significant. To the south-west of this long narrow building was a large pentagonal block 30 metres across; if, with its thirty or so rooms, it was a single dwelling, it was probably the house of the town's leading family. House A's first floor was decorated with frescoes. The family living here may have been responsible for the temple next door. The temple itself was 20–25 metres long and consisted of two main rooms with four smaller rooms opening off them, rather like the Throne Sanctuary at Knossos. There are also the equivalents of bench altars (two stone platforms built up against a wall, again, as at Knossos) and a freestanding stone altar in the middle of the main chamber. Signs of burning suggest sacrificial hearths and there were large numbers of drinking cups implying libations.[4]

Remains of over fifty terracotta figures up to life size show that the temple was dedicated to a goddess. The largest statue shows a mature woman with her breasts exposed, a garland round her neck (like the Theran matron in Figure 8.15). Her face is derived from earlier Cycladic models in being spade-shaped, but she has large eyes and a gentle, humane smile: she is quite unlike the hideous idols produced by the later Myceneans.[5] We shall meet her again on Thera. The idols were not only placed on the stone altars, but repeatedly moved about; they show varying signs of wear and repair. Some are older, some newer. The cult evidently revolved round this steadily growing company of goddesses. A similar collection of idols was found on a bench altar in the Late Dove Goddess Sanctuary at Knossos. The discovery of terracotta feet at Ayia Irini suggests the existence of a major cult statue.[6] The feet are similar to those found at the Anemospilia temple on Mount Juktas in Crete. The evidence overall points to a strong influence from Minoan Crete: the style of the figures, the feet, the stone libation tables, the stone platforms for idols, the shrine with adjacent

Figure 3.2 Terracotta goddess from the Ayia Irini temple

preparation rooms. Terracotta offerings suggest that craft industries nearby manufactured votives and cult equipment, as in the temple workshops in the East Wing at Knossos.

In the 1960s, Ayia Irini emerged as part of a huge, far-flung Minoan empire. If Minoan Crete could be seen as Atlantis, then from its cultural affinities so could Late Cycladic Kea, and by inference at least some, and maybe all, of the islands in between. The scene was set for the recognition of a southern Aegean Atlantis.

MAVOR AND MARINATOS

In 1965, ideas of Atlantis, massive eruptions and subsiding calderas were in the air, and an engineer from Woods Hole Oceanographic Institution visited Athens to enlist support for an expedition to Thera.[7] There, James Mavor met Angelos Galanopoulos, a seismologist who followed Marinatos in believing that the lost civilization of Plato's Atlantis was the Minoan civilization. Galanopoulos made the important additional contribution of reconstructing Plato's story as a story of *two* islands: the larger (Crete) was the 'royal state', the smaller (Thera) the 'metropolis' or capital city and religious centre.[8] In one significant respect this reverses the archaeological findings, which tell us that Knossos on Crete was the capital and religious centre and Thera the outpost and

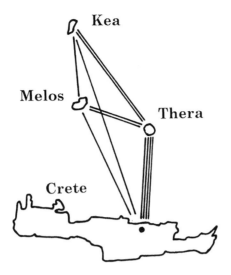

Figure 3.3 Exchanges of ideas among Kea, Melos, Thera and Crete

possession. Galanopoulos circumvented this problem by attributing the trans-position of smaller and larger islands to a simple mistake in retelling: the story may have been repeated orally many times before it was written down.

In July 1966 the Research Vessel *Chain* left Woods Hole for the Mediterranean. Mavor knew of Marinatos' interest in Thera and of his ideas connecting Thera with Minoan Crete. He also knew that Marinatos believed that the fate of Thera was commemorated in Plato's story of Atlantis, so he invited Marinatos to join them. In the first of several communication failures, Marinatos did not reply until the expedition was over. Mavor's lively account makes one wonder whether the invitation was couched in terms that Marinatos would easily understand; he writes excitably of the *Chain* sailing to the Mediterranean, then of flying to Rome to meet the Pomerances of Great Neck before they departed for Crete to meet Nicolas Platon at the newly discovered temple at Zakro, then flying on to Athens where he was diverted to Corinth to see the (unrelated) excavations there. How clear would this breathless itinerary or its purpose have been to Marinatos? It seems that in any case Marinatos was in Australia, returning to Greece only in September.

The arrival of the *Chain* at Thera in August 1966 marked the start of serious data gathering. A seismic profile of the seabed revealed stratified volcanic debris within the caldera, confirming that the void between Thera and Therasia had been created as much by collapse as by blowing out. A series of eruptions lead-ing up to 1520 BC had emptied the magma chamber, then its unsupported vault had collapsed, letting sea water and rock tumble in, causing a violent explosion and tsunamis. The seismic profiler was not operated again until the ship was leaving the caldera, so no second radial trace was obtained, which Mavor hoped

Plate 3.1 Stone mortars were eroded from the ash by stream and wave erosion: Marinatos saw these naturally excavated mortars and knew the settlement must be in the vicinity

would help define his circular harbour. This may have been merciful, as it is unlikely that on the caldera site there were ever concentric channels or harbours as Plato described (*Crit.* 113C, 115D–E). Mavor hoped to find the houses, breakwaters and public buildings of Atlantis, lowered into the Mediterranean as the caldera subsided, but, even if these structures had once existed, he was over-optimistic about their survival in open environments. The survival of part of a bronze age city under pumice and ash at Akrotiri is exceptional and should not lead us to expect that anything recognizable survives on the seabed, in the caldera or in an exposed area subjected to volcanic blast. In fact the seismic profiler could not identify objects smaller than 10 metres across, so even complete houses would have gone unrecorded.

Mavor had two young Englishmen diving to the seabed in search of Atlantean buildings, with no conclusive result. In northern Therasia, Mavor and Loring found the Minoan land surface, with a buried soil 30 metres above sea level containing sherds from the pre-eruption period. Near Cape Riva on Therasia Mavor saw a 'Minoan' anchor. It is not clear how he could have known it was Minoan, although from its shape – triangular with a single hole in it – it might have been. Another curiosity is the report by Abbé Pègues of a marble Egyptian sarcophagus found by labourers in 1836. It was inscribed with non-Greek writing and decorated with figures of birds and deer. The farm workers smashed it up and buried the pieces; Mavor did not rediscover any of them, and given the lack of archaeological context they would not have advanced his argument if he had. The expedition continued with a visit to the Dorian ruins on Mesa Vouno.

Mavor emerged from this tangle of loose ends with his vision of the destruction of Atlantis intact. Galanopoulos left the expedition believing that land excavations on Santorini could contribute little of value in verifying the Atlantis theory: buildings such as palaces or temples in the centre must have been destroyed when the caldera collapsed. Galanopoulos was right, yet Mavor clung to his idea of 'a prehistoric Pompeii. . . . A city preserved under impervious ash would contain many important artefacts that had perished at other Minoan sites – and perhaps Linear A tablets.' Mavor was right, but then the Fouqué, Mamet, Gorceix and Zahn excavations had proved already that Minoan houses were preserved in good order under the ash.

Marinatos wrote to Mavor in April 1967 saying that he, Marinatos, had been appointed director-general for any excavation in Santorini. The Archaeological Service would put up US $2000: would Mavor put up a similar sum? Then came the military *coup* and Marinatos' fortunes changed rapidly with the colonels in charge; in May a letter from Marinatos announced 'the political situation here is excellent'.

Marinatos finally travelled to Santorini with Mavor. In getting Marinatos to Santorini and in particular to Akrotiri James Mavor made a contribution to archaeology that has been insufficiently recognized. Mavor knew he was dealing with a complex, difficult man. But for the moment that was forgotten and all the loose ends were thrown aside. The one firm lead, the discovery of well-preserved houses in the Akrotiri peninsula, was the one Mavor followed through. Unfortunately neither the Fouqué house in the Akrotiri ravine nor the Zahn house in the Potamos ravine could be found again; weathering, slope failure and the resumption of viticulture had obliterated all trace of them. The lower parts of either of these ravines seemed likely to produce good results, but Marinatos was not prepared to dig at random. In 1967 an old mason from Megalochori remembered the floor of a donkey cave collapsing some years before, revealing what looked like a room underneath. Close by, a section of a field had suddenly subsided in a similar way, as if under the ash there were room-like cavities. Marinatos heard these stories and also remembered the Zahn excavation. Mavor and Marinatos found the cave partly filled in by slope wash and other debris. In the valley side the stratification of the pumice could be seen. Close to the cave the strata ran horizontally, but stepped down a metre on each side as if pumice drifting southwards across the landscape during the bronze age eruption had coated a raised, flat-topped block: a flat-roofed house, perhaps.

This was to be the location of one of the first trial trenches. The landowner, Stathis Arvanitis, led Marinatos to a spot in the area where the ground had collapsed and where ploughing was difficult because of masses of stone; these later proved to be the lintel stones of the window above the entrance to Building 4, the West House. Marinatos realized the significance of this local field-lore, and he could see for himself the prehistoric mortars that labourers had pulled out of the ash for watering animals. He had the evidence he needed.

Mavor was uneasy about Marinatos, who seemed to be talking at cross purposes with the rest of the party. Mavor attributed this to an imperfect understanding of English, but Marinatos was exploiting this understandable assumption to pursue his own ends. Marinatos was *thinking* at cross purposes. He was Long John Silver, waiting for the rest of the pirates to unearth the treasure: then he would have it all for himself. He was uninterested in the Americans' magnetometer results. He had already decided where to excavate. It has been said that Marinatos' choice of site was inspired,[9] but it was arrived at by logical inference, schemed out well before the visit to Santorini. The very next year, Marinatos confirmed this when he wrote, 'An archaeological investigation on the island of Thera was planned many years ago by the writer,' with the comment that he had inferred from the work of Gorceix and Mamet that Akrotiri was the best site to investigate.[10]

THE DIG AT AKROTIRI BEGINS

Spyridon Marinatos began his historic excavations at Akrotiri in 1967. One trench was begun at the donkey cave, where the seismograph had indicated an irregular stratum about 4 metres down: this turned out to be a layer of spectacular finds. The workers were scarcely waist-deep when the first bronze age pottery appeared. Marinatos had shown only a passing interest in Mavor's technology. 'Still the best archaeological tool is the shovel', he said smugly. 'It works well and does not speak.' After an exhausting bout of seismic surveying elsewhere on the site, Mavor returned to find Marinatos looking into a pit. 'I do not need you any more', said Marinatos. 'Not you or your friends. But do your tests anyway. Here we have found the walls of a house.' Marinatos at last showed his hand: the dig was his.[11]

Marinatos was keen to have Mavor's help in one further particular. He wanted a seismographic survey of the whole field. If it turned out that the Minoan land surface was fairly level, the site would be a plausible choice for a city. This was the case: the gently sloping bronze age landscape was ideal for urban development. Mavor was keen to find and reopen Zahn's excavation, spending some time trying to rediscover the site, but Marinatos was not interested, sensibly deciding to limit his excavation to the one valley for the time being.[12]

By the second day of Marinatos's excavations an entire upper-storey room was revealed. He had what he needed. He backfilled the trenches for security and a lull followed while he worked on the expropriation of the site. Five days of feverish excavation followed Marinatos's return; he opened nine trenches on both sides of the ravine, each producing evidence of a bronze age township. The workmen were less than a metre below the surface when the shout of 'Wall plaster! Frescoes!' went up. The structure was a building two or three storeys high consisting of small rooms and passages with many of the plastered walls still in place.

Another pit revealed a facade of large limestone blocks in ashlar masonry skilfully fitted together using square dowel-holes for bronze pins to hold the quoins in position, a standard practice imported from Minoan Crete. The facade with its fine Minoan masonry marked the north entrance to a conglomeration of chambers known as Block Delta (Building 12). The 'courtyard' to the north was the Central Square, an almost accidental space bounded by Block Delta to the south, the West House to the west, the House of the Ladies to the north and

Plate 3.2 Minoan masonry techniques in use in Thera: cornerstones were fixed together with square bronze dowel pins, just as at Knossos

another building to the east. Limestone blocks from the top of the wall had come to rest on the ground, where they were covered by coarse pumice, showing that a major earthquake had toppled the upper storey before the major pumice eruption. Nearby, fallen wall stones lay on top of the coarse pumice, so another severe earthquake must have shaken down some more of the wall after the pumice fall had begun. The sequence of events in the destruction of Atlantis was beginning to piece itself together.

Marinatos gives his own account, illustrating his difficult relationship with the American team. He quarrelled with Emily Vermeule about 'the interpretation of certain important passages of the Bible'.[13] What the disagreement was about is not worth pursuing, but he was ready to turn it into a conflict, and dignify it with publication. In his *Second Report on the Thera Excavations*[14] he makes no other mention of the Americans, who were undoubtedly there and helping, and who had contributed financially.

Marinatos appeared cautious in his evaluation of the site, but was in no doubt about its importance. He had found 'remnants of a grand city with numerous palaces and streets and signs of an old culture'. The summer of 1967 ended with Marinatos summoned back to Athens by the colonels, from where he sent Mavor a cutting of his press release. Mavor publicized the 'Minoan Pompeii in the Aegean Sea', truthfully describing it as 'one of the most startling archaeological events of this generation'. Marinatos was nettled by the publicity Mavor had trawled and reacted tetchily when interviewers pressed him to say that Akrotiri was Atlantis; he would say only that the 'palaces' he had discovered could be as important as Knossos. Marinatos was sometimes ready publicly to admit that he thought Minoan Santorini was Atlantis, but in the TV *Chronicle* interview he gave to Magnus Magnusson he was coy: 'It is not for archaeologists to say.' By this he implied that others, media people like Magnusson for instance, could say it for them.

Mavor has tried to make sense of the rift that developed in terms of misunderstandings, but the explanation is simpler. Marinatos was aware early on that he had stumbled on a very important site; he wanted it for himself and did not want to share the glory with others, especially foreigners, and he wanted those foreigners off the site without delay. His only problem was finding a pretext, and a slight over the date of Mavor's press release was just sufficient. Had Marinatos wished to continue to collaborate with Mavor – if indeed he had ever genuinely collaborated – a small matter like this would have been no barrier. The *New York Times* recognized the rift and gave details of Marinatos's accusation that the American team had made its results public before he had made his official report to the Greek authorities. The newspaper noted his promotion to Inspector-General of Greek Antiquities.

Mavor receded from the story of Minoan Thera, bravely trying to come to terms with the way Marinatos had treated him. He paid tribute to Marinatos's ability, 'broader view' and historical insight, but felt betrayed. Jim Mavor's boundless enthusiasm for the Santorini–Atlantis project and his ability to

Plate 3.3 The bronze age city at Akrotiri, general view: the 'torrent' passing intermittently down the ravine eroded the site from bottom right to top left

enthuse others in it counted for a great deal. He persuaded Marinatos to go to Akrotiri, and his ideas had a catalytic effect on him, reconnecting his Minoan researches on Crete in the 1930s with the archaeology and volcanic prehistory of Santorini. He brought Marinatos to the right place to rediscover, for the second time in a century, the lost Atlantean city of Therassos.

4

THE BRONZE AGE CITY OF
THERA EMERGES

'I SEE WITH THE EYES OF MY SOUL . . . '

Marinatos returned to excavate the Akrotiri ravine site in 1968, without the Americans. After a brief experiment with tunnels,[1] excavation proceeded by the normal 'opencast' method. A problem was that the door and window frames had disintegrated leaving only pumice moulds. He found a simple solution: pouring concrete into the moulds and letting it harden simulated the wood even down to the grain, and gave long-lasting support.

Marinatos did not work to the Mortimer Wheeler system of digging in grid squares, so one cannot always be sure how some of the early finds fit into the present site plan. Marinatos's quirkiness extended to a peculiarly inconsistent way of naming the excavated buildings. Some he designated by letters of the alphabet, like Sector Alpha; others he singled out for their fine ashlar masonry, like Xeste 4. One he named according to the frescoes of women on its walls: the House of the Ladies. Another, the West House, he named according to its position in relation to the other houses so far excavated.[2] On a site with only twenty buildings, Marinatos used four different schemes for naming them.[3]

For all his eccentricities, Marinatos produced large numbers of finds: stone tools, pottery, mortars, pestles and negatives in pumice of furniture. The numbers of wall-paintings increased; in 1969 he found a painting of monkeys clambering over what seemed to be the rocky hills west of Akrotiri. Then, in 1970, came the climactic discovery of the Spring Fresco in Room Delta 2, not only a masterpiece of prehistoric art but complete and still in position. It put Minoan Thera firmly on the map as far as the international community was concerned and implied that many more exciting finds awaited discovery, maybe richer, larger and more exotic frescoes that would speak even more eloquently of the bronze age way of life. The double-axe symbol inscribed on the base of a pot in the Spring Fresco Room seemed to sign the culture 'Minoan'.[4]

Marinatos started clearing the lower levels of the room. In the north-east corner was a mass of hardened ash with a hole in it; suspecting it was a cast of some kind, Marinatos had plaster poured into the hole. When the plaster was

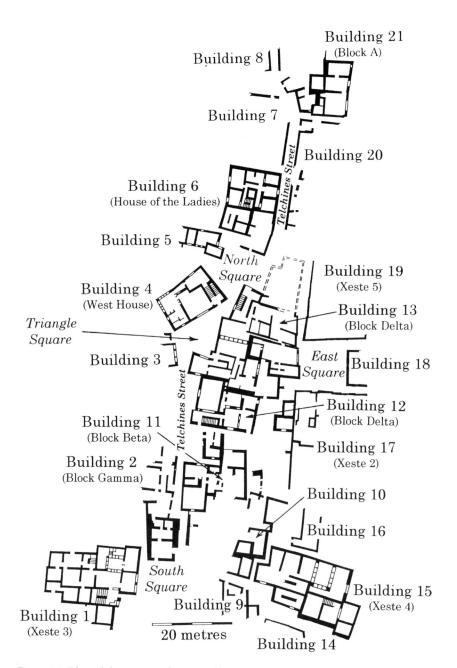

Figure 4.1 Plan of the excavated area at Akrotiri

hard, Marinatos had the ash removed to reveal the shape of a wooden bed. Its legs had not rested directly on the floor: 10 centimetres of ash had accumulated before the bed was taken into the room. This peculiar find was a reminder that the disaster that overwhelmed Thera was not a single continuous event. The earthquakes that preceded the final eruption damaged some houses and not others. Some houses kept their roofs and became refuges for the dwindling number of people remaining in Akrotiri. Perhaps Delta was a refuge. Perhaps someone carried the bed into the Lilies Room and set it down against the wall after ash from an early phase of the eruption had wafted in through a window.[5] But a reconstruction of the fall of Thera should wait until later. The bed had some sort of coverlet, which was pushed back as the sleeper awoke: the bed was left unmade.

In 1971, Marinatos tied the excavation pits together, clearing the central area of Delta, finding the northward extension of Telchines Street, the main road. He also wanted to clear the southern part of the city all the way to the coast. This ambition was never achieved, but the small East Square was discovered at the junction of three roads together with the walls of two buildings fronting its western and southern edges. On the northern edge of a second public square, the Triangle Square, the facade of another important building, the West House, was uncovered. Inside the West House, Marinatos discovered the miniature frescoes that were to tell the world so much about bronze age Thera.[6]

The following year, the rest of the Triangle Square was cleared, revealing evidence that after the first phase of the eruption sequence the Therans had moved debris to clear a way through Telchines Street, building retaining walls to stop debris slumping back across the road. In 1973, Marinatos's last full season at Akrotiri, the ancient city emerged from the ash at a bewildering rate and he realized that he was seeing only a small fraction of it, that it had once stretched from the shore to the south all the way up to the caldera rim. He had no hope, even if he lived to a great age and went on excavating at his present rate, of seeing the city in its entirety. As it was, he had only a year to live. The uncovering of a finely built house at what was and still is the south-western corner of the excavation was the high point of this final season. Xeste 3 yielded so many slabs of fresco that there was not enough room for them in the laboratories in Athens. The discovery of the great female initiation frescoes was a crowning achievement, though it proved an embarrassment to an Archaeological Service unprepared for conservation work on this scale.[7]

While supervising the excavations in 1974, Spyridon Marinatos was characteristically standing on a wall top when he fell backwards and struck his head fatally on a stone in Telchines Street. His work has been continued by Professor Christos Doumas who is clearing the partially excavated buildings to lower levels.[8]

ARCHITECTURE OF A LATE CYCLADIC CITY

The excavations give us a window 150 metres long and 80 metres wide into a bronze age city that may have covered one square kilometre. Plato tells us that the Metropolis of Atlantis was bounded by water and measured 5 stades in diameter, in other words 1 kilometere, just like the city at Akrotiri (*Crit.* 116A). We can make many useful inferences from the excavation-window, but we must allow for the fact that we are seeing only a sample, perhaps one per cent, of the whole picture, and a randomly located sample at that.[9] We do not know whether we are looking at the city centre, a maze of back streets close to the centre, a zone of middle-class housing some distance from the centre, or suburban villas near the city edge. The Minoan houses on the caldera rim to the north at Balos and in the Mavromatis quarry could have been part of the city. Zahn's house, 500 metres away to the east, was probably also part of it. These dimensions imply a city of several thousand inhabitants.

The southern coastline would obviously have been a limit to the town's expansion. The present shore 230 metres south of Xeste 3 is made of ash and stones from the Minoan eruption, and this would argue for a Minoan shore 50–100 metres closer to the excavation. On the other hand, sea level was two metres lower in the bronze age than now, which brings the Minoan shore close to its present map position. An excavation for wells in the area shows that the sea must have encroached significantly further north just to the west of the archaeological site. The flat-floored valley between the hill of Mesa Vouno and the ridge of Mavros Rachidhi is protected from westerly winds by the high ridge; inundated, this would have made an excellent harbour and undoubtedly explains why this location was chosen for the city.[10]

The South Wall Frieze in the West House is a landscape showing a coastal town (Town 5) on the right, a harbour packed with ships on the left and a rocky ridge in the background stepping down in a series of rounded humps ending in a low steep promontory. When the skyline on the fresco is compared with the skyline as seen from the archaeological site, the known site of the bronze age city, the similarity is too close to be coincidental. The wall-painting is a careful depiction of the Theran city as seen from the east, with the harbour beyond. The swirling multicoloured rocks painted on the fresco promontory are a fair representation of the unusual black, green and red rocks to be seen just beyond the real headland at Red Beach. On the third hump of the fresco version of Mavros Rachidhi the artist has painted a large isolated building; at this location on Mavros Rachidhi degraded prehistoric walls of red lava blocks cover an area 40 metres by 15 metres. The location suggests a watchtower, giving warning of ships approaching from the west or south.

The thrust of this is clear. Town 5 is bronze age Akrotiri as seen by a bronze age painter looking westwards across the site; as such the fresco image is of enormous value as a document. It shows a hugger-mugger of close-packed rectangular build-ings with corniced flat roofs at different levels, rectangular windows of different

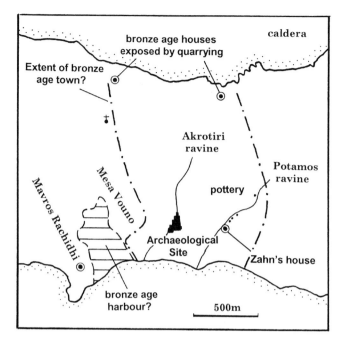

Figure 4.2 The bronze age town at Akrotiri (a large area remains to be excavated)

Figure 4.3 Fresco Town 5 on the South Frieze; this is almost certainly Akrotiri

Figure 4.4 Above: Town 5, ships and skyline from the South Frieze; below: field sketch of the western skyline and coastline as seen by the author from the Akrotiri excavation

sizes and balconies where people stand and look out to sea. Others gather on open ground in front of the town wall with its wooden gate.

Of the town wall and gate there are, as yet, no archaeological traces, but the hugger-mugger of houses is plain to see. Most of the rooms, corridors, hallways and stairways are rectangular or nearly so and the exterior form of the building plan is often stepped where interior spaces push the walls out to varying distances. The buildings are not laid out in any formal pattern: there is no sign of planning. Some of the buildings nest side by side with a parallel-sided road separating them, like Buildings 2 and 11 (Gamma and Beta). Others, like Building 4 (the West House), were built without regard for surrounding buildings. It is very like the city of Plato's Atlantis: 'numerous houses set close together' (*Crit.* 117E), though this could describe a hundred other Mediterranean settlements of other periods too.

The road system consists of narrow alleys grudgingly left between the buildings, their twists and turns probably a deliberate device to check wind speeds. The network is reminiscent of the streets of modern Phira, and it is tempting to see the two towns as part of the same Cycladic tradition. One difference is that Phira's streets mark out blocks comprising several dwellings, whereas in the ancient city the streets mark the boundaries of individual dwellings.[11] The streets teemed with activity. The earth of Telchines Street was pounded and compacted by heavy foot-traffic: lava blocks in the road surface were polished like mirrors.[12] Below this paving ran the city's sewers, narrow ditches lined and covered with stone slabs. They were linked to cess-pits, and took the sewage from lavatories inside the houses by way of clay pipes embedded in the house walls. The arrangement of lavatory and washroom adjacent to cult rooms in the West House is similar to that in the East Wing at Knossos,[13] a reminder that bronze age Therans shared the civilized way of

Plate 4.1 The remains of the Minoan building on Mavros Rachidhi

Plate 4.2 View east from Mavros Rachidhi. The Dexion shed covering the Akrotiri excavation (A) can be seen in the distance, left of centre; the bronze age town probably extended as far as the modern houses. B = bronze age harbour site

49

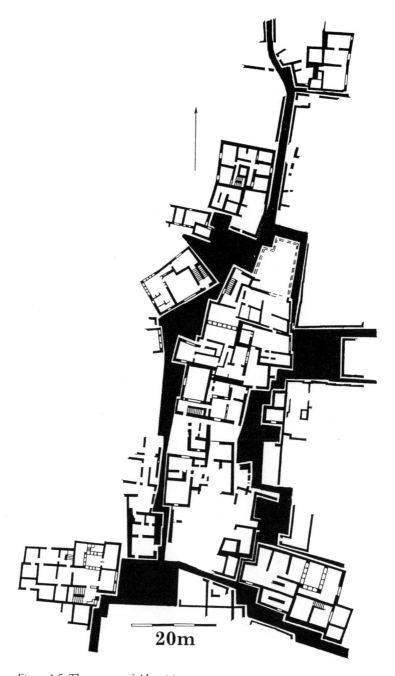

Figure 4.5 The streets of Akrotiri

life devised by their contemporaries on Crete. Sanitation as sophisticated as this would not be achieved in Europe for another 3,000 years.[14] Half-memories of the sophistication of Theran and Cretan water engineering may survive in Plato's description of a system of elaborate land drainage ditches (*Crit.* 118C) ('incredible that it should be so extensive and made by hand'), baths and conduits (*Crit.* 117B) and navigation channels (*Crit.* 115D–E).

Variations in plan and size between the buildings of Akrotiri suggest that each house was built to suit its owner's tastes and specifications, though some details were repeated. The front door was usually flanked by a window to light the hall when the door was shut, and to allow occupants to check who was knocking at the door before opening it. It was also usual for basements to have small windows, possibly to keep food cool, possibly for security. Windows on upper floors where people lived and slept were large. Some large windows were used as workplaces for craft industries in which strong lighting was an advantage: others were used to display wares – practices still common in the Aegean. Window dimensions show that the Therans used a Cretan unit, the Minoan foot of 0.304 metres.[15] In fact, Akrotiri displays many features seen in Cretan buildings: wooden columns on stone bases, masons' marks, ashlar facades, pier-and-door partitions, elaborate wall-paintings, at least one light well, adyta and the development of houses to two or more storeys. Elements of the 'Minoan' architectural style can be seen elsewhere in the Aegean: pillar crypts and wall-paintings at Phylakopi, light wells and wall-paintings at Ayia Irini, and ashlar facades and pier-and-door partitions at Triandha.[16]

Plate 4.3 Telchines Street, Akrotiri: Building 2 to left, Building 11 to right

Plate 4.4 Not Telchines Street, but a similar street in Minoan Gournia, Crete

Most houses were built of unshaped stones stuck together with clay. Timber was embedded in the walls to bind them together and resist earthquake damage, just as they were on Crete. Some believe that the frequent stepping of the wall line was to add strength. The dressed stones (ashlars) used for corners (quoins) would certainly have added strength, but it is just as likely that the projections arose from the internal planning of the rooms within the building and were seen as part of the aesthetic of the architecture. The interest of the exteriors relies on this inadvertence. Even in the great monumental architecture of the period, exemplified by the West Facade of the temple at Knossos, external projections and recesses were allowed to evolve as a result of internal arrangements of chambers; the overall north–south alignment of this wall would also have led to some striking contrasts between light, shadow and reflected light in the after-noon sun. It may have been features like this, inside-out architecture as the later Greeks would have seen it, which caused Plato to describe the Atlantean Temple of Poseidon as 'barbaric [or outlandish] in appearance' (*Crit.* 116D).

Dressed stones were used to frame some doors and windows, and in the case of some special buildings, notably 15, the whole of the exterior was encased in coursed ashlars. On the west front of Building 15, seven courses of very fine masonry have survived: the systematic reduction in course-height from bottom to top to give a good visual effect has been well calculated. Ashlars were also regularly used to make cornices, courses slightly projecting from the general wall surface, at each floor level. The cornices may have had a practical function, to provide a foundation for the rafters supporting the internal floor. It would have

Plate 4.5 North wall of Building 17, still standing three storeys high, showing cornices and casts of timbers

Plate 4.6 Door of Building 4

been useful for maintenance purposes to be able to identify load-bearing courses externally, and setting them proud of the rest of the wall made them easily distinguishable.[17]

The stone staircases were built on wooden frames between parallel walls. A layer of rubble and earth was piled onto the wooden frame and the stone steps set into the earth; this made it easy to replace damaged or worn steps without tampering with the walls. The Theran staircases have resolved an uncertainty about Minoan architecture on Crete. Archaeologists suspected that the two narrow side-by-side spaces found in many Cretan buildings were the shells of returning staircases: the more complete remains at Akrotiri confirmed that this was so.[18]

Floors were of beaten earth or flagstones; if the room was special, flagstones were laid and the gaps filled with painted plaster, just like the Throne Sanctuary floor at Knossos. From the fresco evidence, we know walls projected above the roof to make a parapet: this would have been useful if people frequently went up to walk about on the roof.

Roofs and upper-storey floors were sometimes supported by wooden pillars on stone bases in the centre of a large room. Where rooms were too large for a single pillar to support the ceiling, a pier-and-door partition was built instead: this was as strong as a wall but allowed people to walk through. The lightwells that were such a feature of temple architecture in Crete were generally not needed in the small freestanding Theran houses; Building 6 had the only lightwell known in Thera, and it was very small.[19]

The focal point of each Theran house was a large square room on the second storey. Although structural stability demanded some continuity of walling up through the house, the partitions were varied significantly, so that different spaces were possible on the various floors. A solid masonry wall on the lower level, for instance, might have above it a pier-and-closet partition, a pier-and-window partition, a pier-and-door partition, a thin mudbrick wall, a pier or a pillar: six possibilities.[20] The way space was articulated was both complex and expressive.

The wall-paintings that are the wonder of the site were done when the plaster was dry, and in this Thera differs from Crete. Colours were mixed from red ochre, yellow ochre, Egyptian blue and soot, with limewash added to create a range of paler tones. The images were sketched with diluted paint before the finished picture was painted on. The paintings were built up with translucent colourwashes and many of the Theran frescoes owe their luminosity and lightness of touch to this distinctive technique, which is different from that used on Crete.[21] Theran frescoes are freer than those seen at Knossos, probably because they were not produced under the patronage of a powerful centralized authority but commissioned by individual house-owners. They also show what the earlier, pre-Mycenean frescoes at Knossos may have been like; Cameron saw the Procession Fresco at Knossos as a rigid, formal version of an original that was lighter and more fluid in touch.[22] Life went on at Knossos after Thera was destroyed.

Plate 4.7 Triangle Square, with Building 4 to the left

The work of different painters can be recognized. The person who painted the miniature frescoes in Building 4 used a different style from all the others. Hockman believed he was a Theran trained in Crete, summoned to decorate Building 4 by the owner.[23] The magnificent religious paintings in Building 1 were the work of a different artist, who handled paint with breadth and clarity, like a great nineteenth-century watercolourist. The subjects of these paintings tell us much about the tastes, beliefs and concerns of the Therans, and are best left for a later discussion.

THE ISLAND: BRONZE AGE THERA

When the bronze age city at Akrotiri was overwhelmed by the eruption, it was already ancient,[24] and this chimes in well with Plato's Atlantis, which had an advanced ancient civilization ruled by a succession of kings (*Crit.* 114D).

The physical geography of the island on which Akrotiri evolved was more ancient still, just as Poseidon adopted Atlantis and carved out its concentric shape long before there were ships. The lava cone had been building up from the seabed for over a million years.[25] The gradually accumulating cone initially had a circular coastline, but before 54,000 BC an eruption blasted out the south-west basin: the north-west basin was created in about 18,300 BC. After that, a long sequence of smaller eruptions gradually refilled the crater. The existence of the South Bay in Minoan times raises several questions. Such a bay might have

55

Plate 4.8 A fallen staircase, showing how stone steps were mounted on timber

been seen as a more attractive location for Thera's metropolis than the Akrotiri site, but the opening of the harbour entrance to the west-south-west was a major disadvantage, in effect trapping vessels there. Bronze age ships could only sail before the wind. Even so, there must have been a settlement of some sort on its shore, perhaps Town 4 on the Building 4 fresco, which is smaller than Town 5.[26]

Parts of Minoan Thera were much as today, but over the site of the North Bay volcanic peaks rose to heights of 400 metres. That some sections of a vertical caldera wall were visible in the bronze age is suggested by Plato: 'the land rose sheer out of the sea to a great height' (*Crit.* 118A). The volcanic complex occupying the site of the North Bay is also suggested in Plato's description: 'near the centre [of the island] at a distance of about 50 stades [from the coast] stood a mountain that was gently sloping on all sides.' Fifty stades are 9 kilometres, and the low peaks in the North Bay area would have been 9 kilometres from the east and south coasts of Thera, a little closer to the north and west coasts, but then Plato is careful to say that it was *near* not *at* the island's centre (*Crit.* 113C).

Sections of buried Minoan landscape exposed in the caldera rim to the north of Imerovigli suggest the rocky landscape of the Spring Fresco. The Minoan cliffs remain round Mesa Vouno and Mikra Profitis Ilias and can be seen running inland from Perissa and Kamari. They can be seen, buried by pale pumice and half the height of the modern cliff, below the town of Oia. The same can be seen on the west coast of Therasia. The Minoan coastline was dominated by low cliffs, with little in the way of beach. An attraction of the Akrotiri site was that there the land shelved gradually into the sea, enabling sailors to haul their

56

vessels out of the water; along the harbour waterfront to the west of the excavation, there were probably Cretan-style shipsheds.[27]

Minoan Thera was about 110 square kilometres in area; the islands of modern Santorini have a total area which is just 10 per cent less than that. Of the present land area 65 square kilometres was already in existence in the late bronze age, 43 square kilometres were lost from the interior in the caldera eruption, 25 square kilometres added round the edge. Minoan Thera was small, and for many this has been a stumbling-block to the hypothesis that Thera was Atlantis, which Plato described as a large island. The problem is resolved by seeing Atlantis as a group of islands, with Crete the largest of them. The description given by Plato is compressed, and contains details plainly located in Thera: this acknowledged that, though small, Thera played a special role in the economy or religion of Atlantis. Galanopoulos' idea that Plato's description is really an account of two of the islands in the Atlantean archipelago is a very fruitful one.

5

ATLANTEAN ARTS AND CRAFTS

POTTERY

Akrotiri's sudden burial under a blanket of ash means that an unusually detailed record of the Aegean culture has been preserved, far more complete than anything found on any of the other islands, including Crete. Akrotiri offers us a window onto Atlantis.

Recurring pot sizes show standard measurements of volume, a liquid measure of 12 litres and dry measure of 28.4 litres.[1] The potter's wheel came into use on Thera in 1570 BC, when it was introduced from Crete, bringing an explosion of new pottery shapes. Before that time, potters occasionally put their own distinctive marks on pots, regarding each as an individual creation. Once the wheel came in and it was possible to make several pots a day, the potters' marks disappeared along with the feeling for pots as individually crafted pieces.[2] By 1570, almost all the pottery made on Melos was modelled on prototypes imported from Crete, but the Theran potters were still developing their own native tradition.[3]

The clay came from two main sources, one local, one on Crete. Eighty per cent of the pottery was either made on Thera or imported from a supplier on Crete; two stirrup jars are chemically identical to jars found at Knossos. The remaining 20 per cent came from a variety of sources, reflecting Thera's trading contacts across the Aegean.[4] Some came from Kos;[5] breasted ewers were imported from Phylakopi.

Much of the pottery was ornamented. Storage jars were often given plastic decoration, such as the rope motif covering the join between the bands of clay of which the jar was made.[6] Theran pottery painting technique followed two distinct traditions. One, the arrangement of motifs in horizontal zones, was borrowed from Crete. The other, covering the vase with a free design, was local. The two contrasting systems favoured the use of significantly different motifs. Circles, running spirals and other geometric designs lent themselves to the discipline of zoned patterns; pictures of plants and animals to the open spaces of the Cycladic tradition. The decoration was often free and confident. A flower vase and a strainer show flowers rather like the lilies in the Spring Fresco but

Figure 5.1 Courting swallows from the Spring Fresco

painted much faster. A breasted ewer shows the swallows from the Spring Fresco. Another piece, a jug with a plant motif, is even more rapid in treatment, almost like a Picasso sketch. The freest painted decoration is the splash of paint running from the rope-lugs of storage jars. At first glance the motif, more Pollock than Picasso, looks like a tatter of string hanging from the lug.

Other pieces were decorated with care, the most elaborate piece being an offering table decorated with dolphins swimming through a seascape of weed and rocks. The offering table was for religious cult use, but most of the pottery was everyday ware, like the barbecue for grilling souvlaki.

STONE

Though one might have expected metal tools and artefacts to dominate, the Cycladic stone-working tradition was kept alive. One reason was the availability of raw materials on Thera. The Therans, like Plato's Atlanteans (*Crit.* 116A–B), were great users of stone. The main types of stone implement were pestles, grinders, polishers, millstones, hammers, anvils and big hammer stones for knocking down walls. Lava mortars, a Theran speciality, were exported to Crete. Most of the stone implements at Akrotiri are of local rock,[7] but fine stones were also imported. An unfinished jar was made of Laconian stone, probably imported by way of Crete.[8] Other imported raw materials include alabaster, gypsum, Parian marble, serpentine and several types of limestone. A similar range of exotic stones was collected on Crete: blocks of Spartan rock still lie waiting to be worked on the floor of the temple workshops at Knossos. Obsidian found at Akrotiri, like that found at Knossos, came from Melos and Giali, but the discovery of an obsidian core suggests that some obsidian objects were made at Akrotiri. Some stoneware was imported ready manufactured, such as the blossom bowl and marble chalice – recognizably Cretan vessels. The web of relationships between Thera and the other islands, Crete especially, becomes ever more close-knit.

METAL-WORKING

Plato says the Atlanteans were great metal-workers, working gold, tin and silver on a large scale (*Crit.* 116B). The bronze age reality was that Crete was the major metal-working centre. Therans and other Cycladic traders acted as entrepreneurs in the important new industry, and the wealth and prosperity of Thera may have originated in this trade. Metal items were luxury goods and therefore systematically removed when the city was evacuated. A small amount of bronze was left,[9] including sickles, knives, daggers, chisels and fish-hooks, braziers, frying pans, tripod cooking pots, ewers and a pair of scales. A bronze jug was a Cretan import.[10]

A set of lead balance weights shows the Therans using the Cretan system of weight measurement. An examination of weights from eight Aegean sites shows that symbols were used (though not consistently) to denote multiples and fractions of two units, of 62 and 496 grammes. The latter is the Minoan mina, and is equivalent to eight of the smaller units. There are nevertheless also weights belonging to some other system based on a unit of 180 grammes.[11] These rogue weights may represent an Anatolian or Near Eastern system.

Although no metal-working site has been proved at Akrotiri, there is some evidence that silversmiths operated in the basement in Building 4. Traces of crystalline lead monoxide have been found there. The isotope composition shows that the lead came from Laurion on the Greek mainland which later became famous for its silver mines: Therans were already importing from Laurion in the bronze age.[12] Some rings of silver wire were left in Building 12. The only gold left was a piece of gold leaf and two rings.[13] All other portable objects of high value were taken away.

TEXTILES

No cloth has survived, but the wall-paintings give a clear picture of the different and sometimes elaborate styles of clothing worn by Theran men, women and girls. Loom weights show that weaving went on in upstairs rooms; groups of people can be imagined arriving from other houses nearby, getting together to spin, weave and gossip. The work probably involved all the women of the immediate neighbourhood, and formed an important part of the domestic economy. Textiles were needed for sacks, garments and sails. Probably wool from local Theran sheep was used, and flax for linen could easily have been grown on the island.[14]

The looms are likely to have been of the ancient warp-weighted type, with the warp threads suspended vertically from a bar and stretched taut by weights. The weights found at Akrotiri were grooved along their upper edges, so they must have been tied to a suspended horizontal slat. Over 950 weights have been found, more than 450 in Building 4 alone, compared with 185 in contemporary levels at Ayia Irini. Room 3 in Building 4 was big enough to hold five looms. As on Kea, weaving went on in some rooms in some Theran houses. The looms were dismantled when not in use so the weaving rooms could be used for other purposes, but the absence of wall-paintings in Room 3 suggests that it was designed for weaving, with maximum light reflecting from white walls.[15]

The wall-paintings show some figures naked, but it can be assumed this was not usual. The nakedness of the drowning sailors, for instance, is probably a convention; in Aegean, Egyptian and Near Eastern art it was a common short-hand for depicting warriors in defeat.[16] Nakedness also indicated involvement in a religious ritual. Boys and young men probably did strip naked for rites of passage, to symbolize the shedding of boyhood in preparation for a new role in the community. The baring of women's breasts, in the popular mind the hall-mark of the Minoan civilization, and also seen on Thera, was done for major religious observances. In everyday life, breasts were covered and everyone wore clothes.

To judge from the paintings, fashions on Thera, even for ceremonial occasions, were simpler than those on Crete. The Therans created startling effects by placing bright, contrasting colours and tones side by side, usually in horizontal, vertical or zig-zag stripes. What the garments had in common with those of Crete was the sewing of separately woven strips of cloth onto the edges of garments, so that the lower edges of dresses, sleeve-ends and the cleavage edges of bodices always had a coloured hem. The main purpose was to stop the edges fraying and wearing excessively, but they also had a decorative value that was incorporated into the design texture. The hemming strips were woven on portable hand-looms.[17]

Men wore a variety of clothing. A long white garment, a cloak or djellaba of sun-bleached linen, was worn by men of high rank or men performing special ceremonial functions. Double vertical lines down the front may represent the hemmed inner edge of the cloak, which was fastened at the neck with strings. A second garment worn by men was a smock or poncho in white, grey or red ochre. A third was a fleecy smock; its fabric was woven with large loops to make it bulkier. Clothes made of this material were worn by shepherds and warriors. The fleecy look was common in Minoan Crete: a figure on the Harvesters Vase from Ayia Triadha wears this type of coat. Its use was doubtless widespread in the Aegean region, including the Greek mainland: it was worn at Mycenae,[18] and Aegean shepherds wear similar coats to this day. Of the three garments, the white robe seems to have been the Sunday best, worn by processional figures such as those in the Meeting on the Hill in the miniature fresco in Building 4. As this robe covered the arms – it is always shown enclosing the arms – it

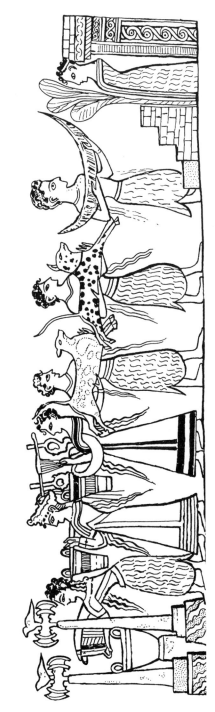

Figure 5.2 Agia Triadha sarcophagus, Crete; the three men and one of the women wear kilts made of the fleecy material

must have been taken off for any kind of work. Probably a loincloth was worn underneath.[19]

The loin-cloth, again using the wall-paintings as evidence, was a length of cloth, either rectangular or with curved ends, tucked between the legs, pulled up at the front and back, held tight to the body by a belt, and with the ends hanging loosely like aprons fore and aft. It was the everyday garment for men doing physical work. The frescoes show several variations, which can be explained simply by variations in the length of cloth used and the amount of tucking in that was done: these in turn may have been dictated by considerations such as safety in some occupations, fashion or personal preference. A long squarish apron hanging down front and back, with dyed hemming strips, made the loin-cloth into a kilt.

The women of the pastoral communities wore a white bodice with bicep-length sleeves and an opening down the front: the breasts were covered. They also wore an ankle-length skirt in the looped, fleecy material. The women of the town wore dresses which were in effect extensions of the bodice: the braids used to edge the two front edges of the bodice were sewn together to make a double decorative line right down the front. Some of the townswomen's dresses seem to have been striped, and this simple pattern was probably woven into the cloth. Something similar appeared in mainland Greece in LHIII figurines, though not in Crete, suggesting that it originated in the Cyclades, perhaps in Thera itself, and later spread to Greece. It is interesting to reflect that fashions followed by fourteenth-century Mycenean women may have originated in sixteenth-century Thera.[20]

One of the most memorable features of the Minoan civilization in Crete is the spectacular ceremonial dresses of the women.[21] Thera too had its ceremonial costume. The basic garment was the townswoman's dress, which swept fairly broad and full to the ankles, sometimes incorporating a couple of broad horizontal decorative stripes above the hem, probably sewn on like the hemming-strips. The flounced or layered effect, such a feature of depictions of Minoan priestesses, was achieved by adding a short overskirt. This had decorative zoning built up in two or three overlapping layers and was tied on round the waist, covering the undergarment between waist and knee.

The inner edges of the bodice were normally pulled modestly together but for religious ceremonies priestesses and other female celebrants pulled them back to expose their breasts. A scene in the vestibule of Room 1, Building 6 shows a standing woman handing an overskirt to a seated woman wearing only the plain dress or undergarment. Robing ceremonies like this were an integral part of Minoan religious ritual, and as in many other religions which garments were worn and in which way mattered a great deal. The exposure or concealment of various body parts was of prime importance.

Bodices were sometimes decorated. The woman in Room 3b in Building 1, for instance, has small lilies embroidered on hers. The overskirt was also given embroidered lattices, criss-cross designs that enclosed dots or crosses. Much of this could be seen in Minoan Crete too, though not the translucent veil that envelops one of the girls in the initiation rite in the adyton of Building 1. It is shown by a pale yellow colour wash covered with red dots.[22] This can only be embroidered lace, still made by village women all over the Aegean. The other two females on the same fresco have lace overbodices, one embroidered with a lattice pattern, the other with crocuses, the flowers dedicated to the goddess. These lace garments were probably specially made for particular people for particular rites of passage, rather like the christening gowns and wedding dresses of later times. Plato mentions Atlantean clothes only in connection with the rituals of the ten kings in the Temple of Poseidon. They wore azure robes while deciding judgements at night, then offered their robes up to the deity (*Crit.* 120B–C). This is reminiscent of a practice at Knossos, where both actual dresses and miniature dresses made of faience were left as offerings to deities.[23] As we shall see, wall-paintings at Akrotiri show that ceremonial clothing was either offered or received during initiation rites.

Purple powder made from the murex mollusc shows that purpura was extracted for dyeing. Smashed murex shells were found at Akrotiri, so dye was manufactured there. The purpura was probably used for face-painting, for which there is fresco evidence. The central figure of the goddess in Building 1, Room 3a has two red crocus symbols 2–3 centimetres long painted on her left cheek; the two women on the walls of Building 6 are shown with 'rouged' cheeks.

The techniques of weaving were applied on a coarser, rougher scale for the manufacture of floor matting. As early as 2500 BC, Theran pottery was made on mats, so that wheel-less potters could easily turn them on the work surface; mat impressions survive on the base of the pots, disappearing in 1570 BC when the potter's wheel was introduced. It is also from this time that the first actual matting has survived; it was used as a floor covering in Building 4.

FURNITURE

As the pumice drifted into the Theran houses, it settled round the furniture, making moulds which have survived even though the furniture itself has long since disintegrated. The first major discovery was the bed found in Building 12.[24] This wooden divan had legs that were square in section and relatively thick to give them strength where they were jointed with the frame, but tapered downwards into a roughly circular form; the shape is reminiscent of a Minoan pillar and capital, and may have been absorbed unconsciously from Knossian architecture. The result is pleasantly functional, striking the modern eye as not unlike mid-twentieth-century Danish stick furniture. Three more beds were stacked in the open space west of Building 12, apparently saved from a collapsing house.[25]

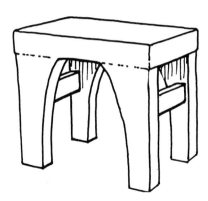

Figure 5.3 Reconstructed stool

The cast of a broken stool was recovered from the same room.[26] Casts of a chair and parts of other stools have been found at various points round the city. The finest piece of furniture is a three-legged round table. The legs were not only fretted into intricate silhouettes – surprising enough – but relief-carved as well in a design centring on a large crocus blossom (dedicated to the goddess). This single object hints at what may have been lost in the way of carpentry and woodcarving in Thera.

The evidence points to a rich and ambitious civilization pervading the Aegean in the late bronze age.

6

THERAN FOOD AND TRADE

AGRICULTURE AND PASTORALISM

The rural population living outside Akrotiri in a dense scatter of hamlets suggests Plato's 'many rich villages of country folk' (*Crit.* 118B), though these may instead have been on Crete, since Plato says they were situated on the slopes of mountains of surpassing magnitude and beauty. The south-west of Thera would have been the area most favourable to agriculture. It was the lowest, flattest and easiest to cultivate; the volcanic peaks on the site of the North Bay sheltered it from cold northerly winds; the southerly aspect made it a sun-trap; it would have been amply watered by south-westerlies. Since this part of the island also offered two fine harbours it was destined to become the most dynamic area economically. Favoured for food production, a natural focus for trade and therefore also for settlement, the growth of the city further stimulated food production, so in and round Akrotiri there was an upward spiral of economic activity.[1] Plato tells us that on Atlantis '[the Plain] faced towards the south and was sheltered from northern blasts' (*Crit.* 118A–B), although this seems more likely to apply to the Plain of Mesara on Crete.

The hill slopes were the natural focus for animal husbandry and pastoralism still underpinned the bronze age economy. Large numbers of animal bones were found at Akrotiri. The prime source of meat was sheep and goats. The cattle were raised mainly as draft animals and perhaps as milk cows: the bones show little evidence of butchering. The emphasis on sheep and goats was typical of the bronze age Aegean. An animal fold is shown on one of the miniature frescoes as a hedged enclosure. A goatherd and a shepherd tend their flocks on a nearby hillside, suggesting a summer scene. Both animals are brought down to low ground in winter months. The flocks were probably kept mainly for their milk and wool, only surplus lambs being slaughtered for meat.[2] Dairy products were vital as a source of protein for Therans. Today in the Aegean, sheep and goats' milk is made into cheese and yoghurt, and certainly cheese was made in the bronze age.[3] Sheep's wool was the main raw material for the textile industry. The Theran landscape was unsuitable for large-scale cattle-rearing, and relatively small numbers were needed for drawing carts.

66

Crops included various types of legumes, possibly lentils and chick peas. Barley flour, barley grains and milling equipment in several basements confirm barley as the major food crop.[4] The olives, almonds and pistachio nuts consumed could have been grown on Thera or imported from Crete.[5]

Miniature wall-paintings provide some of the evidence. Inside the animal fold described earlier are two fig trees, which grow well in stony soils and Thera's must always have been stony. The fig is often planted where shade is wanted, beside a well or in a courtyard, as its thick foliage casts dense shade. In the fresco it provides shade for the sheep and goats. It yields two harvests, in June or July and between August and November.[6] Marinatos found a dried fig at Akrotiri.[7] The careful portrayal of big black fruits in the fresco implies that the fruit was important to the Therans.[8] Therans ate almonds, which they preserved in earth-filled jars.[9] They grew vines, and the grapes were eaten as fruit and probably pressed for wine. Bees were kept, as a beautifully painted hive shows, so honey too was part of the diet.[10]

The crocus featured again and again in Theran art is *sativus*, an autumn-flowering type that produces saffron. Saffron could be collected from the wild, but some *sativus* was cultivated. In wall-paintings crocuses are often shown in clumps, suggesting that several bulbs have been planted together to make collection of stigmas easier; in the Crocus Gatherers painting in Building 1, they are growing in pots. The stigmas were collected in baskets by girls, then dried and crushed to produce the yellow dye. As many as 140 stigmas were needed to make one gramme of saffron, which made it a luxury product. It had several uses: to colour and flavour food, to colour textiles, and as a sedative. Since saffron was also made in Crete, Syria, Cilicia and Egypt, it does not look as if the Therans manufactured it for export. On the other hand, the major symbolic value given to both saffron and crocuses in the Minoan world suggests that saffron was made for use within that world. The fact that girls depicted in the religious paintings in Building 1 are shown collecting crocuses and offering them to the goddess proves that the crocus was considered to belong to the goddess. This is corroborated by the Priestess Fresco in Building 4, where the priestess wears a saffron-dyed gown. One of the ships' hulls in the Ship Fresco bears paintings of crocus blooms, and more crocus flowers deck the ship's rigging. Perhaps the ship carries a cargo of saffron to one of the other Aegean islands. Much later, Pliny wrote of the saffron flowers of Cyrene, Mount Olympus in Lycia and Centuripa in Sicily: none could compare with the saffron of Thera.[11]

TRADE

The Building 4 wall-paintings give the Atlantean economy its key signature: bustling, thriving walled seashore towns with their inhabitants looking seawards, the Aegean Sea dotted with ships plying between the towns, carrying passengers and cargoes from island to island. One passage in Plato's *Critias* (117E) describes such a scene:

The whole of the wall had numerous houses built onto it, set very close together; while the seaway and the largest harbour were filled with ships and merchants coming from all quarters, which cause clamour and tumult of every description and unceasing din night and day.

The Therans were above all traders. Their position on the closest of the Cyclades to Crete made it ideal for entrepreneurial activity; they were well placed to act as intermediaries between Minoan Crete and the Mycenean mainland: the presence of Mycenean cups shows that contact was made.[12] Thera's zenith coincided with the final period of Minoan greatness and its trading thrust outwards across the Aegean: it also coincided with the rise of a new culture on the Greek mainland, the Mycenean. Thera was the pivot of the see-saw, prospering from its trading and cultural contacts with both old and new civilizations.

The full extent of Thera's trading contacts is not known, but it was certainly at the centre of a complex web of trade routes. It lay on a major north–south route joining Crete with the Greek mainland silver mines, an island-hopping

Figure 6.1 Minoan trade routes in the Aegean

route from Knossos by way of Amnisos to Thera, Naxos, Siros, Kea, Laurion and Thorikos. The link with Cretan ports such as Amnisos would have meant tapping into other Cretan trade routes, such as the one from Zakro in eastern Crete to Karpathos, Triandha on Rhodes, Cyprus, Ugarit in the Levant and from there on to Mari. Given the east–west current along the south Anatolian coast, it is likely that this route was more often used by vessels sailing westwards. A north-west–south-east current from Crete to Egypt offered an alternative way of reaching the eastern shore of the Mediterranean.[13] A triangular trade route suggests itself: from Palaikastro or Zakro to Egypt, north to Ugarit and from there west along the Anatolian coast to Rhodes, back to Palaikastro.

There was another African link too, from Marsa Matru in north Africa to Kommos on the south coast of Crete, and from there by way of Khania, Zakro or Palaikastro to Thera, and on to Mycenae. Routes within the Aegean included an easterly route from Thera via Astipalaia and Kos to Bodrum on the Anatolian mainland and a westerly one linking Thera to Tiryns and Mycenae on the Greek mainland by way of Folegandros, Phylakopi on Melos, Andimelos and the islets of Parapola and Spetsai.

The overall distances covered were enormous. Islands thought of as near neighbours in the Cyclades, Naxos and Melos, were 90 kilometres away. Amnisos in Crete was 110 kilometres: the Greek and Anatolian coastlines (Laurion and Bodrum) were 240 kilometres away. Libya was an incredible 740 kilometres sailing away, and Egypt and the land of Mari must have seemed positively mythical. How much of this trading was peaceful is impossible to tell, but from later times we know that piracy and warfare were the rule. Thucydides recorded a tradition that most of the Aegean islands were colonized by Phoenicians and Carians and that Minos king of Crete organized a navy and drove them out because piracy was endemic among them.[14] He went on to relate how this could be proved:

> during the present war when Delos was officially purified by the Athenians all the graves were opened up. More than half the graves were Carian, as could be seen from the types of weapon buried with the bodies and from the method of burial, some as is still used in Caria.[15]

The bones unearthed on Delos were, he believed, those of the enemies of king Minos' *pax minoica*, the Anatolian enemies of peaceful trading in the Aegean.[16]

The role of Crete in organizing and controlling trade in the Aegean will be considered later, but it is certainly true that in the two centuries leading up to 1500 BC, Minoan trade spread far afield, and Theran seafarers played a significant part in that operation. Recently Minoan stone anchors have been discovered in Bulgaria, proving that traders sailed northwards past Troy, through the Hellespont and along the Black Sea coast, a journey on the same scale as the voyages east to Ugarit.

Figure 6.2 The Tomb of Rekhmire wall-painting (detail); Minoan gifts to Egypt above, Nubian below

One exotically furnished Theran house contained a Canaanite jar which can only have been imported from the Levant.[17] Similar jars found in Egypt can be dated to the reign of Tuthmosis IV and Queen Hatshepsut (1520–1457BC), which ties in well with a date of around 1520 BC for the destruction of Thera.[18] More of these jars have been found on the Anatolian coast, Crete and on the Greek mainland, pointing to a vigorous Aegean trade in exotic imports. A tripod stone mortar found at Akrotiri was probably imported from Syria, to judge from the running spirals carved on it. No raw elephant tusk has been found and very little in the way of worked ivory, suggesting that the Therans had less contact with north Africa than the Cretans, who did import tusks. According to Plato, Atlantis contained 'a very large stock of elephants' (*Crit.* 114E). This and other remarks imply a huge latitude spread, and we can reconstruct Atlantis as not so much a landmass as an elaborate network of sea trading links. Ivory-producing regions in Africa were economically tributary to the Minoan trading empire. Two rhyta made of ostrich eggs may have been made in Egypt and imported as finished goods. At present, only twelve ostrich egg rhyta are known, one each from Phylakopi, Palaikastro, Knossos and Dendra, six from Mycenae and two from Thera. On the paintings in the Egyptian tomb of Rekhmire, in the zone below the famous procession of Minoans is another, of Nubians carrying ostrich eggs, ostrich feathers and elephant tusks, conveying the message that the Minoans and Myceneans got their materials from Africa as a result of Egyptian mediation.[19] It is nevertheless also possible that ostrich eggs were traded directly across the Libyan Sea without the involvement of Egyptian middlemen. Peter Warren has drawn attention to the bronze age port at Marsa Matru, well to the west of the Nile delta, where there is a bronze age depiction of ostrich eggs: perhaps the eggs were exported direct from here to Crete and the Aegean.[20]

Urbanization on the scale seen at Akrotiri must have consumed large quantities of timber for doors, windows, staircases, floors and roofs, to say nothing of the ships. A small island like Thera could not have supplied more than a fraction of the timber needed. Presumably it was imported from Crete or Anatolia.[21]

Access to key raw materials (stone, timber, copper, gold, silver) was as important to economic well-being as access to energy sources is now. Thera's trading position was the key to its wealth. In much the same way today, a small Gulf state may prosper mightily because of its key location on an oilfield. Weapons buried with Minoan warriors in the Mesara tombs in southern Crete were from Kythnos in the Cyclades to the north-west of Thera, presumably transported by a ship island-hopping from Kythnos to Serifos, Sifnos and Folegandros and from there to Thera, the natural last port of call before the open-water voyage to Crete. The copper needed for Cretan metal-working probably came from Laurion. Again, islands (Kea, Naxos and Ios) would have been used as navigational stepping-stones to reach Thera. Alternatively, the copper used in Crete may have come from Mesopotamia. The earliest ashlar masonry in Crete dates from 1900 BC, when ashlar masonry was being built in Ugarit, implying that Minoan traders from Crete imported copper and architectural ideas at the same time. Whatever the truth about the copper trade, the overall picture of trading and cultural relationships among the evolving bronze age communities was extremely complex.[22]

Thera had little to offer Crete in the way of trade goods or raw materials. The only identifiable commodity Thera offered which Crete did not have already was tripod mortars made of volcanic dacite, and these were certainly exported to Crete.[23] It is therefore hard to find archaeologically verifiable arguments for a Cretan interest in Thera. The idea that Thera or indeed the Cyclades generally offered opportunities for Crete to unload its excess population is unconvincing because of the smallness of the islands: Crete was huge – well able to accommodate its own population growth.

A second possibility is that Crete needed Thera as a military outpost. The Greeks later saw Minos as the founding father of the navy and the idea of the Cretans surrounding themselves with a ring of protective naval bases of which Thera might have been one certainly accords with that view. A third explanation is that Crete's interest was purely commercial, that it suited the Cretans to have Cycladic trade funnelled through Thera, handled by Theran merchants, transported by Theran sailors. So far no sign of any defensive works has been seen at Akrotiri or any of the other bronze age sites on Santorini, and it has been argued that Thera was defended by a Cretan navy;[24] it may be that the protection was a confederate navy policing the Aegean and Libyan seas, defending

Figure 6.3 Reconstruction of the east gate of Akrotiri, based on fresco evidence

all the trading partners from piracy. Against this idea, we must acknowledge that other important sites that might have been part of this 'Cretan League' (Ayia Irini and Phylakopi) had defensive walling, in each case in a distinctive local style, not a standard one supplied by Crete. If fresco Town 5 is Akrotiri, it too had a curtain wall with an imposing gate. This evidence might be taken to suggest that the Cretan or confederate navy was ineffective in repelling raiders, but the walls are all on the towns' *landward* sides.

Cretan stirrup jars have been found on Thera, implying that the Cretan oil trade was in the hands of Theran merchants acting as middlemen between Crete and the rest of the Aegean. It seems reasonable to assume other commodities were handled in the same way and that some sort of 'special relationship' existed between Crete and Thera.[25] As far as Crete was concerned the trading went on under the aegis of the temples, but it is not yet clear who on Thera was making the decisions. There was one unexpected benefit from conducting trade by way of Thera. A nineteenth-century traveller reported that a ten-day stay in Theran waters cleaned a ship's bottom beautifully, saving a good deal of hard work; this feature would have made Thera an attractive port of call in the bronze age too.[26] The archaeology shows Therans to have been proud of their sea-faring tradition, and most likely it was this the Cretans valued. The commodities for trade were supplied principally by Crete and, increasingly in the late bronze age, Mycenae, but Thera supplied the navigational skills to handle the trade.

The precise nature of the socio-political relationship of Thera with Minoan Crete may never be known, but Professor Branigan has gone a long way towards clarifying the alternatives.[27] In the neolithic, Crete stood apart from the rest of the Aegean but by 2300 BC sailing ships had appeared, important harbourside towns began to develop at Mochlos, Palaikastro and Zakro in eastern Crete, and trading on an ambitious scale with the Levant began with the importing of Egyptian and Syrian goods and the exporting of Middle Minoan wares. Cretan pottery was exported throughout the Cyclades, and also to Lerna on the Greek mainland, and Kos and the ports of Anatolia in the east.[28] It was shortly after this, and perhaps in part *because* of this, that in about 2000 BC the great Minoan temples were built. At that early stage the trading was probably free-lance, handled by resourceful, independent merchant-mariners. By the late bronze age, from 1550 BC onwards, it had become more complicated. Probably free-lance trading still continued between Crete and the Levant, but a new exchange mechanism had come into play, the formally structured exchange of prestigious gifts between elites. The Theran operation has to be fitted into this more complex phase of development.

Thera may have functioned as a commercial outpost of Crete, but it is not yet clear whether that means Thera was a Cretan colony. The colonial idea is an old one; Herodotus expressed the view that Minos reached out and colonized the Cyclades.[29] If Thera was a colony, it could have been a governed colony, a settlement colony or a community colony. A governed colony is an existing settlement of indigenous people with a foreign administration imposed by force, the settlement being run for and in the interests of the foreign power, like Gibraltar in the nineteenth century. A settlement colony is a township founded by foreigners on otherwise unoccupied land, like the English colonies in America in the sixteenth century: the result is a distinct and obviously foreign culture. In a community colony, foreign immigrants comprise a significant proportion of the settlers, often forming a distinct social enclave within the settlement. The enclave-group promotes trade with and for its parent country by residing in a foreign city, rather like the Chinese communities scattered round South-East Asia.

With such an incomplete picture of the bronze age city at Akrotiri it is not possible to be sure which type of colony, if any, we are looking at. The area exposed may be a Cretan mercantile quarter of an otherwise Cycladic city, or it may be representative of the city as a whole; it is too early to say. What is clear is that the area we see is much more Cretan in its architectural and decorative style than either Ayia Irini or Phylakopi, which were major trading posts in the Minoan commercial system, but none of the towns has been completely explored; the implication is that when a complete picture is assembled they might all turn out to have similar proportions of buildings with Cretan affinities.

Significantly, all three towns developed over a long period before the ascendancy of Crete, which rules out the settlement colony idea.[30] Nor is there any sign at any of the three towns of the administrative centre that would go with a governed colony. So, if the Theran city was a colony at all it must have been a community colony, and the same would apply to Ayia Irini and Phylakopi.[31] So far, Kastri on Kythera and Triandha on Rhodes are the only sites outside Crete with any credentials as Minoan colonies in the fullest sense: they seem to have been purely Cretan foundations dating from 1550–1450 BC.[32] On balance it seems more likely that, although a few Cretans may have lived there for commercial reasons, most of the inhabitants of Thera were indigenous, but many adopted those Minoan customs, fashions, artefacts and designs that they chose. In other words, Thera was inherently Cycladic but adopted a strong Cretan accent, just as many British pop groups sing with an American accent out of deference to an implicitly stronger culture. Even though, according to Apollonius of Rhodes, some islands in the Cyclades were actually called Minoan islands, we need not believe that they were colonies. There were 'Minoas' on the coast of Syria, near Gaza, on Corfu and far to the west on the south coast of Sicily. The names certainly prove familiarity with the Minoan world (although it was Evans who coined the name 'Minoan' for it, not the Minoans!), and a wish to be associated with it, but not necessarily political domination by it.

As we saw earlier, the Therans were using a Minoan system for weighing commodities. Regular trading between Thera and the neighbouring islands would have necessitated standardizing weights and measures, and it is significant that the Therans followed a Minoan system. Professor Chadwick has pointed out that the Mycenean system was not based on Minoan units, with talents of around 32 grammes and minae of around 520 grammes, and it would be difficult to reconcile the two systems. Significantly, it was lead weights of the Minoan system based on a unit of 65 grammes that Caskey found on Kea.[33]

This is not to say that the Therans were not trading with the mainland of Greece – they were – but rather that from the evidence available they were oriented towards Crete and conducted their operations with a Minoan perspective. Nevertheless, the zenith of Thera's activity coincided with the shaft graves of Mycenae, the royal graves from which Schliemann produced unprecedentedly rich grave goods. It would seem that no comparable artistic tradition existed on mainland Greece at the time, and that craftsmen trained in Crete or the Cyclades were commissioned to produce pieces for the Mycenean royal family.[34] Some artwork at Akrotiri closely resembles work from Mycenae. The swallow jugs from Mycenae and Phylakopi have been proved by analysis of the clay fabric to have originated in the Cyclades: it is also likely on stylistic grounds that they were made by the same potter. Gold earrings found in a shaft grave at Mycenae are identical to those worn by one of the Saffron Gatherers in the Building 1 fresco at Akrotiri.[35]

This does not prove, as Marinatos suggested, that some of the people in the Theran frescoes are Myceneans, but that the Therans and other dwellers in the Cyclades provided Mycenae with styles, patterns, ideas and craft skills and maybe borrowed mainland fashions in return. The art of seventh-century BC Etruscan cities showed a powerful Greek influence, yet it is known from documentary sources that the Greeks had no dominion over Etruria. The warriors on the North Frieze in Building 4 are wearing boar's tusk helmets, often associated with Mycenaean warrior graves on the mainland, but this type of helmet was also used in Crete and it may simply represent a fashion that originated on the mainland. It is going too far to say that the wearers of the helmets must be Mycenaean; not every soldier who carries a Kalashnikov is a Russian. The Shipwreck scene is reminiscent of the battle scenes shown on Mycenaean silver vases, and this too is likely to be an example of Thera borrowing from Mycenae. Those who prefer a 'hard' view of prehistory may see Akrotiri as a native Cycladic town conquered and taken over first by Minoans, then by Mycenaeans. Marinatos, Negbi and Iakovides were all persuaded that Mycenaeans had settled at Akrotiri at the time of the shaft graves; Iakovides saw them as dominating Theran socio-politics, taking over key positions, such as the 'admiral of the fleet' who, according to Marinatos, lived in Building 4.[36]

Naturally, as the new culture took root on the Greek mainland and became more vigorous, more distinct from the Minoan, more of the new elements surfaced in the Cyclades. Maybe there were Mycenaeans travelling to Thera and other parts of the Aegean, sailing on ships that were Cycladic or Minoan, and that underlines the eclectic nature of life in the Cyclades. Maybe the same navigational skills that had brought such benefit to the Cretans in their trading enterprises were now exploited by mainland Greeks to supplant them. That could explain the rapid extension of Mycenaean trade impact throughout the eastern Mediterranean.[37] It is not known how the trading activities of the Cretans and Therans were seen by the Mycenaeans. The reading of the Atlantis legend being developed here is that the Aegean islanders were seen as threatening the Greek mainland: it was this memory that led to the Minoan-Atlanteans later being remembered as aggressors and invaders, people who posed a real military and political threat to the mainland communities in general – not just to Athens.

SHIPS

For Thera to have developed a key mercantile role in the prehistory of the Aegean, Theran ships must have been designed well and Theran mariners must have known how to get the best out of them. The style and construction of Minoan ships has been known for a long time from representations on Cretan sealstones and other artwork, but the miniature wall-paintings in Building 4 have added enormously to our knowledge. Because the ships are painted in such detail and several are shown together, with crews and passengers added to give scale, we can tell that several types and sizes of vessel were made.

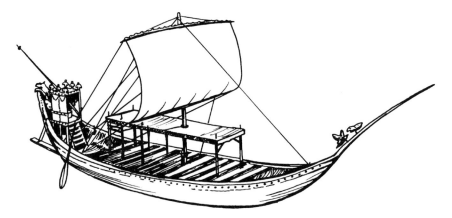

Figure 6.4 Reconstruction of a Theran ship, based on fresco evidence

A small boat is paddled by two men. Another, larger, vessel with a higher freeboard has five men, representing five pairs of oarsmen, rowing under a light frame designed to carry an awning while a steersman stands in the stern holding a long steering-oar: beside him sits the captain. Still larger vessels were apparently paddled by up to forty-two men in spite of the much higher freeboard which made it hard for the paddlers to reach the water. These larger vessels had a single central mast, a long bowsprit carrying symbolic devices, space amidships for up to thirteen pairs of passengers to travel in seated comfort under an awning, and a cabin for the captain on the poop. This consisted of a wooden frame with cowhide stretched and nailed over the back and sides and an awning over the top. The cabin was installed originally to give protection from wind, rain and sun, like the wheelhouse on a modern fishing boat, but the amount of decoration added by 1500 BC shows that it had become a status symbol; it is not by chance that the cabin on its own is repeated again and again in the decor of Building 4, Room 4. Nor is it by chance that it looks like a Minoan litter: litters are known to have been reserved for high-status people.[38]

The larger vessels were substantial ships 30 or 40 metres long, as impressive as anything built in Europe until the Renaissance. They were long, broad vessels with a shallow draft, designed to sail in shallow water and to be easy to beach. The graceful curving profile swept up at the front into a long bowsprit whose only function seems to have been to carry insignia. The Atlanteans as described by Plato also had great oar-powered galleys. He says the shipyards were 'full of triremes, all amply equipped' (*Crit.* 117D, 118E).

It is impossible to discuss the ships in the Ship Fresco without speculating about the scene as a whole. It makes a significant difference whether we see it as an everyday scene or a ceremony. People involved in a ceremony do not dress or behave in a normal way. Bunting is shown on the ships' rigging, elaborate insignia are fixed to the bowsprits and painted on the hulls, leading several commentators to infer that the fresco shows a Nautical Festival. The ships may be travelling a short distance from one harbour to the next: this would explain why they are being paddled, an inefficient method of propelling a large vessel, rather than rowed or sailed. Perhaps this was the major Spring Festival to mark the resumption of navigation.[39]

In the classical period in both Greece and Rome the Isidis Naviguium, dedicated to the Egyptian god Isis, was held on 5 March to inaugurate the new season's sailing. Although it was a popular festival, little information has survived. The most detailed is from Apuleius:

> The chief priest uttered the most exalted prayers over a ship that had been built with exquisite skill and decorated with wonderful Egyptian paintings. With a bright torch, with an egg and sulphur he purified the ship so well that it was purity itself. Then he publicly named it and dedicated it to the goddess. The gleaming sail of this auspicious barque bore golden letters woven into its texture; these signified the inaugural prayer for fortunate sailing in the new year's commerce. Thereupon all the people, both devotees and unattached alike, vied in loading the ship with baskets heaped with spices and similar offerings and they poured on the waves libations of meal mixed with milk until the ship, laden with gifts, was freed from its anchor and launched into the sea with a favourable breeze that blew especially for it. When it faded from view, the bearers of the images took up their loads and made their way back to the temple, processing in the same order.[40]

Although this account is from the second century AD, it describes so well the feeling and the detail of the South Frieze Ship Fresco that the two events, the one described, the other painted, might be part of the same tradition, even if 1,700 years apart.[41] The Theran ship was in fact related to a type used by the Egyptians. The retractable mast raised through a central awning was rare in the Aegean, though common in Egyptian ships of the Eighteenth Dynasty; this period in Egypt's history began in 1570 BC, so it is contemporary with the painting.

All the Theran ships were steered with the Aegean-style oar rudder. The sailing ship, needing extra control when powered by a strong wind, had two rudders. All ships were rigged with rectangular sails that could only be filled by a following wind, a serious limitation to navigation, explaining how early sailors became trapped in harbours, and why ports often developed adjacent to harbours facing in two different directions.[42] To judge from the one ship with its sail up, there was no standing rigging; rather surprisingly there were no forestays or back-stays to hold the mast rigid. It may be that on longer voyages on open sea forestays and backstays were added, and that their absence on the Ship Fresco indicates, again, that the journey was a short one, perhaps from one bay to the next, possibly just round the Akrotiri peninsula. The method of propulsion used drives us to the same conclusion. The paddlers bend low to reach the water with their paddles, an uncomfortable position to work in for long. Paddling was a common method of propulsion a thousand years earlier in Egypt and the Near East, but an old-fashioned way of getting about by 1500 BC. It is significant that, when the Ship Fresco was painted, paddling was only used in Egypt for ship processions during major annual festivals, occasions when an obsolete practice was an appropriate reminder of the past. Ritual usually involves archaic practices. So it was in the Theran nautical festival.

The larger fresco ships on the South Frieze are elaborately decorated, like a fleet on review. The most elaborately decorated of all, probably the flagship, has lions and dolphins painted on its hull and three or four huge rosettes mounted on its prow, and dress-ship lines of festoons with pendants of huge gold imitation crocus blossoms sweeping from stem to stern by way of the masthead. Until the discovery of the Ship Fresco, no-one had suspected that Aegean ships' hulls had been decorated with painted designs. The practice was nevertheless common in Egypt at about this time, especially on ships used for ceremonies. Perhaps the ships were normally undecorated. For everyday use we may imagine garlands, rosettes and bunting removed, the painted emblems washed off. The shipwrecked vessels and harbour boats are shown in plain undecorated wood. The three-dimensional emblems attached to the prow included birds, dolphins, butterflies. All the ships, whatever other insignia they carry, have a rosette. The device is painted on the hull of the flagship and it has been suggested that the rosette was the fleet's emblem, whereas the other devices refer to the names of the individual ships; we can easily imagine these graceful vessels bearing names like 'Dolphin,' 'Lion,' 'Butterfly,' 'Swallow'.[43] The sterns of the larger ships carry figureheads, a lion, or a leopard. These may be incarnations of the courage needed to venture out to sea.

The projecting timbering at the waterline behind the ship has been explained in various ways. There are ropes holding it up, suggesting that it might be removable or at any rate lifted as the vessel beached. Probably it was the gangplank, and this fits in with the Aegean custom of beaching ships stern first; a carving from Naxos shows a man stepping onto this boarding platform.[44] It is also possible that it doubled as the ship's lavatory. If so, the ropes would have been necessary for people to hang onto while relieving themselves into the ship's wake.

Whilst the theory of the seasonal nautical festival has much to recommend it, there are those who prefer to see the miniature fresco scheme as a narrative, a piece of Theran history. The narrative began with the West Frieze, the first part of the scheme a visitor entering the room would see. Unfortunately, almost all of the West Frieze was destroyed, but there was evidently a town, Town 1, presumably a place visited by the Theran fleet. In the North Frieze the fleet approaches a second landmass where people are conducting a ceremony on a hill, possibly a purification preliminary to battle. A sea battle or shipwreck follows and soldiers with shields and spears advance on Town 2. The East Frieze is dominated by a river flowing through a tropical landscape, a third landmass, with a third town along its banks. On the South Frieze, the triumphant fleet sets sail from Town 4 to Town 5, which can only be 'home', Akrotiri itself. In this interpretation, the festive bunting on the ships can be seen as part of a victory celebration.[45] The problem with this is the civilian appearance of the robed passengers on the ships and the general lack of weapons, shields and helmets – apart from the helmets which hang as if suspended from the awning above the robed passengers on board one of the ships. Are these after all, in spite of appearances, 'the mighty host' (*Crit.* 24E) of Atlantean warriors that once threatened Athens?

7

WRITING AND WALL-PAINTING

As well as being a very ancient people, the Atlanteans had a form of writing and advanced forms of figurative art: in both respects they showed the precocity of the people of the bronze age Aegean. The kings of Atlantis inscribed laws and oaths on a pillar in the Temple of Poseidon (*Crit.* 119E). This is reminiscent of the sacred double-axes carved on the two pillars in the crypts at the centre of the Knossos Labyrinth (see Plate 10.4). The Atlantean kings wrote their judgements on tablets, recalling the clay archive tablets found at Knossos. The Atlanteans sheathed important walls in different coloured metals, while the Cretans, Melians, Keans and Therans coloured their walls with paint. The Atlanteans decorated their temple with 'golden' statues of Poseidon and nereids on dolphins: round the temple there were statues of princes and their wives (*Crit.* 116E). The Cretans in their turn were credited by the ancient Greeks with devising the first modern images of gods: they certainly made huge statues with metal fittings. One larger-than-life goddess is known to have existed at Knossos[1] and another at the peak sanctuary on Mount Juktas. The Therans may have made statues, although no remains have yet been discovered. We do however know that they made many noble fresco images, some of deities.

WRITING

The bronze age people in the Aegean used both the Cretan scripts, Linear A and Linear B. As early as 1867, Fouqué found a piece of Theran pottery with an inscription later identified as Linear A, the script used in Crete from 1700 BC until 1450 BC.[2] Most of the inscriptions discovered so far are lists of produce and offerings, sometimes with the names of gods.[3]

Both language and writing must have been used for things other than these lists, but no religious texts or poems have been found. Therans and Cretans must have written poetry: the people of neighbouring cultures wrote poetry and it is reasonable to assume that the Minoans did so too. The wall-paintings prove that they had music. Purely instrumental lyre music seems to have been a later idea than the lyre itself, so the gilded lyre shown being played by a monkey was almost certainly used to accompany song, and there cannot be songs without lyrics. The Minoans probably performed poetry with a musical accompaniment.

Evans argued that the images on the silver rhyton from Mycenae and the Town Mosaic from Knossos proved the existence of epics.[4] Hesiod and Homer describe epic scenes depicted on the shields of Heracles and Achilles.[5] It has been said that Evans's description of the Town Mosaic reads like a description of the North Frieze from Building 4 at Akrotiri.[6] Possibly the wall-painting scheme in Building 4 was intended to show seasonal rituals, communal rites of passage like the Spring Nautical Festival, but later on, perhaps when the original impulse had been forgotten, became a trigger for the composition of an epic. In other words Therans, or Cretan or Mycenean visitors, invented stories to explain the images on the walls and this was how a whole imagined history came into being. It has been suggested that the Homeric sagas are really Minoan sagas, originally told in the Minoan tongue and later translated into Greek. If hexameters are alien to Greek, as has been alleged, the metre too may have been imported from the Minoan culture.[7] Possibly whole verses in Homer were lifted from a Minoan original.

In support of this idea is the notion that the epic poem *Gilgamesh* was originally told in Sumerian and later translated into the Accadian and Hittite languages. It is known that Minoan names were transcribed from language to language. There is a writing tablet from the reign of Thutmose III, 1483–1450 BC, which is headed 'The Making of Keftiu [Cretan] Names'. In about 1500 BC, the text of a medical papyrus was taken to Egypt from Crete and transcribed into Egyptian. It was a magic spell:

SANTI KAPUPI WAYYA AJAMANTA RAKUKARA

This is a pentameter, not a hexameter, but it is interesting that it breaks into feet that are regular dactyls, as used in Homer. The galloping six-foot dactylic line was preferred for epic verse, and it looks as if dactyls may have been a Minoan invention.

But this line of thought runs on ahead of the evidence so far available from the Cyclades or Crete. Poetry chanted or sung to the accompaniment of a lyre almost certainly existed, whether short lyrics, ballads or long epics; all the wall-paintings can tell us is that the material and ideas were available for the construction of epic poetry. The concrete evidence is disappointing. Given the story of Cretan bronze age archaeology, it seems unlikely that any creative writing will ever be recovered at any bronze age Aegean site.

It may be, in the end, that there are no writings recording the thoughts of the bronze age inhabitants of Crete or the Cyclades.[8] It will be one of the great archaeological disappointments if the Minoan civilization should prove to have made no record in words of its ideas. As an old scribe of the Fourth Dynasty wrote to his son a thousand years before the zenith of the Minoan civilization, 'If only I could make you love books more than you love your mother! If only I could make you understand their beauty! The scribe's is the greatest of professions.'[9] The Minoans, so far as we can tell, thought differently.

WALL-PAINTINGS

If they left little in the way of written documentation about themselves, the Minoans left a rich collection of eloquent images. The wall-paintings of Thera are the finest surviving creations of a bronze age society anywhere in the Aegean world. They are snapshots of life before the eruption, and show what may have been lost at Knossos. They show what people looked like, what Therassos itself looked like when complete. There are hints at refined and complex social differentiation among people in their clothing, hints at values, hints at something indefinable that we might call tone or atmosphere.

Painters used yellow, red, brown and black pigments, achieving a rich variety of colour and tone by mixing and diluting. A little black was mixed with blue to make a light grey, black with red for brown, white with red to make a range of pinks. Cretan painters mixed yellow with blue to make green, but Theran painters, on present evidence, did not. It may be that the colour green was only 'discovered' after the time when the Theran frescoes were painted, in other words too late for the Theran painters to have adopted its use.[10] Green can never have been a conspicuous colour on the island. Whatever the reason, yellow ochre was used to represent light greens and blue to represent dark greens. In a similar way, polished white plaster was used for female flesh tones, red for male flesh tone. The colours are not natural, though the eye quickly accepts them as such. We know dolphins and monkeys are not really blue; we learn to read the blue as grey.

Variety was also achieved by using space in different ways. Sometimes a design was allowed to spread freely across unbroken areas of wall, continuing round room corners, as in the Spring Fresco in Building 12 or the Blue Monkeys Fresco of Building 11. This broad, free approach may be associated with Thera's alfresco position, open to sea and sky, open to social and cultural influence from all sides. The Spring Fresco spreads right across jambs to the very edges of openings to emphasize this panoramic effect.

Sometimes walls were divided into panels for a repeating design, like the cabins in Building 4. Sometimes a design was adjusted to exploit the breaks created by door and window openings. In Building 11, antelopes faced one another across a large window space, while the narrow space between a room corner and a door in the same room was used for the Boxing Boys Fresco. We have already seen another compositional technique in Building 4, where the strips of wall above windows, doors and niches were used for a narrative frieze; the dado below the windows was painted with panels of imitation marble. Usually Theran painters liked to emphasize the upper and lower limits of their compositions by drawing in horizontal coloured bands.

Several distinct characteristics speak of a Theran, in contrast to Cretan, style of painting. The untouched white plaster background is one. Another is the single background undulation above the figures. In Minoan pictures there are often several undulations, known as 'silent waves', passing behind the figures. The implication is that Theran artists took the undulation idea, adapting it in a way that made a better pattern. Theran painters generally show more interest in the figures than in their setting, more interest that is than Cretan painters. They used clear outlines, then applied colour washes in a watercolour style, which incidentally allowed them to paint translucent material such as lace. The fragments of wall-paintings found at Ayia Irini and Phylakopi also exhibit this 'watercolour' technique, implying that what we are seeing is a Cycladic wall-painting tradition that is recognizably different from the Cretan tradition, however much was borrowed from Crete.[11]

A final Theran characteristic is the absence of a hanging inverted landscape border along the top of the picture.[12] There are exceptions such as the rock work above Town 5 in Building 4 and above the Wounded Girl in Building 1. In other words, Theran artists imported Cretan conventions when it suited them, in this case to establish the strong sense of scenic setting the client evidently wanted. It is also significant that in the major religious fresco of the Goddess the scene, an elaborate outdoor altar, is set very carefully and formally: possibly a deliberate reference across to the formal temple-art of Minoan Crete.

Several artists were at work in Thera, sometimes on the same painting, where one artist corrected the work of others. Themes were dictated by the client, presumably the house owner, but painters had considerable freedom in the way they interpreted them. The artwork is free, with plenty of scope for individual expression. The effect of this artistic freedom is a remarkable exuberance, the excitement of creativity still communicating after over 3,000 years. It is very different from the formal style of the Cretan frescoes, where the oppressive control of the temple priestesses and their bureaucracy is evident. The explanation may simply be that the 'house art' at Akrotiri was commissioned by the more prosperous house owners in the community, not by the priesthood. If and when a Theran temple is unearthed, it may be that its decor will prove to be of a more formal, politically correct type, closer in style to that of the Knossian wall-paintings. It may alternatively be that Theran society as a whole was freer of control by temple authorities, and that what we will see will be the result of the prevailing 'free market' spirit of merchants and middlemen operating within a competitive economy. It may be that these expensive-looking art works were commissioned to impress social peers and business rivals just as modern businessmen adorn their homes and offices with Bacons, Hockneys and Frinks.

The freedom and competition encouraged by patrons produced a panorama of Theran society. Some paintings have an obvious religious content. Some were found with religious cult equipment, showing that the rooms they decorated were used for religious ceremonies, though not necessarily exclusively. In this respect the Therans may have been more flexible than the Cretans, who set aside suites of rooms exclusively for religious use.[13] Here we see another way in which Therans were borrowing Cretan customs and using them rather freely. The art is nevertheless never purely decorative in intention, but magico-religious, and in this the art of Thera is the same as that of Crete and Egypt.[14]

The Theran paintings are the culmination of a long evolution. The first attempts at wall-painting in the Aegean were very simple. In early bronze age Cretan villages, house walls were painted Pompeian red; this practice is still evident in the decorative schemes of late bronze age Knossos, where red is often the background or dado colour. The early all-over red walls gave way to a period of experimentation with geometric patterns painted on walls and floors at Phaistos in the Old Temple Period. Then, in the late bronze age, there was a flowering of wall-painting in both Crete and the Cyclades, establishing a tradition of pictorial art that spread at once to the Greek mainland[15] and was to become one of the most distinctive threads in European culture from then on.

Of the schemes of decoration belonging to the final stage, those in Buildings 1 and 4 have the most to say about Theran religion and society. They will be discussed last, in Chapter 8.

FRESCOES OF BUILDING 6
(THE HOUSE OF THE LADIES)

Excavation of this three-storey building is still in progress, so the contents are incompletely understood. One chamber on the second storey was decorated with clusters of large flowering plants which Warren identifies as papyrus. The Papyrus Room Fresco showed low hillocky terrain with clumps of papyrus growing on it against a white background. Above, a broad frieze of blue, white and red bands ran round the room. A corridor from the south-east corner led to the Papyrus Room and it was the walls of this corridor that carried the famous frescoes of 'Ladies'. The lady on the south wall faced east, as did the one on the north wall. Both were reaching out and should be seen as part of a three-dimensional composition, a pair of mature female worshippers or attendants approaching a person, goddess or object of veneration painted on the east wall, now lost.

There is no obvious reason for supposing that the Papyrus Room had any religious significance, although it may, like the landscape of lilies in the Spring Fresco, have had a covert symbolic value. The fact that papyrus probably did not grow on Thera and artists must have borrowed the iconographic image from Egypt, perhaps via Crete, suggests that it had a symbolic religious value, associated with the griffin,[16] which was seen as inhabiting papyrus swamps. It was also seen as the familiar of the Minoan goddess. In the Throne Sanctuary at Knossos, the presence of griffins implied that an epiphany of the goddess was imminent; in creating a papyrus swamp in a room on Thera the artist was conjuring, luring griffins and thus creating a spirit landscape in which the goddess could manifest.

Both Spyridon Marinatos and his daughter Nanno have drawn attention to four repositories under the floor of the Papyrus Room,[17] citing them as evidence of a religious cult use for that room, but this is a second-storey chamber and the boxes are really cupboards in the first-storey room below. The contents of the cupboards look like household utensils. The damage suffered by Building 6 during the eruption was unusual in that the walls of the lowest level of the building on the east side were blasted out and the upper storeys sank, almost without distortion, onto the debris of the ground floor.[18] Cult equipment in the adjacent Room 7, on the other hand, is evidence of cult activity in the Papyrus Room: there were rhyta, triton shells and nippled ewers.[19] Room 7 was not directly accessible from the Papyrus Room, but a window between them might have been a serving hatch.

The two women in the frescoes are mature. One, leaning forwards, has large pendulous breasts hanging out of her bodice. Both women have dark wavy hair reaching their waists. Although mature, they are not old enough to have their hair tied into buns. The woman on the south wall is stooping reverentially and holding a flounced overskirt, which she is offering to a missing (seated?) figure to the east; this is probably a robing ceremony and the missing figure was a priestess being prepared for a religious ceremony. The adjacent bathroom suggests that preparation and dressing went on in this area in reality, not just on the walls, and it is important to recognize that often wall-paintings, here as at Knossos, sign the use of the rooms they decorate. Indeed, their purpose is to signal and reinforce function. The ceremony the three women were preparing for probably took place in the Papyrus Room.[20] But, most significantly of all,

Figure 7.1 A female 'presentation' scene, based on fragments of wall-painting found in the Pillar Crypt, Melos
Source: Morgan 1990, p. 259

female presentation ceremonies of this kind were seen not only in Thera, but at Ayia Irini[21] and in the Procession Fresco at Knossos;[22] they were part of a pan-Aegean culture.

FRESCOES OF BUILDING 11
(BLOCK BETA)

Rooms 1 and 6 in Building 11 produced important paintings. Room 6, of which the north-west corner survives, had an all-over design of monkeys scrambling over a rocky landscape. Monkeys also featured in the Cretan frescoes, such as the Saffron Gatherer from the temple at Knossos, where they attended the Goddess; the same is true in Theran frescoes. One fragment from Building 21 shows an altar supported by columns topped by papyrus capitals and a monkey with its arms bent in a Minoan worship gesture. Another monkey, playing a gilded lyre, was painted on a wall in Building 1. The Building 11 design spread round at least two walls; the other two were badly damaged, but seem to have had additional features. Nanno Marinatos notes that, as in the Nature Fresco in the House of the Frescoes at Knossos, there were monkeys, swallows, crocuses, myrtle and goats: probably both frescoes, the one Theran, the other Cretan, illustrated the same spring theme.[23]

Room 1 was better preserved. Its upper storey was divided by a north–south brick partition, creating an eastern chamber with five openings. Two doors flanking a niche in the south wall left a narrow panel, used for the beautiful painting of the Boxing Boys. The boys' heads were shaved; many of the children in the frescoes had nearly all their hair shorn off to emphasize their status in the community, and in particular to show which rites of passage they had or had not passed through. Far from being a game, the boxing match was a central act in a rite of passage.

The other three walls of Room 1 were covered with paintings of antelopes. The pair on the west wall showed what Marinatos thought were courtship gestures. Doumas in his turn saw no connection between the boys and the antelopes,[24] but the key lies in the interpretation of the antelopes' behaviour. Marinatos thought the animals were engaged in courtship, which the boys clearly were not, but since the paired animals are the same size they are probably all male and engaged in competitive behaviour: gazelles are well known for being competitive and territorial. More aggressive behaviour – confrontation and head-butting – might have been depicted, but it was competition not conflict that the artist wanted to show. In exactly the same way, boxing is competitive, not aggressive, a ritualized status struggle, and it now becomes clear that we are being shown parallel situations from the animal world and the human sphere as the Therans saw them. The 7- or 8-year-old Boxing Boys are, in a controlled and ritualized situation, struggling for status in the same way that animals compete

Figure 7.2 The Boxing Boys fresco

with one another for mates or territory. It is a decorative scheme with a specific social, ethical and religious story to tell, and the fact that the same red silent wave flows behind boys and antelopes emphasizes that they are to be seen in parallel.[25]

The boys are shown naked but for a belt. Their heads are shaved but for two long tresses at the back and two small locks above the forehead, and each wears a single boxing glove on his right hand. One wears jewellery – none is visible on the other boy – and the jewelled boy may be older or for some other reason hold higher status. The combination of jewellery-wearing, nudity and shaved head indicates that this is a ceremonial occasion. The wearing of the belt may be significant, in that Cretan males regularly wore a belt and loincloth for ceremonial games such as bull-leaping or boxing, and also when attending religious ceremonies.[26] The Theran boys are nevertheless not wearing loincloths, possibly to emphasize that they are mere boys.

The test represented by the boxing match is a classic rite of passage, reminiscent of a whole string of tests that boys have been subjected to in ancient and modern Europe. What we see in Thera, as in ancient Egypt, is the attainment of higher social status by a public display of physical strength, skill and courage.

Figure 7.3 Two fresco antelopes challenge one another

Figure 7.4 One of the Boxing Boys (fresco detail)

FRESCOES OF BUILDING 12
(BLOCK DELTA)

Room 2 is the only room in Building 12 to have had wall-paintings, so they mark it out as a room of special distinction. Fortunately, the paintings were found still attached to three walls and in a marvellous state of preservation. The fourth wall consisted of a niche, a window and a door. The painting shows a rocky mountainside composed of multi-coloured rocks in red, blue, grey and yellow ochre, just the sort of terrain seen west of Akrotiri. Only 1 kilometre from the archaeological site it is possible to see lava coloured black, red and yellow, with the jagged contrasts shown in the fresco; it is part of the old Minoan land surface and must have been even more conspicuous before it was smothered in ash. The colours and forms in the fresco arise directly from the artist's observation of the landscape.[27] These are the multi-coloured rocks, 'some white, some black, some red', described by Plato as being available on Atlantis for building (*Crit.* 116A–B).

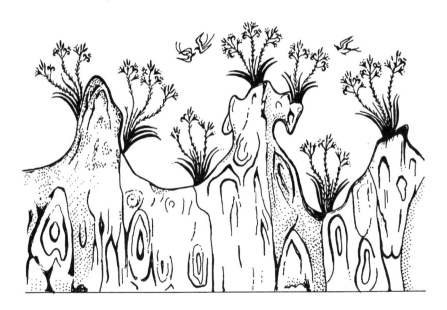

Figure 7.5 The Spring Fresco: this scene covers an entire wall

The painting as a whole is a portrayal of the Spring Festival under the patronage of the spring goddess, a primitive Easter; the swallows have returned to mate. It is said that swallows no longer nest on Thera, that they have shunned Thera ever since the eruption, which covered any deposits that might have been used for nest-building – but I have seen swallows on Mavros Rachidhi, and just a week before Easter.

8

ART, RELIGION AND SOCIETY

The fresco schemes in Buildings 1 and 4 at Akrotiri are crammed with evidence of the nature of Theran society and ritual, though the emphasis is different, and we see two different sides of the culture. In Building 1 individual Therans are involved in religious ceremonies in what may be an imagined or supernatural landscape where meetings with gods and goddesses were possible. In Building 4 there is a more literal approach to what seem to be the physical, everyday landscapes of the Aegean islands; we also see the whole community turning out for major social events, a prehistoric equivalent of Frith's 'Derby Day'. After exploring these images, it should be possible to pull the threads together and make a reasoned assessment of the true relationship between Plato's description of Atlantis and the prehistoric realities of the Aegean.

A PANORAMA OF ATLANTIS

The upper-storey room in the north-west corner of Building 4 contained a frieze of miniature frescoes running continuously round the walls above doorways and windows. Ceiling beams ran west–east across the ceiling, with sockets in the east and west walls, which is why the frieze on the east wall is shallower than those on the north and south walls;[1] very little of the west wall frieze remains because most of that fell outwards into the street during the catastrophe, but the fragments that survive show that a narrative extended round all four walls.

At the middle level, the level of the windows, there were two panels with paintings of naked youths carrying fish. They are shaven-headed apart from locks at front and back, as well as naked, and these features suggest that they are engaged in a religious ceremony: they are not just fishermen, any more than the Boxing Boys are just boys boxing. There can be little doubt that the strings of fish they carry are offerings.[2] The placing of the two boys is significant; one is in the south-west corner walking northwards, the other in the north-east walking westwards. On the window sill in the north-west corner, where the two boys were heading, was an offering table decorated with dolphins, rocks and seaweed. The table and the paintings show not only that offerings were made in the room,

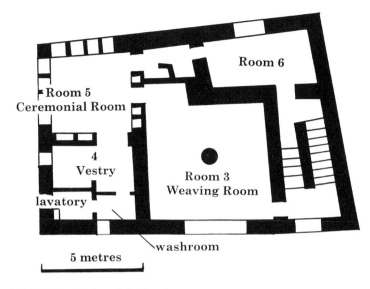

Figure 8.1 Building 4: plan of the first floor

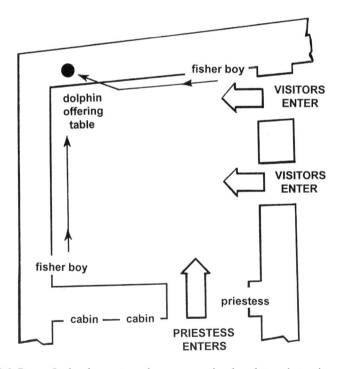

Figure 8.2 Room 5: the decorative scheme at eye level and its relationship with the room's function

but where and how. This line of thought becomes even more productive when we look at the fresco scheme in Building 1, still more at Knossos, but we must first turn our attention to the friezes.

Visitors would have entered through one of the doorways in the east wall, so the west wall frieze is the first thing they would have seen and that is where the painter will have begun his narrative.[3] Town 5 at the western end of the south wall frieze therefore marked the climax of the story, confirming the earlier conclusion that Town 5 was intended to be Akrotiri itself. Only tiny fragments of Town 1 survive, so we must move on to the north wall, where the Meeting on the Hill and a Shipwreck scene survive. A flotilla of ships is shown, one with its bowsprit broken, either by colliding with another vessel or by running onto the rocks, both common mishaps.[4] Some have suggested that because a man standing on one of the ships wears a Minoan kilt and others, in the water, are naked two different peoples are represented, supporting the idea of a sea battle.[5] But nakedness was a pictorial device to indicate death or defeat – in this case both, as we are looking at shipwreck victims floating in the Aegean Sea. The depiction of the corpses in the water is very accomplished, with some acutely observed detail. The hair of one corpse is shown sticking out radially, which is exactly what happens to a head of long hair when immersed.

Close by the rocky shore is a curious building with a flat roof and a row of huge doors, two of which open to reveal dark empty spaces inside. This is a ship-shed.[6] Some men in knee-length tunics above the shipshed are not watching the shipwreck: one crouches on his haunches, a characteristic 'prehistoric' resting position. It is likely that these men are part of a separate event, a procession to the Meeting on the Hill. Two women in long coloured skirts and white bodices pointedly go about their everyday work of carrying in vases on their heads water from a rectangular well-head: two more vases on its parapet wait to be filled. Their activity is markedly separate, at least on a superficial reading, from the male procession and the shipwreck.

Further up the hillside is a hedged enclosure, a fold for livestock with shade trees. Herdsmen drive flocks of sheep and goats along the hillside. Below is a line of warriors armed with long spears, rectangular shields covered in dappled cowhides and plumed boar's tusk helmets. They have knob-kerries tucked through their belts, probably for hand-to-hand fighting after the spears had been thrown. Whether these warriors were enemies attacking the civilians just described or members of the same community returning from battle is hard to judge. The fact that the civilians are going about their daily business in a normal relaxed way suggests the latter, and it may be that the 'message' is that a strong military force makes possible the normal idyllic way of life shown; the warriors are there to protect the civilian population.[7]

On the hill top to the left is a meeting of men dressed in two distinct ways. Two men wear only kilts, leaving their arms free to make a Minoan gesture of adoration, upper arms extending forward slightly, lower arms pointing vertically upwards with the hands open and thumbs pointing back at the face.

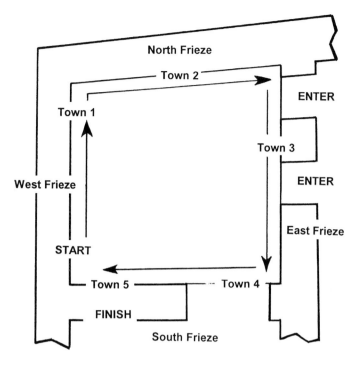

Figure 8.3 Room 5: the decorative scheme at frieze level

Figure 8.4 North Frieze detail: shipsheds, women collecting water, herdsmen, soldiers

The painting is indistinct, but it looks as if these two worshippers are making the adoration gesture with the right arm only. The left elbow is held at the side, with the forearm extending forward horizontally, palm upward. We see this in more detail in a fresco fragment from the temple at Knossos: a woman on a balcony above the Tripartite Shrine makes the same gesture.[8] Other men on the hill are enveloped in white robes that make saluting impossible. Whether this means they were of higher ranking is difficult to tell. Two of them have additional hemming strips, suggesting a pecking order. The men on the hill have no ostensible purpose; they are doing nothing other than meeting and have no equipment: there are no altars or shrines, so there is no proof that this is a gathering at a peak sanctuary.

There is archaeological and iconographic evidence of peak sanctuaries with shrines and altars on Crete, such as Juktas above Knossos and Petsofa above Palaikastro, and a few have been identified from the late bronze age in Laconia, Messenia and Argos on the Greek mainland. There is less evidence from the Cyclades, though it may be that the building on the Troullos hill near Ayia Irini on Kea was a focus for ritual activity, and the late bronze age building on Mavros Rachidhi may have been the peak sanctuary for Akrotiri. Low hilltops within sight of the sea and within easy reach of the town were favoured, and we are shown a procession of men going up the hillside from the settlement itself.

The apparently disconnected snapshots of Theran life must be thematically linked and the ceremony may be the key. Peak sanctuaries were located in the summer pastures and were thus a focus for shepherds; the elevated position suggests an appeal to whatever deities controlled the weather, and this would be a major concern to the herders. In rural Greece, 23 April is celebrated as the beginning of summer, when the flocks are moved to the high pastures. At Arachora, a rite in which the men of the village run to the top of a hill is still performed. Is this shown on the south wall, where youths run to and from the building on Mavros Rachidhi? The Meeting on the Hill may be a statelier version of this, with men walking solemnly to the summit to inaugurate the summer grazing season. The herders on the same hillside take their flocks to the summer pastures.

What of the women? Summer was a time when water levels in streams and wells dropped and the work of fetching water from the well was harder and more critical to the domestic economy: that is why women bringing water from the well are shown – it was an activity that became more conspicuous in summer.

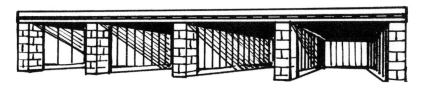

Figure 8.5 Shipshed at Kommos, reconstructed from excavation

The shipwreck takes its place as a summer risk. Navigation resumed following the Spring Nautical Festival, making the resumption of trade possible, but also maritime disasters like the accident we see on the fresco and the activities of pirates. Piracy made it necessary for the island community to defend itself, hence the soldiers.[9]

A gap to the right of the shipwreck and warriors makes it impossible to reconstruct the way the north wall frieze connected with the east wall frieze. A new reconstruction by Televantou is persuasive; she adds a town on the strength of fragments showing buildings.[10] The subject of the east wall frieze is a landscape with a meandering river, on the face of it a pastoral without human drama.[11] Televantou believes that the north wall sea stretched all the way to the room corner with the river on the east wall emptying into it; probably there was a harbour town at its mouth.[12] Beside the river are palms and papyri, ducks, a wildcat, a deer and a griffin. The griffin is shown in its mythic wetland habitat, running at full gallop after the deer: the wildcat stalks a preening duck. In spite of the apparent lack of narrative, a theme of hunter and hunted emerges, possibly a commentary on the theme of victory and defeat on the north wall.

Is this a real river? If so, it cannot have been on Thera: even with its centre intact, Thera could only have fed a few small streams. If a fully fledged river is intended, it might have been on Crete. It could alternatively have been the Menderes or the Nile: we know Theran navigators sailed to Anatolia and Egypt. If the river is the Menderes, Town 3 readily identifies itself as Miletus, a known Minoan trading post. A simpler explanation for the interlude of the river landscape between two Aegean panoramas is that it was a genre painting borrowed from elsewhere. 'Nile Scenes' were common in Egyptian art and they were borrowed by Minoan artists, who changed them to suit Minoan interests. Of five Nile Scenes known from the Aegean, this is the best preserved, but they share a de-emphasis on human activity. The hunting theme is conserved, only now the animals are the hunters.[13] Even though the concept of a river landscape was imported, the east wall frieze may be a near-authentic landscape. Since palms and papyrus plants occur singly along the river banks, not in clumps, it has been suggested that this was a deliberately planted water garden, with native and imported species.[14] Against this idea is the population of the garden with griffins, deer, ducks and wildcats; this is more like a safari park, to say nothing of the supernatural element. It should also be borne in mind that fragments not incorporated into the museum reconstruction show buildings, so a town[15] formed part of the composition and the landscape is not, after all, empty of human activity.

The river may have its source in the land shown on the eastern side of the south wall frieze. This is a representation of a specific inhabited landscape: the narrative sense returns in strength. Its composition falls into three. On the left is a rocky mountainous land, possibly an Aegean island, possibly part of the Greek or Anatolian mainland, the setting of a coastal town, Town 4. On the right is another mountainous land, with a larger coastal town, Town 5.

Between them a fleet sails, filling the sea in the centre of the panel. This composition has excited a great deal of speculation. The towns and skylines have a very specific feeling about them. As we saw earlier, Town 5 is Akrotiri.[16] Where Town 4 is cannot be ascertained. The dressing of the ships, the use of paddles, the ceremonial nature of the event – all suggest that a short distance separates Towns 4 and 5, so Town 4 may have been on another island in the Cyclades, such as Melos or Kea (still a day's journey away), or it may have been another settlement on Thera, perhaps in the South Bay; if so, we may be seeing the town of which Fouqué found traces on Therasia. The flora and fauna surrounding Town 4 are consistent with the Aegean. The mountainsides are clad with umbrella pines,[17] contrasting with the treeless 'Arrival Land'. 'Departure Land' is less variable in colour than Arrival Land. My impression is that Arrival Land is densely settled and deforested Thera, while Departure Land is a different island, less densely settled, less intensely used, probably limestone, probably not far from Thera. This argues for one of the nearby islands, Naxos perhaps. A river runs into the sea beside Town 4.[18]

The people are differentiated by style of dress. Rustics on the hillside wear fleecy ponchos; ordinary townsmen wear tunics; youths standing in a line in front of the wall are either naked or wear only loincloths; others similarly undressed run to and from the building on the hill, perhaps to get a better view of the ships arriving. Another group separating itself by style of dress and size is the older women, who wear white dresses with black stripes and have their hair in buns. Groups of these high-status women congregate on roof tops. Their larger size shows their importance. One has a balcony to herself with sacral horns

Figure 8.6 Town 4 (Departure Town) on the South Frieze

mounted on the parapet in front of her and a young naked male attendant standing on a lower level behind her: she is probably the high priestess. In Town 4, a smaller, less sophisticated settlement, there seems to be only one woman depicted but, significantly, she is alone on her roof whereas there are four men on the neighbouring roof.

Another striking difference between the two towns is that Town 4 has no curtain wall – it rises out of a coastal reed-bed – whereas Town 5 has a substantial wall, apparently of ashlar masonry, with an elaborate city gate and what looks like a guardroom with barred windows above it. Since the picture shows a view towards the west, the town wall must have run along the town's eastern boundary, defending the city on its landward side, very much the fortification pattern at other key Aegean towns such as Ayia Irini and Phylakopi.[19]

It was not only people but settlements that had varying status in this society. The late bronze age 'Minoan' settlements of the Cyclades, Anatolia, the Dodecanese and Crete were complementary components of a large-scale Aegean society. Their areas give a good indication of likely relative importance.

Akrotiri appears to have been ten times as important as Phylakopi. In population too it would have been impressive. It is difficult to estimate prehistoric population, but Sinclair Hood's estimate that late bronze age Knossos had a population of 12,000 seems sensible. This gives a population density of 160 per hectare if we assume no-one lived in the temple, and this estimate may be too low. Modern European sensibilities – the perceived need for personal space, for instance – may cause us to underestimate bronze age urban densities. Estimates of a thousand people per hectare derived from analyses of Amerindian pueblos may be nearer the reality. If we allow for some open spaces in Minoan towns, a figure of 500 per hectare is reasonable. That being so, Knossos would have had a population of 20,000, Palaikastro 18,000, Mallia 12,500, Phylakopi 2,000 and Akrotiri 10,000–15,000, about the same as Ugarit.[20]

Table 8.1 Size of 'Minoan' settlemnts

Town	Island	Area (hectares) [mainly Wiener 1990]	
Knossos	Crete	75	
Palaikastro	Crete	36	
Mallia	Crete	25	
Akrotiri	Thera	20	(Warren 1979) or
		30	(Castleden this volume)
Triandha	Rhodes	15	
Zakro	Crete	9	
Gournia	Crete	3	
Phylakopi	Melos	2	
Pseira	Crete	2	
Ayia Irini	Kea	1	
Pyrgos	Crete	0.5	

As well as supporting the town at Akrotiri, Thera sustained numerous outlying settlements. The list of known Late Cycladic sites in Santorini is impressive: Davis and Cherry list fourteen.[21] Other Cycladic islands gathered their populations into a single settlement; although Akrotiri must, from its size and sophistication, have been the main settlement on Thera, many lived in farming hamlets dispersed round the island, with an average spacing of 2 kilometres, giving a settlement pattern much like that of today.

The ship procession passing between Towns 4 and 5 was, as we have seen, the annual inauguration of navigation. All eyes turn to the sea, all watch the procession – except two fishermen with nets over their shoulders and they, significantly, are part of the maritime life which the fresco celebrates. They are full-grown versions of the fisherboys shown in the room corners. The two young fishermen are a reminder that there may be other layers of theme and meaning behind the fresco sequence. The excavators of Palaikastro in eastern Crete drew attention to the similarity between the remains they uncovered and Town 5.[22] Whilst I think it unlikely that Town 5 *is* Palaikastro, there may be a link of a different kind between the two places. In the Hellenistic and Roman periods there was a Spring Festival at Palaikastro celebrating the rescue of the infant Zeus by the Kouretes. The rite probably had its beginnings in the Minoan period, when Palaikastro was known as Dikte after its association with Diktaian Zeus. Perhaps boys from Thera and elsewhere in the Minoan world travelled to Palaikastro as one of their rites of passage. Perhaps this is why one line of youths waits eagerly at the harbour side for the fleet's arrival and another runs excitedly up and down the hill. Perhaps, alongside the earlier interpretation we may place a second, a narrative of the spring or early summer expedition taking boys to Palaikastro and possibly other locations. Perhaps the sons of the wealthier Theran families were treated to an educational cruise, and Building 4 was a feasting place for the young aristocrats once they returned.[23]

The fragmentary west wall frieze included a ship that had some characteristics of the processional ships on the south wall, but also some features of the north wall ships. What this combination of features signified is hard to guess without any contextual detail, but it implies a narrative connection between the three walls.[24] Two more fragments show part of a town, the most distinctive feature of which is a large triangular projection sticking up from each of the roofs. This feature is not shared by any building in any other town in the sequence, so it was intended to indicate a different town in a different place. Interestingly, the same architectural feature appears in a fresco at Ayia Irini, so perhaps this is a Kean house design. The narrative clearly begins in a town other than Akrotiri. In all, we are dealing with five towns: Town 1 may be Ayia Irini, Town 3 may be Miletus, and Town 5 is certainly Akrotiri.[25] The linking of the towns by navigation carries a suggestion of the Minoan trading empire with Thera as its fulcrum. This is reminiscent of the ten city-states of Atlantis with their ten kings; perhaps each of the larger Aegean islands was an early city-state, like the temple-centres on Crete. Seen in this light, the frieze is a panoramic view of Atlantis.

The east wall frieze is a landscaped version of the *agon*, the classic Minoan theme of confrontation and struggle. The north wall shows a festival heralding summer, which carries with it a hint of struggle: the struggle for water, the struggle with the elements at sea, the struggle against pirates or invaders. The south wall shows the Nautical Procession in which similar oppositions are tacit, but the prevailing mood is one of people on top, on both land and sea – the struggle won.

Next to Room 5 is the Room of the Cabins, which had a related ceremonial use. Painted on the door jamb connecting the two was a saffron-robed priestess carrying an incense burner into Room 5. Her head is shaved except for a few long tresses on top. Her ears and lips are reddened with red ochre and she wears big earrings. She represents the priestess who passed through the door in real life: the portrayal in paint freezes the ritual for all time, ensures that its efficacy is endlessly renewed.[26] Room 4 was subdivided, with a lavatory in the south-west corner and a washroom with a bathtub in the south-east corner. These features mark Room 4 out as a vestry or preparation area. The bowl of pigment found in the bathroom was presumably used for face-painting and applied to the living priestess's ears and lips before she stepped into Room 5.

The decoration of Room 4 was unusual. Above a marbled dado the walls were divided into rectangular panels filled with images of stern cabins from ships. The cabins were seats of honour for the captains. In some, the captain's spear was fixed behind and his helmet mounted on top, to emphasize his warrior status. It is likely that the cabin was detachable: off the ship, it became a palanquin (palanquin frescoes and models were made at Knossos). The cabin thus became a symbol of high social status, of Theran command of the high seas, and also possibly of human supremacy over the elements. The decorative scheme of the house as a whole set the scene for male induction ceremonies, and the cabins were there to emphasize that the youths undergoing the rites of passage would one day become captains or would in some other capacity, perhaps as merchants, share in the Theran lordship over the seas.

GROWING UP

Sixty metres south of Triangle Square is another square with another fine ashlar building fronting it on the west side. This, Building 1, was the scene of more elaborate ceremonies, the nature of which is explicit in the wall-paintings. Six rooms on the ground floor and another six on the floor above were used for initiation ceremonies, and the architecture implies that the entire eastern half of the building was given over to cult use, while the western half was a conventional dwelling, a home for a priestess's household, who acted as care-takers and officiants for the cult rooms. The emphasis on initiation rites is significant, in that it was shared by Minoan Crete; the fresco schemes in the temple at Knossos show a variety of religious rituals including a communion rite.

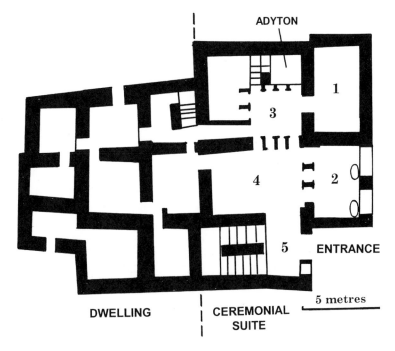

Figure 8.7 Building 1 (Xeste 3) at Akrotiri

Plate 8.1 Building 1 at Akrotiri: entrance to the left, Room 2 to the right

The tradition of initiation rites was to outlive the Minoan civilization, and was later lifted by the Spartans.[27]

The east wing was entered by way of a monumental doorway in the south-east corner of the building. The plan is designed to control people's movements and what they could see. Two of Room 4's walls were pier-and-door partitions, which meant that any paintings on those walls had to be fitted into friezes running above the door spaces. The slow pace of conservation work does not permit an overall reconstruction yet, but the subjects include swallows feeding their young, monkeys playing a lyre and brandishing a sword, presumably the otherworldly monkeys attending the goddess. One of the sets of double doors opened into Room 2, a preparation room containing bathtubs. Significantly, it was not decorated with mythic imagery, but with spirals and rosettes. A second set of double doors opened into a square concourse, Room 3, the focus of the cere-monial activity. The cultic nature of Room 3 and the adjacent chambers is proved by the strongly ritualistic nature of its lavish beautiful paintings.

Here too is the only adyton so far discovered at Akrotiri. There are four in the temple at Knossos, and because the Akrotiri adyton is embellished with fres-coes illuminating its use it is a crucial example, throwing light on the way the four adyta at Knossos were used. The adyton is a small square paved area, sunk below the level of adjacent rooms and reached down an L-shaped staircase. A pier-and-door partition controls visibility into the adyton. In spite of the small window in the north wall, it is a claustrophobic space separated from the rest of the building, and this seems to have been the intention in the design of every adyton – to create a space that feels entirely separate from everywhere else. Whatever rite took place in it can have involved only one, two or three people. The lower parts of the adyton walls are decorated with a dado of local andesite slabs mounted between wooden uprights. The decorative use of stone facing slabs was a recurring feature of Theran architecture. The painted dado in Building 4 shows slabs of different coloured veined marble alternating with vertical timbers. This was a feature of Plato's Atlantean architecture too: 'Some buildings were formed of one colour, others . . . of many colours by alternating the stone for the sake of ornament' (Crit. 116B).

Above the stone dado was a zone of important paintings. The north wall shows a rocky landscape with tussocks of vegetation and three female figures. The one on the left, who is visible from the top of the adyton steps, and was therefore the first in the narrative, walks elegantly and confidently towards the adyton, carrying an offering of a necklace in her right hand. Her bodice front is open, so that her breasts are showing: this tells us she is engaged in a ceremony. Her bodice is nevertheless made of translucent lace. She wears both underskirt and flounced overskirt, emphasizing that this is a ceremonial act. Beyond the small square window lighting the adyton steps, a second girl comes into view. Dressed like the first, she sits on a rock with a myrtle branch in her hair. Her right hand reaches down to her left foot which is cut and bleeding. Faint with pain, she supports her head with her left hand. The pose was borrowed from

Egyptian tomb art, where lamenting women were shown kneeling with one hand touching the ground and the other raised to the forehead; the Therans imported an Egyptian image to portray sorrow or pain.

The second figure became visible when the visitor started descending the steps, but it could also be made visible to onlookers assembled in the concourse by opening the westernmost pair of double-doors.[28] A third girl is walking back towards the injured girl but looking over her shoulder towards something beyond the end of the fresco. She is wearing the same clothing as the other two girls but with the addition of a diaphanous veil, which she is drawing away from her face. Her hair has been shaved off but for two long tresses at the crown and a small lock above the forehead. All who have studied the fresco agree on its ritual character: it shows a ceremony of female initiation.

The three girls are progressing, as real initiands entering the adyton progressed, towards the sunken area and its east wall. On this wall was an architectural composition consisting of walling on each side and a higher structure in the centre framed by running spirals. In a double panel within, rather like one of the double doors ranged round the concourse, there were red lilies, evidently a painted decoration applied to the doors. Above this doorway was a cornice carrying a forbidding pair of sacral horns. Dribbling down the horns, over the cornice and down the doors were splashes of blood. There is iconographic and archaeological evidence that blood from sacrifices was collected to offer at altars.

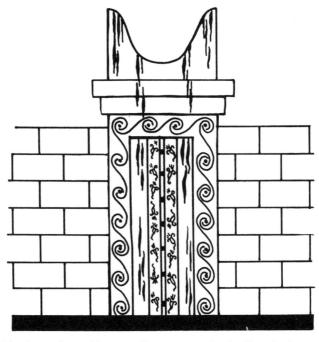

Figure 8.8 Bloodstained sacral horns: wall-painting in the Building 1 adyton

The Ayia Triadha sarcophagus shows a bucket near a trussed bull to collect the blood from its cut throat; on the other side of the sarcophagus we see priestesses carrying buckets to an altar and pouring libations into a large vessel. The finds at Anemospilia on Mount Juktas above Knossos imply that the trussed boy sacrificed on the altar in the northern chamber was also killed by having his throat cut and that one of the attendants was carrying a bucket of his blood to offer before an image of a deity in the room next door at the moment when the temple roof collapsed, shaken down by an earthquake, killing the three responsible for sacrificing the youth.[29]

The sacral horns tell us that this is a surrogate altar, that those entering the adyton and standing in the sunken area were in effect standing before an altar where blood offerings had been, or were to be, made. The composition is neatly linked to the north wall scheme. The girls are making their way towards the altar: even the third girl, who has momentarily turned back, perhaps for the aesthetic purpose of making the composition pivot about the injured girl, is looking over her shoulder at the bloodstained altar: she pulls aside her veil to see the altar more clearly.

The other link between the north and east wall schemes is the injury and bleeding experienced by the central figure. Is hers the blood we see on the altar? The two schemes are clearly one single scheme, however we interpret them in detail, and the three girls on the wall represent a succession of real girls who went down into the adyton for some formative, life-changing experience. It may be that they were actually cut in some token way, possibly even underwent circumcision, and therefore made a literal blood offering. Alternatively, it may be that the bleeding from the injured foot and the associated pain may be metaphorical, that the onset of menstruation is what is really meant, and that the rite of passage is a puberty rite.

Double doors opened westwards from the concourse into 3b, where fragments of another scheme have been found. A big window in its north wall made it a less secret place than the adyton. On the west wall a man wearing a white loincloth sits holding a ewer on his knees, poised to pour its contents. This master of ceremonies is the only adult in the 3b scheme. He is the focus of an all-male ritual, the equivalent of the female rite of passage. Approaching from the north along the west wall is a naked boy carrying a large one-handled bowl. His hairstyle is unusual, cut uniformly short all over the top, with the lower parts shaved neatly up to a straight edge. Also approaching the seated man, along the south wall, are two delightful figures, a euphoric older boy looking over his shoulder as he walks along followed by a younger boy. Both are naked. Both have their heads shaved apart from topknots growing from the crown. The older boy carries a length of patterned cloth, which is probably to be his loincloth or kilt.

This scene is reminiscent of one reconstructed by Mark Cameron from the wall of the Grand Staircase at Knossos.[30] Cameron reconstructed the Knossian procession – seven men and a boy – as a happy, informal group carrying rhyta,

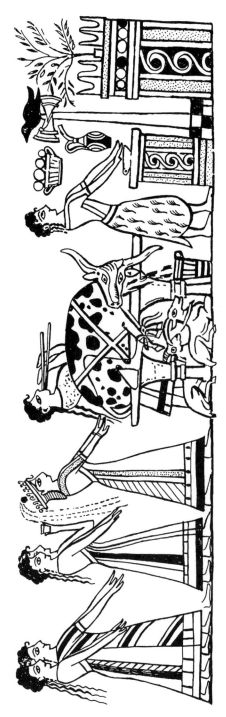

Figure 8.9 Agia Triadha sarcophagus: animal sacrifice

Figure 8.10 Boy carrying bowl

Figure 8.11 Boy carrying robe

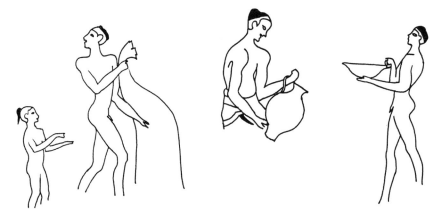

Figure 8.12 Boys' initiation ceremony: the surviving figures

pitchers and lotus blossoms. The Knossian boy is kilted, possibly having completed his initiation rite. Like the older Theran boy, he turns to look behind him, down the stairs towards a man standing on the lower level from which he has climbed; this man may be the master of ceremonies or the boy's sponsor. The atmosphere is livelier than the formal scene in the Procession Corridor, though still more formal than the Theran scene: Cameron is right to see it as pure Minoan, pre-dating Mycenean influence and, it should be added, pre-dating the destruction of Thera. The fresco fragments surviving at Knossos suggest that rites of passage similar to those illustrated at Akrotiri took place there too.[31] As if in confirmation, an upward procession of men similar to the Knossian Grand Staircase procession has been discovered on the staircase of Building 15 at Akrotiri.[32]

Incomplete as the Building 1 fresco is, there can be little doubt that it shows a boy's initiation ceremony. A man presides over the cleansing ritual, probably to take place in Room 2, and then the boy will be dressed in the kilt as a token of manhood, rather like the 'manly gown' signalling arrival at adult status in ancient Rome. It is the older boy who is the initiand: he is the biggest of the three boys, he is speaking or laughing, he clutches the loincloth, and the artist has portrayed him with particular zest; in terms of shape and rhythmic line, it is one of the most beautiful of the Theran fresco images. The varied hairstyles shown in the frescoes speak of a finely stratified social hierarchy. Very young children probably had their heads completely shaved. As they approached puberty isolated locks of hair were allowed to grow long; then the hair was allowed to grow all over, though still in styles tightly controlled by etiquette. Hairstyle indicated status, at least in the social stratum using the cult rooms, and it may be that these nuances of status were affected by an elite group rather than by the population as a whole.[33]

The double doors permitted those standing outside the room to see some, all or none of the wall images, according to the wishes of those officiating. In the

Figure 8.13 Procession on the Grand Staircase at Knossos; this portrays what was actually to be seen on the staircase – a clear indication of the cult activity that went on in the East Wing

Source: After Cameron 1987, p. 587

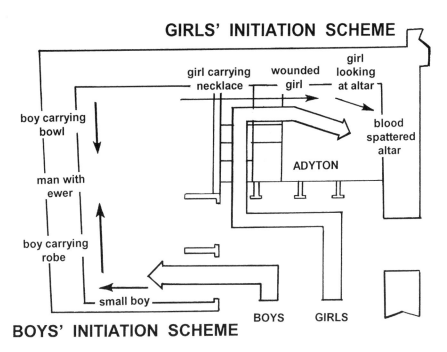

Figure 8.14 Room 3, Building 1: ground floor; the decorative scheme and its relationship with the room's function

same way, those standing in the concourse would always be able to see the first of the girls, but the injured girl only if the first pair of double doors was opened and the girl in the veil only if the second pair was opened; the altar would become visible only when the third pair was opened. Doubtless family members stood in the concourse waiting for the stages in the ritual to be emblematically revealed.

The room plan on the second storey was very similar, except that the adyton was not sunken, as in the East Wing at Knossos, so the use of the rooms must have differed to some extent, but the upper adyton was still the focus of an important scheme of paintings. In the room above the Naked Boys Fresco the image on the west wall was a fowling scene, a genre borrowed from Egyptian art. Ducks were shown in a landscape of reeds. This was not merely decorative. Marshes were the habitat of the mythic griffin, the goddess's familiar, so showing marshland was a way of setting the scene for an appearance of the goddess. Architect and painter together created a mythic landscape that would attract the goddess's griffin; when the griffin appeared, the goddess would not be far behind. The same sympathetic magic was practised in the Throne Sanctuary at Knossos.

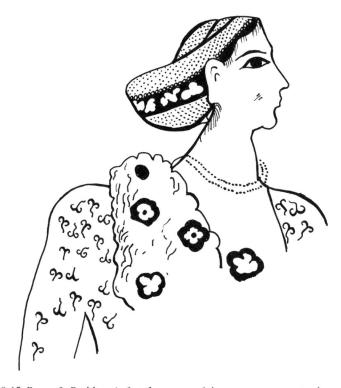

Figure 8.15 Room 3, Building 1: first floor; one of the mature women in the procession

On the south wall of 3b Minoan women processed towards the marshes of the goddess. Matronly age is indicated by buns encased in elaborately decorated hats. One woman wears a garland like the terracotta goddess at Ayia Irini. One carries a bunch of wild roses, an offering to the goddess and a reminder that the dedication to the goddess made in adolescence was life-long: the older women in the community were her servants and adorants just as much as the girls on the ground floor. Not that these matrons were old by modern standards; in the poor-diet, low-hygiene conditions of the Aegean bronze age average life expectancy was 35 for men and only 30 for women.[34] The procession on the wall echoed processions of real women in the space in front of it, just like the painted processions on the walls of the Procession Corridor and Grand Staircase at Knossos. The paintings show us not only what people did, but exactly where. The high status of these women is evident from the way they are painted. The same impression of high status is given by the Grandstand Fresco at Knossos, where priestesses form a central elite group. Minoan society was, unlike Plato's Athens, one in which women could aspire to the highest status. This is reflected in a little-noticed passage in Plato (Crit. 110B–C) where the participation of Atlantean women in warfare is mentioned, 'testimony that all, male and female, may if they please practise excellence in common'.

In the adyton area, as on the floor below, we find the focus of the decorative scheme. Directly above the central figure of the injured girl, the initiand who is at the crucial point of her rite of passage, we see the Minoan goddess seated in all her glory on her altar-throne. This consists of a seat on a corniced platform, the edges of which rest on the edges of two lower corniced platforms, each in turn standing on two incurved altars.[35] The throne is chequered black, blue, white and red. The components of this distinctive structure are purely Minoan: similar altar-thrones are shown in Cretan works of art,[36] proving that this is part of the mainstream of Minoan religious imagery. Presumably the platforms would have been built of timber, which makes it unlikely that any trace would survive in the archaeological record; it is significant though that incurved altars made of stone were found at Arkhanes near Knossos.

The goddess rests one foot on the uppermost platform, the other on the platform below, adding a touch of relaxed informality; this too is seen on Cretan seals. She wears a layered dress and a bodice with the front open to show her breasts. She is festooned in jewellery: bracelets, beads in her hair, huge beaded earrings, a beaded necklace. The necklaces of ducks and dragonflies are reminders of her marshland domain. There can never have been marshland on Thera, so this must be an import from Crete or even Egypt. On her cheek are two forked marks, painted in red: these beauty spots represent the crocus, sacred to the goddess. This is the most detailed as well as the most beautiful portrayal of the Minoan goddess that has survived anywhere.

The manner of the goddess is gentle, unassuming, sympathetic. She may be the same goddess worshipped in the temple at Ayia Irini. She relaxes, bows her

Figure 8.16 The Minoan Heaven: the goddess enthroned, with attendant monkey and griffin, and girl offering crocuses

head slightly to look at the monkey who has mounted the shrine-platform to give her some crocuses from the basket at his feet. The monkey's posture is more human than simian, putting him firmly in the world of the supernatural. He too, as we have seen before, was often seen in the Minoan world as the goddess's servant, collecting crocuses for her in Crete as well as in the Cyclades. On the goddess's other side, disregarded for the long-suspended moment and begging to her like a dog, is her griffin. The scene is one of great delicacy, refinement and tranquillity, yet it also has an heraldic quality, as if we are seeing the Queen of England imagined conferring with her lion and her unicorn on a throne among the oaks of Windsor Great Park.

Behind and all round the goddess crocuses are growing. To the left of the altar-throne a girl gazes up at the goddess and empties a basket of crocuses onto the lowest platform. To the right of the griffin another girl approaches with a basket. The idyllic scene continues without a break onto the east wall; there on a hillside two more girls collect crocuses. The girls make the link with the scheme on the floor below. The girls going through the adolescent initiation rite on the ground floor are here imagined collecting crocuses in the Theran equivalent of Heaven and offering them in person to the epiphany of the great goddess. There is also a clear difference between the two floors. Whereas the images on the ground floor stayed fairly close to rites that real Theran boys and girls underwent, those on the upper floor are elated images of a dream world of fecundity and renewal, a dream world no-one could actually enter.

Figure 8.17 The face of the goddess

Ultimately it is the marvellous image of the goddess that captures the imagination – now, as then. This goddess of Thera was seen as dwelling on Thera, even by the Cretans. There is tablet evidence that the Cretans venerated a goddess called Therasia, 'the goddess from Quherasos', as it was written in its Mycenean form. The word *Quherasos* was formed from a basic word *Quhera* in Linear B. This word became *Thera* when transliterated in the post-Mycenean period. *Thera* was the name given to the island or islands of Santorini at that time, and apparently earlier too. Thera was known as *Thera* at least as early as 1500 BC, and probably before, and it is probable that the bronze age town at Akrotiri was called *Therassos*. So when Minoans at Knossos wrote about Therasia,[37] 'She-from-Therassos', they were referring to the goddess we see in the fresco. Maybe the Cretans knew her name but referred to her obliquely out of respect; maybe they did not know it; maybe the Theran priestesses concealed it to protect the mystique of her cult. It must be significant that at Knossos she was often listed just before or after the entry of offerings 'to all the gods', the catch-all dedication to the deities whose names the Cretans did not know.[38]

Proclus, writing in the fifth century AD, quotes a lost book, the *Ethiopic History* of Marcellus, which described Atlantis as having seven islands sacred to Persephone, and three much larger islands sacred to Pluto, Ammon and Neptune (= Poseidon).[39] According to Plato the gods were allocated particular regions by lot (*Crit.* 109B), so Thera may have 'belonged to' a particular goddess. A later passage seems to rule out an identification of Thera as Atlantis as it states that Atlantis was Poseidon's (*Crit.* 113C), but then it emerges that the principal temple of Atlantis was dedicated jointly to Poseidon and his beloved 'mortal' wife Cleito (*Crit.* 113D, 116C), so it may be that the goddess Therasia's realm was the human hearth, the flowered hill slopes of Thera, while the rumbling volcanic forces beneath and the sea surrounding Thera were Poseidon's realm. In the matter of religious observance Plato's Atlanteans do not sound much like the Therans. Plato describes the Atlanteans as having fallen from grace; once they had walked with the gods and had carried a portion of the divine within them, but now, as they faced impending destruction, 'the portion of divinity became faint, they had . . . lost the fairest of their possessions. They were filled with lawless ambition and power' (*Crit.* 121A). The Therans were still in touch with their gods. In this, Plato was wrong, but perhaps only because he made the common teleological mistake of assuming that because the Atlanteans were destroyed they must have deserved destruction. Diodorus, perhaps feeding off the same tradition that Plato had drawn upon, said that the Atlanteans excelled their neighbours in their reverence towards the gods: 'The gods, they say, were born among them.'[40] This is more in line with the Akrotiri frescoes and the Cretan tradition that the goddess Therasia was a native of Thera's city.

Therasia ruled the city of Therassos as far as the devotees of her cult were concerned: in the spiritual world, the world of dreams, she held sway, presiding over the initiations into different grades of the social order. Theran society, we see from the frescoes, was finely stratified and ordered, but who presided over it in the secular sphere? In the ancient world there was less distinction between secular and spiritual, but it is obvious that Theran society could not have been ordered by a wall-painting, however beautiful. It is likely that the priestesses held an important position in Theran society, given the evidence from Crete,[41] and the prominence of the priestess in the Town 5 Fresco from Thera itself. Priesthoods could exert enormous power in ancient societies. What other power or powers there were can only be guessed on the evidence we have. The variations in design among the buildings suggests a lack of central control; the informality suggests either weaker or less autocratic control than seen in Cretan cities such as Knossos or Palaikastro. Some have gone as far as proposing that Thera was a republic, which is possible: with power in the hands of priestesses and a 'chamber of commerce' composed of the city's leading merchants, something like an early form of republic could have evolved. There may have been loose political control of a sort from Knossos. Perhaps the sons of the wealthier families were taken to Knossos to be educated and conditioned, within a kind of Minoan public school tradition, as happened in contemporary Egypt.[42]

9

THE LAST DAYS OF AKROTIRI

According to the *Timaeus*, Atlantis was lost in a major geological convulsion, a series of earthquakes accompanied by a massive subsidence that took the land area below sea level. The longer and more detailed account in the *Critias* promises more detail on the destruction, but breaks off just before Zeus passes sentence on the ancient civilization.

The destruction of Atlantis has often been seen as a memory of the desolation of Thera. The Late Cycladic town of Akrotiri came into being after the Middle Cycladic town was damaged by earthquake in 1580 BC.[1] After a period of stability, the beginning of the end of the city was signalled by another series of earthquakes in about 1525 BC. Initial earth tremors warned the Therans to leave, gave them time to gather their treasured possessions and escape the city to neighbouring islands, perhaps Ios, the nearest, as a first stop. The sequence of tremors culminated in a big earthquake that shook down many houses; their ruins are often found under layers of rose pumice ejected during the eruption that followed, showing that they were felled by the earthquake before the eruption.

Then the earth stopped shaking and some of the refugees returned. Special work teams went in to the make the city safe. Unsafe buildings were demolished to prevent them from collapsing into the streets, exactly as was done after the 1580 BC earthquake. The work teams cleared as much as they could of the popcorn-like pumice: knee-deep, it represented a large volume of material to clear. In some places the pumice had drifted like snow, with well-developed wave forms where the blast of the eruption had bounced off walls and created eddies in the pumice. These wave forms can be seen (in a section) where the high north wall of Building 17 bounced southward-travelling shock waves back into the East Square. The work teams cleared paths through the debris, a mixture of fallen house walls, roofing material and pumice: some was retained behind drystone walling to stop it falling back across the streets. In the East Square an east–west wall was built to keep the pumice back from the north wall of Building 17, creating a split-level square and necessitating major changes to heights of doors opening onto it. Generally, the work teams smoothed debris out in the roadways, leaving them higher than before, and making ground floor

114

Plate 9.1 Staircase in Building 13 crushed during an earthquake: view from North Square

rooms into semi-basements. Now there was a step down from Telchines Street into Building 2, which the workmen used as a workshop.

How many Therans returned is not known. Presumably after the first year of repair work, the city could have begun to function again and 'civilian' families returned. The lull as a whole probably lasted 2–5 years: although exposed wall stumps of ruins were not weathered there was enough time for soil to form,[2] and therefore enough time for significant numbers of citizens to reoccupy Thera.

After the evacuation and delayed return, the Therans must have been disappointed and frustrated when the island began to shake again. In 1520 there was a series of earth tremors, probably of increasing severity, Plato's 'portentous earthquakes', and the Therans knew that either a major earthquake or a volcanic eruption was coming. Probably the final signal to leave was the emission of steam, gas and smoke from the volcanic cones beyond the South Bay. As clouds of sulphurous vapour drifted across the city, the last inhabitants of Akrotiri left for the last time. The earthquake damage during the build-up to the catastrophic eruption was considerable. Staircases were shaken down, tipped sideways, stone steps tilted and broken. Horizontal courses of large, well-laid ashlars were tilted. The quoins of the porch in Triangle Square were buckled into a curve.

Workmen laid aside their tools on the rubble and ran for their lives to the harbour.[3] Only a few – in these situations it is usually the foolhardy and the old – remained on the island and they perished in the holocaust that followed. The eruption sequence was under way. It began with a massive eruption of steam and a fountain of fine white pumice that covered the island to a depth of 2 centimetres. This new material, spread across the island like a light fall of snow, was in effect lava with millions of tiny gas bubbles in it, thrown up from 10 kilometres beneath the island.[4] After this came a pause, time for large quantities of basaltic stone weathered from the crater's sides to roll down onto its floor; fragments of this basalt were later embedded in the lower layers of the pumice after they had been catapulted out in a later phase of the eruption. During this respite, possibly lasting several months, the Therans were for some reason not tempted to return. Probably there were continuing earth tremors as the huge vaulted magma chamber under Thera changed its shape; perhaps there were emissions of warning smoke and steam.[5]

Then another fountain of pumice was sprayed from the vent, pea-sized pellets that covered the island to a depth of 10 centimetres. At the same time basalt

Plate 9.2 The interior of Building 17 is still entirely buried. Below the surface seen here, three storeys of the building are filled with ash

fragments were blown out, landing on top of the pumice layer. The pumice went on fountaining from the vent, the pellets now larger and forming a layer twice as deep as before. There were fewer rock fragments in this layer, showing that the crater was now cleared of infalling rock debris and that the pace of the eruption was increasing to the point where material was being thrown out at a faster rate than the rate of slope failure in the crater walls.

The great volcano was not only reawakened. It had cleared its throat. A huge eruption cloud towered several kilometres above the island, darkening the sky: the rest of the eruption sequence happened in a monochrome twilight. From the eruption cloud a new layer of still larger pumice rained down on the beleagured island, covering it in still deeper drifts. The pumice now lay a metre deep in places, and completely clear of basalt fragments. The pumice eruption had gone on without any significant break. Certainly there was no pause long enough to allow any erosion to take place. In the build-up of the pumice layers that followed some sections of walling sprawled sideways. The roofs may have collapsed as a result of the earthquakes and the buildings had filled up with pumice, causing the walls to fall outwards under the weight. This would have been assisted by the earthquakes that must have accompanied the pumice erup-tion. Many walls tend to be broken off about 2 metres above their foundations, which suggests that the lowest 2 metres were protected by burial in pumice. Either way the bronze age city was suffering serious damage as its streets and squares became choked with drifting pumice. A huge column of steam, gas, smoke, pumice and ash towered 35 kilometres into the air,[6] and the pumice – possibly as much as 5 cubic kilometres of it – fell from it like snow.[7]

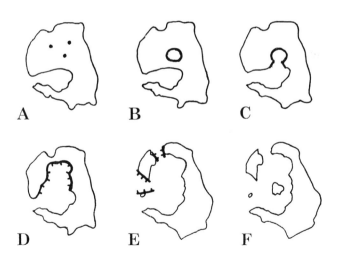

Figure 9.1 Stages in Thera's development
Note: A: before the Minoan eruption, with three volcanic peaks, B: crater opens on site of North Bay, C: seawater enters crater, triggering base-surge eruption, D–E: caldera collapse, F: post-bronze age cone forms

Plate 9.3 Minoan ash lines a ravine eroded west–east across the Phira Quarry

Plate 9.4 Cliffs south-east of Akrotiri, showing chaotic ash with black fragments of the bronze age crater walls

The crater had enlarged to 160 metres across and sea water from the South Bay seeped into it. Then the water touched the hot lava, and the resulting violent horizontal blast changed the nature of the eruption drastically. The base surge was the most violent event in the sequence so far; ash wetted and weighted with sea water shot horizontally from the vent at 300 metres per second,[8] sweeping huge volumes of wet ash outwards into horizontal layers 7 metres thick. The crater in the hills north of the South Bay grew larger and larger. Huge boulders were ripped from its walls cannoned outwards in all directions. One of these stone bombs, 1.5 metres across,[9] scored a direct hit on Building 6. The force of the eruption's lateral blast was enormous. The lower walls of Building 6 were by now buried and therefore protected, but the upper part of the building collapsed as it was subjected to enormous pressure thrusting from the north-west through the house. The stone steps of the staircase next to the lightwell were rammed through the window in the south wall of the light-well as they sank and rotated clockwise, as if the whole building was being screwed into the ground.[10]

The eruption deposits above the base surge layers followed on relentlessly with only a short break, but long enough for a ravine to be eroded across the site of the Phira Quarry; horizontal layers of grey ash were eroded to form a ravine at least 15 metres deep and 20 metres wide. The ten or more ash-fill layers that line the ravine behaved differently, wrapping themselves over the new terrain like blankets.[11] The layers of 'chaotic ash' directed mainly towards the east and south-east by the wind reached a thickness of 50 metres and may represent an eruption lasting several weeks or months.[12] Massive explosions rocked the wide, funnel-shaped vent which was filled with a slurry of ash and rocks. The old shield volcanoes built up inside the pre-Minoan caldera dis-integrated, their remains hurtling out in all directions. The amount of erupted material may have been great enough to dam back the sea for a time during this stage.

The present-day cliffs south-east of Akrotiri offer a superb natural section through the chaotic ash layer. Most is pallid ash, but within it can be seen hun-dreds of roughly broken pieces of black lava blocks, the remains of the ancient volcanic peaks that stood in the north of Thera in Minoan times. The walls of the crater disintegrated, collapsed into the inferno and were blasted to the edges of the island,[13] enlarging the crater to a diameter of 500 metres as little as two days after the eruption started.[14]

The pumice and ash layers covering the city are thinner than those at the Phira Quarry. The city was 3 kilometres further from the main vent; in addition, the wind carried much of the ash east and south-eastwards. It is also likely that the caldera rim north of Akrotiri stood a little further north than it does today, offering some protection from a blast across the South Bay. Owing to these factors, the eruption blast did not completely destroy the buildings. White pumice and ash settled on the city like deep snow. We know from modern eruptions that it takes surprisingly little volcanic ash to make a gently sloping house roof collapse; probably as little as 20 centimetres of pumice were enough to break the flat roofs of Theran houses, leaving them open to the sky for most of the eruption. Unroofed buildings that were both filled and surrounded by pumice and ash were actually protected from the later, more destructive, eruption of coarse black tephra, which lashed the island like shrapnel. The wall-tops of Building 1 were left unprotected by ash and were blasted off. The steam generated by the eruption condensed in the cloud column above the island, reducing the island to darkness. Rain fell in torrents. Overland flow on the new lava surface produced gullies, alluvial fans, landslides, mudflows.

By now some 30 cubic kilometres of magma had been thrown up.[15] This left the huge magma chamber beneath Thera empty, a yawning cavern hundreds of metres deep. The island sagged down into this vault and networks of ring fissures and radial cracks developed like a huge spider's web over the whole of the centre. What remained of the 500 metres high volcano that had torn itself apart in the eruption collapsed vertically into the abyss below. The seabed is now 480 metres deep in the deepest parts of the caldera. Unsupported, successive blocks slid into the caldera one after the other, allowing sea water to flood into the hot magma chamber. This caused more violent eruptions and probably generated huge high-energy waves that sped out through the widened entrance to the South Bay and the expanse of water separating Thera from the northern end of Therasia. The progressive collapse of the volcano into the chamber created the North Bay. The large bite-shaped bays in the caldera walls have been linked to this slope failure.[16]

Marinatos believed that the upper parts of the caldera walls, which often have a gentler slope than the cliff-like lower walls, were eroded back by a type of eruption called *nuée ardente*. His theory is supported by new evidence. The south wall frieze in Building 4 was pitted by the impact of thousands of tiny hot grains from a *nuée ardente* (literally 'burning cloud') eruption. The pitting was in patches that lined up with windows on the opposite side of the room. By joining the edges of the patches with the window jambs on a plan it is possible to reconstruct the direction of the blast: it came from a point 18 degrees west of north, probably in the western half of the North Bay.[17] The deposit of base-surge tephra across Thera from Balos to Cape Exomiti confirms that the eruption blast in the Akrotiri area was north-north-west to south-south-east. This layer is 9 centimetres thick at its maximum and only 2 centimetres on the city itself, but it shows that the vent was on that axial line running 18 degrees west of north from the city.[18] The collapse of the volcano must have been accompanied by colossal shallow-seated earthquakes measuring as high as 10 on the Richter Scale. Ear-splitting explosions were heard as deafening roars all round the Aegean, and would have been audible 4,800 kilometres away. People in Pakistan, Zaire and Egypt heard them. People living in the shadow of Stonehenge, then recently completed with its bluestones reinstated, heard the rumble of Thera's spectacular implosion, and will have thought no more of it than distant thunder.

There is a tendency currently to reduce the spectacle, to try to tone down the severity of the Thera eruption, by spreading the time-scale and seeing it as a number of much smaller events, by making the collapse of the North Bay gradual and piecemeal, by reducing the severity of the eruptions, by proposing that there were no tsunamis. One reason for doing this is an embarrassing fact of prehistory: the survival and partial recovery of the Minoan civilization on Crete.[19] The Minoan civilization continued to function for a hundred years after the eruption. If ashfall from a huge eruption reached Crete and coated its fields the agricultural economy would have been crippled. If tsunamis had been generated, all the low-lying and coastal Minoan settlements on Crete's north coast – and there were many – should have been destroyed.[20] Yet the Cretan economy weathered these hardships and made a recovery. Late Minoan Ib pottery was manufactured on Crete and exported to Melos, immediately after the ashfall, which occurred in Late Minoan Ia; the eruption therefore did not stop trading for long.

Nevertheless, the caldera itself, the enormous quantities of almost contemporaneous ash and pumice on Thera, the huge area of seabed coated with ash – all indicate a volcanic eruption that was relatively fast and on a very large scale, in fact an eruption of a violence and intensity probably not since equalled.[21] The nearest parallels, referred to by many scholars including Luce and Marinatos, are the eruptions of Krakatoa in 1883 and Tambora in 1815.[22] The result at Krakatoa is remarkably similar to that at Thera, even to the 'post-eruption' cone building up in the centre of the old caldera. The area of the Santorini caldera is

Plate 9.5 The caldera wall

about twice that of the Krakatoa caldera, and we can be sure that more energy was released in the bronze age Thera eruption, that it was more violent, that like Krakatoa it did produce tsunamis. The Krakatoa tsunamis drowned 36,000 people.

It is difficult to reconstruct the size or behaviour of the tsunamis generated by the Thera eruption, partly because it is impossible to be sure which parts of the caldera wall had collapsed to give access to open sea at the times when seabed eruptions and earthquakes occurred, or precisely how much energy was injected. It would appear that if the eruptions in the centre of the North Bay were the starting-point for tsunamis, the waves could only have left Thera by the north-north-west and south-west, where there were, as now, broad breaches in the caldera wall. The situation is complicated further by the phenomenon known as wave refraction. In open water of constant depth, a wave front can move forward at constant speed and therefore remain straight, but if at one end it moves into shallow water close to an island, that section slows down and the wave front curves, wrapping itself round the island. So, even though the tsunamis may have had restricted egress from the caldera, it was still possible for them to fan out and affect large areas. It may also be that 360-degree tsunamis were generated by shallow-seated earthquakes vibrating the seabed round the island as the caldera collapsed.

Positive evidence for huge waves that can only have been tsunamis comes from the nearby island of Anafi, and also distant Tel Aviv: pumice which must have floated ashore is now stranded high above present sea level. There is also pumice at present sea level amongst the ruins of a Minoan house at Amnisos on Crete. The height of the pumice on Anafi and at Tel Aviv can be used to calculate the likely height of the tsunami at its source and along the north coast of Crete. One calculation is that the tsunami that deposited the pumice on Anafi must have been 63 metres high when it left Thera.[23] There are problems

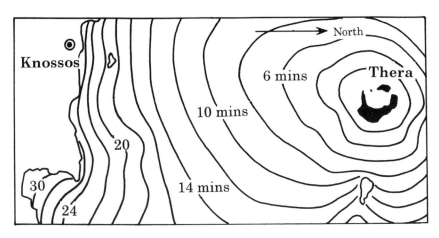

Figure 9.2 Tsunamis took 25–30 minutes to reach Crete (note wave refraction)

Figure 9.3 A nineteenth-century reconstruction of the 1755 Lisbon earthquake, a triple catastrophe of earthquake, fire and tsunamis

with the 11-metre wave extrapolated for Amnisos. Although the wave must have lost energy by 'stretching' as it spread outwards, there is another factor, the shape of the seabed. The water between Thera and Crete is very deep. The tsunami would have raced across the Cretan Sea at 300 miles per hour as a broad low wave, but when it reached the shallow coastal waters of Crete it would have towered up into a tall, narrow wave, slowing down as it toppled onto the coastal towns. Eleven metres may therefore be a serious underestimate of the height of the tsunamis that struck Amnisos and Mallia 25 minutes after the eruption.[24]

There are problems in any case in drawing inferences from Anafi pumice, which has been found at heights of 50 metres 350 metres inland, 160 metres 750 metres inland and 250 metres 1,650 metres inland. These are separate deposits of pumice from different tsunamis, although a quarter of a century ago the potassium content was taken to show that all relate to the Minoan eruption sequence.[25] They probably relate to earlier eruptions of Thera: the fact that their refractive index is 1.514 compared with the 1.508 or 1.509 for the Minoan pumice found on Thera supports this.[26] Radiocarbon dating of the calcium carbonate cementation of the Anafi pumice confirms that it dates from at least 18,000 years ago, and therefore may have been blasted out during the eruptions of 18,300 BC or 23,000 BC. The Anafi pumice has also probably been lifted by land movements.

In spite of the collapse of the Anafi evidence, it is certain that there were tsunamis in 1520 BC, and that they had devastating effects on coastal settlements on the Thera-facing coastlines of Crete and other Aegean islands. The effects on the Aegean economies can be imagined. Proof that tsunamis reached Crete and made an impact on the Cretans comes from Amnisos and Nirou Khani. The seashore villa excavated by Marinatos had several huge blocks in its foundation course shoved sideways – they can still be seen today – and the only way they could have been displaced is by pushing or dragging by a very large volume of water. Since the Minoan coastline was probably 50 metres away, only a tsunami could have had this impact on the house. Pumice deposited among

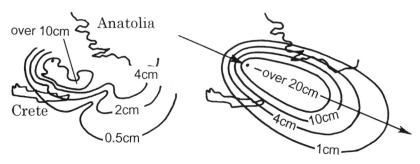

Figure 9.4 Left: thickness of surviving ash layer on seabed; right: reconstructed ash footprint, with inferred wind direction
Note: dot = Thera

the foundations adds corroborative evidence that it was tsunamis at the time of the Thera eruption that were to blame. Theran pumice has recently been found 10–15 metres above sea level behind the villa.[27] A shrine in the small temple at Nirou Khani contained tiny offering cups; the Minoans had put pieces of pumice in them, presumably as offerings back to Poseidon. Here we glimpse the primitive terror inspired by the arrival of the Theran pumice. Why would it have inspired this response unless it had arrived with a tsunami?

Similar uncertainties surround the ashfall, though a great deal of ash has survived, most of it on the seabed, where it marks out a Poseidon-sized footprint with its heel on Thera and its toes pointing towards Cyprus. Early reconstructions of this footprint give it a north-west to south-east axis, showing that ash would have covered central and eastern Crete. This is significant, because even thin falls of ash may have decisive social and economic effects. A layer 7 centimetres deep is enough to cause farms to be temporarily abandoned in Iceland, 15 centimetres to lead to permanent abandonment.[28] More recent reconstructions of the ashfall pattern show it with a west–east axis, taking the ash towards south-west Anatolia, away from Crete altogether.[29] It can safely be assumed that of the original thicknesses of ash perhaps half remain in the sedimentary record and that in some places, such as to the east of Crete, seabed currents have swept most away. Making due allowance for these changes, it is possible to reconstruct a more likely ashfall footprint halfway between old and new reconstructions, implying a west-north-west wind trailing a plume of ash across eastern Crete.[30] Given that 2 centimetres of ash survive in eastern Crete as well as on the adjacent seabed it is reasonable to assume that in 1520 BC there was a coating on average 4 centimetres thick and in places it will have been twice as thick as that, which would have caused more than a brief nuisance. The ash evidence implies a major economic setback for the eastern third of Crete. The effects of ash in a modern eruption of comparable size can be seen in the Tambora eruption on Sumatra in 1815, when the after-effects of fall-out caused 50,000 people to starve to death.[31]

High-level winds may have carried ash to China. The Bamboo Annals for 1618 BC record 'yellow fog, a dim sun, then three suns, frost in July and the withering of all three cereals'. The annals are authentic, but the date is unreliable because they were lost for a time and some miscounting of years is likely; the effects described are exactly what might be expected in the way of atmospheric pollution. Ash in the upper air will have caused temperatures to fall 1 degree Celsius globally and as much as 5 degrees locally, which would have had a major impact on food production.[32] Low-level winds carried ash towards Egypt, where the sky was darkened and there were terrible storms that struck awe into the pharaoh Ahmose himself. Ahmose had a memorial pillar raised at Thebes describing the destruction.[33]

> The gods expressed their discontent . . . a tempest . . . caused darkness in the western region. The sky was unleashed . . . more than the roar

of the crowd, . . . was powerful . . . on the mountains more than the turbulence of the cataract of Elephantine. Houses and shelters were floating on the water like the banks of papyrus outside the royal palace for . . . days, with no-one able to light the torch anywhere. Then His Majesty descended in his boat, his council following him. The people at the east and west were silent, for they had no more clothes after the power of the god was manifested. His Majesty set about strengthening the two lands, providing them with silver, gold, copper, oil, clothing, all the things they desired; after which His Majesty rested in the palace – life, health, strength.

The Egyptians were familiar with Nile floods. This was something exceptional, and that suggests a tsunami rather than a river flood. The Tempest Stele was probably inscribed between 1540 and 1517 BC, in the reign of Ahmose, a period that includes the date we have been considering as a likely one for the eruption. If the inscription describes ashfall and tsunami damage it helps to date the eruption to around 1520 BC. An inscription in the temple at Medinet Habu describes a tsunami even more vividly, but this is believed to date from the reign of Ramesses III, about 1200 BC: 'The might of Nun [Ocean] broke out and fell on our towns and villages in a great wave . . . and the head of [the Sea Peoples'] cities went under the sea; their land is no more.' The principal city of the Sea Peoples is said to be on 'the sacred island', and Plato specifically describes a 'sacred island' at the heart of Atlantis.[34] This apparent reference to the tsunami and the loss of Thera is puzzling: it seems to be 300 years too late. The Medinet Habu inscriptions nevertheless confirm the truth of another passage in the *Timaeus* (23A), in which the Egyptian priest told Solon:

> Whatever happened either in your country or in ours, or in any other region of which we are informed, if there were any actions noble or great or in any way remarkable, they have all been written down by us of old, and are preserved in our temples.

AFTER THE ERUPTION

The eruption left Thera unrecognizable. The volcanic mountains that had formed the island's centre had gone, and in their place was a yawning flooded crater 700 metres deep.[35] Sections of the caldera rim had foundered, creating the islands of Therasia and Aspronisi. On the east side of Thera huge accumulations of pumice and ash had built the coastline out into the sea. Where a relatively fertile hinterland had been was now a ragged bay 10 kilometres across, walled by the rim of the eviscerated crater. Where there had been fertile and accessible slopes with farms and villages were now sheets of pale grey dust. Sea round Thera that had been deep was choked with shifting reefs of eruption debris and mud,

Figure 9.5 Sites showing evidence of destruction in 1520 BC (Late Minoan IA)
Source: from Marketou 1990; Woudhuizen 1992

and difficult to navigate; the *Critias* (108E–109A) speaks of a 'barrier of impassable mud which prevents those who are sailing from proceeding further'.[36] Euripides seems to have access to a tradition of this event in *Hippolytus*:[37]

> O to escape! . . .
> And reach that shore planted with apple trees [= the Garden of the
>   Hesperides at the pillars of Heracles]
> Where the daughters of evening sing,
> Where the sea-lord [= Poseidon] of the dark shallows [= shoals round
>   Thera]
> Permits to sailors no further passage [= unnavigable waters round
>   Thera],
> Establishing the solemn frontier of heaven
> Which Atlas guards [= the pillars of Heracles].

Where there had once been a great, bustling, noisy, prosperous, civilized city and a harbour full of commercial activity was now a featureless carpet of silent

127

grey ash. As Plato said, 'the island of Atlantis was swallowed up by the sea and vanished' (*Tim.* 25D). Of the handful of people who stayed on the island, none survived: only a few charred bones and teeth remained, deeply buried in the ash, to show where they were overwhelmed. The partial skeleton of an old man was found on the south coast of Therasia. Human bones and teeth were found in the Phira Quarry in 1956; two of the teeth were burnt, showing that the victims had been scorched to death by the ash.[38] At Herculaneum, very few human remains were found until 1982, when the whole population was discovered on the beach. At Akrotiri the picture is as yet incomplete[39] and it may be that some grisly discoveries will yet be made. No-one lived on Thera now. No-one could have lived there in the first few decades after the catastrophe.

Stream erosion soon cut radial gullies in the ash and re-deposited it along the coast, forming features like the little delta at the mouth of the Potamos valley. These deposits gradually filled up the channel between Thera and Monolithos – and it was there, at Monolithos, that the first attempt at recolonizing the island was made, though not for 200 years. The pottery found there is Mycenean (Late Helladic IIIB) and dates from 1320 BC. This may be seen as part of a pattern; the Myceneans took over Triandha, the Minoan trading post on Rhodes, in about 1430 BC and establishing a base on the uninhabited island of Thera would have been a natural progression. It is the succession of the Mycenean traders and colonists following the physical collapse of Thera and then the economic and cultural collapse of Crete that are remembered in the Platonic tradition as the victory of the Hellenic peoples over the Atlanteans (e.g. *Crit.* 108E and *Tim.* 25B–C):

> Then it was, Solon, that the manhood of your city [Athens] showed itself conspicuous for valour and might in the sight of all the world. For it stood pre-eminent in gallantry and warfare and . . . defeated the invaders . . . saved us from slavery.

But the Mycenean empire did not last long. Only a hundred years after the founding of the trading post at Monolithos, the region was invaded by the 'Sea Peoples', and the Aegean trading system was disrupted.

The eruption had been a turning-point. Just as much earlier Thera had turned away from mainland Greece towards Crete for cultural influence, now it turned back again. By 1320 BC the great Cretan trading operation was over. The Minoan temple civilization had continued for another century after the eruption, Knossos and its Labyrinth rising briefly to even greater pre-eminence, but the capacity or ambition for overseas extension had gone and in 1380 BC the Labyrinth was destroyed. Knossos gave way to Mycenae.

But what happened to the Therans, the thousands who had inhabited the great city and its outlying villages? They evacuated the city, systematically removed nearly all the valuables and set off in their ships. Only a few of the rural dwellers risked staying, and paid with their lives. Where did the evacuees go?

Figure 9.6 Early fifteenth-century Anatolian colonies may have been founded in Crete, exploiting the weakened state of the Minoan empire following the Thera eruption

Did they sail to the coastal towns of northern Crete – Amnisos, Khania, Mallia? Did they go to nearby islands in the Cyclades – Ios, Sikinos, Amorgos – or further north to Naxos or Paros? Did they reach the mainland of Greece? Wherever they made landfall, it seems all trace of them has vanished. It would be pleasant to think of the Therans founding a civilized colony somewhere in the Cyclades and that one day we will find archaeological evidence of it, but it is more likely that they perished. They would have landed on some Thera-facing shore, drawing their ships onto the beaches, imagining themselves safe, watching the eruption column growing over their one-time home. They would have unloaded their belongings, making themselves as comfortable as possible in makeshift shelters.

Then the tsunamis came to claim them.

Spyridon Marinatos homed in on the Aegean folk memory of the disaster.[40] Praising the island of Kea, the poet Pindar drew on a distinct Cycladic tradition when he wrote darkly, 'Zeus and Poseidon once sent a land together with a countless host of people right to the depths of Tartarus.' Was he referring to a long-lived Cycladic oral tradition of the sinking of Thera and the loss of

Figure 9.7 The spread of Mycenean control during the fifteenth century; the Minoans retained the eastern Aegean, and probably Crete too

life inflicted by tsunamis?[41] At the end of the *Critias*, Zeus gathers the gods on Olympus to arrive at a judgement on the Atlanteans. We know from the *Timaeus* in general terms what the sentence was, but it is likely that the source Plato was drawing on contained crucial extra detail, and had Zeus commanding Poseidon to destroy Atlantis with earthquake and flood. The partnership of Zeus and Poseidon mentioned in Pindar may therefore have been recorded in a document subsequently lost; perhaps it was Solon's poem that survived not just to be a source for Plato, but for Pindar a hundred years earlier too.

Maybe the Therans reached Rhodes. North of the Late Minoan town there is a cemetery, close to the seashore and unusual in having no grave-goods at all. This suggests burial in some traumatizing emergency. Were these unfortunate people refugees from the Thera disaster camping on the beach and hoping for Triandhan hospitality, yet pursued, caught and wiped out by the tsunamis?[42]

The consequences of the Thera eruption and the destruction of the entrepreneurial community on the island were far-reaching. Few now seriously attribute the termination of the Minoan civilization to the eruption. There was always a problematic gap between the proposed date for the eruption in around

Plate 9.6 Agia Triadha: in 1300 BC (LMIII) the Minoan town was completely rebuilt by Mycenean colonists; this Mycenean staircase led down into an arcade of shops

1520 BC and the fall of the Knossos Labyrinth in 1380 BC; the recent proposition that the eruption occurred one hundred years earlier makes a connection even less probable. It is nevertheless possible that the eruption seriously damaged the Minoan economy and infrastructure, by removing altogether the key trading station on Thera, flooding and damaging settlements and harbour installations on the north coast of Crete, and probably destroying shipping; after those impacts the trading operation will have continued in significantly weakened form. The post-eruption period on Crete was one of regrouping, centralization, introversion, with a focus of power on Knossos. Without a strong Cretan control over the trading operation, without Thera as a fulcrum, the Aegean islands fell one by one under Mycenean domination. Both Ayia Irini on Kea and Phylakopi on Melos lost their Minoan character in favour of Mycenean traits towards 1450 BC.[43] The Minoan mansion at Phylakopi was replaced by an unmistakably Mycenean megaron at that time.

Renfrew sees no effect other than temporary disruption, but there is archaeological evidence of significant ashfall in eastern Crete.[44] In 1989, a layer of volcanic ash 5 centimetres deep was found at Mochlos, in a staircase cage that was sealed in before the house was substantially rebuilt; the ash was sealed between LMIA and LMIB floors, proving that ash fell over Crete at the close of LMIA.[45] The rebuilding confirms that civilization did not come to an end on Crete, but together with the ash it also confirms that the eruption did cause physical damage. Doumas reports a layer of well-packed ash 10 centimetres thick at Triandha,[46] while a ditch nearby at Rhodes airport exposed a layer 1 metre thick. Another report is of an ash layer as much as 3 metres deep at Triandha.[47] It becomes very clear that the ashfalls reconstructed by McCoy must be treated as minimum thicknesses, that locally far greater thicknesses accumulated, and that far more than temporary disruption will have resulted.

Minoan trading may have revived for several decades, but the progress of Minoanization of the Aegean region and its possible eventual spread throughout the Mediterranean power and culture vacuum was checked.[48] We know from the goods and materials traded that the Minoans, using Theran and other Cycladic navigators, were ambitious traders. Unchecked, they might well have Minoanized the entire Mediterranean basin, in the same way that later the region was Romanized. Checking the progress of the Minoan civilization meant permitting the development of alternative cultures. The Helladic civilization developed in its place; that in its turn was a key formative influence on the Roman civilization, with all the effects that both of these have had on the shaping of modern western society. The rise of mainland Greece was a key step in the evolution of that society, and it was only possible in the absence of a strong Minoan civilization: that is the underlying thrust of Plato's story.

We could speculate endlessly about what might have happened if the process of Minoanization had continued, if all Mediterranean communities had become something like Thera. The Minoan civilization was enormously complex, its people lovers of nature, natural beauty, sport, public ceremonies and rituals, with no interest in history, royal power or great heroic deeds.[49] In Minoan art

Plate 9.7 Leaving Thera for the north: Thera to the left, Therasia to the right

everything floated in endless extension; time ceased in a continuous ecstatic awareness of the present. Art and architecture were atectonic, with no overall symmetry. Above all, there was a powerful female deity. The Minoan ideals were fundamentally different from those of the Helladic civilization. The Helladic or Graeco-Roman world was symmetrical, square, seen from outside, objective, and its principal deity was male.

We can explore ideas of alternative universes, alternatives pasts in which different principles and belief systems prevail. It is plainly impossible to speculate where, after three thousand years of European history, an alternative Minoan past would have brought us.[50] Nevertheless, when looking at the images in the Theran and Knossian frescoes, especially at the portrait of Therasia, it is impossible not to wonder what a Minoan Europe might have been like. It did not come about, yet only the wind separates us from it. If the ash plume had instead been blown from the east-south-east, things might have turned out differently; if the ash had been carried towards mainland Greece and covered Mycenae instead of eastern Crete, the young Mycenean civilization might have been severely disadvantaged from 1520 to 1400 BC and the mature Minoan civilization might then have prevailed.

10

ATLANTIS DESTROYED

The earlier chapters in this book pointed towards the Cyclades, including the key island of Thera, as components of Atlantis. Plato tells us Atlantis was an island group that included one island larger and more important than the others. That large island was Crete. As we have seen, because of its position and the entrepreneurial tradition that developed there, Thera was, in spite of its small size, second in importance to Crete. Although much has been made of Atlantis as a huge land mass, its size was exaggerated in the retelling, and the idea of an archipelago is in any case explicit in the *Timaeus* 24E, where the islands are used as stepping-stones, and 25E, where we are told that Atlantis was 'a wonderful empire which had rule over the whole island and many other islands also and parts of the continent'. This could easily be a description of the Aegean region in 1600–1500 BC – Crete, Thera, the Cyclades and parts of Anatolia and the Peloponnese – the area encompassing the Minoan trading empire at its fullest development in about 1550 BC.

THE MINOAN TRADING EMPIRE AS ATLANTIS

This book has so far occupied itself largely with Thera. As many as one-third of the specific references in Plato that can be attached to an ancient civilization can be matched by bronze age Thera: almost half the references can be related to Crete, some necessarily overlapping.

Among the exclusively Cretan references one or two are outstanding. The *Critias* (113C) says that 'halfway down the length of the island there was a plain . . . very fertile'. This implies a long narrow island, not circular as other Platonic descriptions insist, and supports the idea that Plato was conflating descriptions of more than one island. Crete is very conspicuously long and narrow; halfway along it is a very fertile plain, the Plain of Mesara. That Mesara was meant is confirmed by the longer description later (*Crit.* 118A–B), where we are told of

> a level plain, smooth and even, oblong in shape, extending in one direction 3000 stadia, but across the centre of the island 2000 stadia.

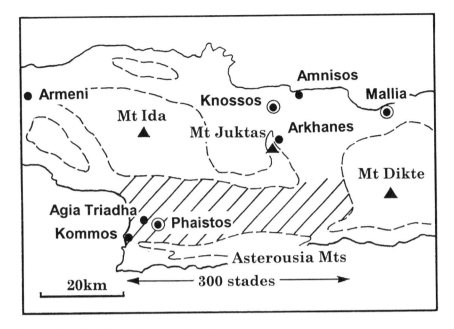

Figure 10.1 The Plain of Mesara (shaded)

> This part of the island looked towards the south and was protected from the north. The surrounding mountains were celebrated for their number, size and beauty.

This describes well the Plain of Mesara, which is rectangular, with its shorter dimension across the centre of the island; from it one can see the mountains of the Ida range to the north and north-west and Mount Dikte and Lasithi to the east: all much more imposing than anything elsewhere in the Aegean. The Mesara has a southerly aspect, and is sheltered from north winds by the island's main watershed. Only the distances are exaggerated. The Mesara is not 550 kilometres long from east to west, but the distance is exaggerated exactly tenfold, and the error may have crept in during the translation of the story from Egyptian to Greek, or during transliteration in Egypt.

The *Timaeus* (25) says Atlantis disappeared abruptly 'in the depths of the sea, for which reason the sea in those parts is impassable because there is a shoal of mud in the way, and this was caused by the subsidence of the island'. Much of Thera literally disappeared overnight, and what was left would have been unrecognizable. A large part of Thera did subside: the site of the bronze age volcanoes in the North Bay is under 480 metres of water. The trading network, the invisible threads connecting harbour to harbour round the Aegean and across to Crete, also disappeared, albeit temporarily, after the eruption; probably many merchant ships were lost to tsunamis that swept across the Aegean. The whole web of economic activity was figuratively swallowed up by the sea: it disappeared as suddenly and completely *as if* it had sunk beneath the waves. The shoal of mud is easily understood when we realize that immediately after the eruption ash and pumice covered the surviving parts of Thera to depths as great as 200 metres. Similar quantities were deposited in the water round Thera, and it will have taken many years for wave action and currents to disperse it. The seabed for a kilometre or two round Thera will have been noticeably shallow and muddy for a long time afterwards and navigation in the area will have been difficult: it was a century before any resettlement was attempted.

Before the destruction of Thera, the scale of the Minoan trading operation was very ambitious. 'Because of the greatness of their [the Atlanteans'] empire many things were brought to them from foreign countries' (*Crit.* 114D). The claim that there were 'great numbers of elephants in the island' (*Crit.* 115A) is false, in that there were no elephant herds in Crete; trading nevertheless reached out to north Africa, which supplied Crete with tusks for ivory carving. Plato emphasizes that Atlantis provided 'all sorts of animals . . . whatever

Figure 10.2 The Minoan trading empire
Note: recent evidence suggests a Minoan trading station on Samothrace, way off the map to the north; there were probably others too

Plate 10.1 Mochlos, a Minoan port on the north coast of Crete: the leaning pillar was tilted and the wall on the left fell over during the earthquake that destroyed the town

fragrant things there are in the earth . . . fruit . . . nuts . . . pleasant kinds of dessert' (*Crit.* 115A–B). Here we have a clear statement of the motive for creating the huge trading system: to establish the most diverse resource base possible for the citizens of Atlantis. Plato goes straight on to say 'meanwhile [the Atlanteans] went on constructing their temples, palaces, harbours and docks', as if acknowledging that the creation and maintenance of this theocratic infrastructure were essential to the working of the trading empire.

THE KNOSSOS LABYRINTH AS THE ATLANTEAN TEMPLE OF POSEIDON

From its location the large island of Atlantis was undoubtedly Crete, even though one sentence of Plato's throws us off the scent. The *Timaeus* tells us that the large island was 'in front of the straits you [Athenians] call the pillars of Heracles; the island was larger than Libya and Asia'. Although many scholars have acknowledged that the pillars supporting the sky were thought to be in different places at different times, and therefore do not have to be at the Straits of Gibraltar, the huge size of an island larger [μειζων] than Libya and Asia seemed to exclude a location within the Mediterranean. Solon's original text may nevertheless have read not 'μειζων' but 'μεσον', meaning 'a middle point between Libya and Asia' (i.e. between Africa and Anatolia), which describes the location of Crete perfectly. The alternative pillars, at the edge of the early Athenians' world, were the two southernmost headlands of the Peloponnese, Cape Tainaron (Matapan) and Cape Malea; Crete was indeed a large island with one extremity not far outside *these* pillars of Heracles. Plato may have felt that the huge dimensions Solon gave for Atlantis meant that the description 'midway between Libya and Asia' had to be a mistake and altered the text accordingly.[1] Plato assumed Solon's pen had slipped. It is nevertheless clear from the climate – warm wet winters and hot dry summers (*Crit.* 118E) – that Atlantis must have occupied a location within the Mediterranean basin; the significance of this detail is usually overlooked.

As we saw earlier, the large fertile plain of Atlantis is identifiable as the Plain of Mesara. That Crete and the Mesara were in Plato's mind is suggested by another work written at about the same time, the *Laws*, in which a utopian state called Magnesia is set up in the Mesara as a Knossian colony. Book I opens in Knossos, and one of the protagonists is Cleinias, a citizen of Knossos.[2] Although Plato may have known nothing of the very specific historic connection between the Minoan civilization and the origin of Solon's Atlantis account, he nevertheless refers back to the laws of Minos as being god-given,[3] and to the tribute demanded of mainland Attica.[4]

In Cleinias' time, the painted ruins of the Labyrinth were visible in the south-east corner of Knossos – Pliny was still able to describe them 400 years later – and stories about the Labyrinth's past were in circulation. There can be little doubt that the Labyrinth was the original of the Temple of Poseidon at the heart of the capital of Atlantis.

> In the centre [of the Royal City] was a holy temple dedicated to Cleito and Poseidon, which remained inaccessible. Here was Poseidon's own temple, which was a stadium in length and half a stadium in width and of a proportionate height, having a strange barbaric appearance. The outside of the temple, with the exception of the pinnacles, they covered with silver and the pinnacles with gold.
>
> (*Crit.* 116C–D)

The Knossos Labyrinth is roughly square and rather larger than Plato's temple, one stadium each way. By ancient standards it was a lofty building; the East Wing, built into a specially made cutting in the tell, was four or five storeys high, the floor of its third storey level with the Bull Court. The Labyrinth would have looked strange and barbaric to foreigners, and also to those who saw its ruins in later times. The building lacked symmetry, indeed denied it at every opportunity. Doors were positioned near the corners of rooms as if to provoke curiosity. Everywhere there was something unexpected to look at, drawing the visitor deeper into the building. Like the cult rooms on Thera, it had pier-and-door partitions and sunken adyta. Corridors and stairs twisted and turned, roof lines

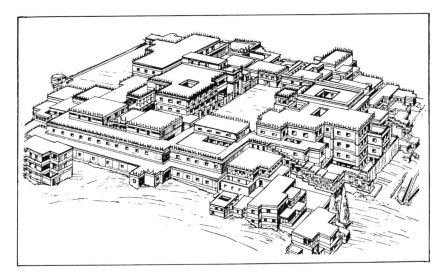

Figure 10.3 The Knossos Labyrinth: a reconstructed view from the south-east

rose and fell, and the skyline was broken by jagged lines of sacral horns – the pinnacles, or double pinnacles, of Plato's description. It was built on totally different lines from the temples of the classical period. Like a ghost train, it was intended not so much to be looked at as to be experienced, to be wandered through. To the classical Greeks it was very strange, outlandish and foreign.

The double dedication of the temple to a god and a goddess at first seems curious, but it is clear from Linear B tablets that Poseidon was the most powerful of the Minoan gods, just as he was later to be respected in the Mycenean world, though nowhere at Knossos is a representation of him in human form to be found. By contrast, the goddess Potnia, literally 'The Lady', is shown repeatedly. In ceremonies in the Labyrinth, and probably other temples too, a priestess dressed up as the goddess and, after appropriate rituals, became a living manifestation of the goddess. Poseidon's epiphanies were more complex. In the Minoan cosmos there were three worlds, heaven, earth and underworld. In the sky, Poseidon could manifest as the sun; in the underworld he was earth-shaker; on earth he could manifest as a bull. This explains the Minoan obsession with bulls, bull-leaping and bull sacrifices; these rituals were part of the dialogue with their principal god. The fact that the bull-leaping ritual, the bull dance, almost certainly took place in the central court at Knossos (and in the central courts of the other temples) confirms the dedication of both the act and the building to Poseidon.[5] Poseidon's trident is a common mason's mark, cut into many of the wall stones; Potnia's double-axe is also common.

What Plato says about the history of the temple also conforms with what is known of Knossos. 'At the very beginning they built the palace in the habitation of the god and of their ancestors, which they continued to ornament in successive

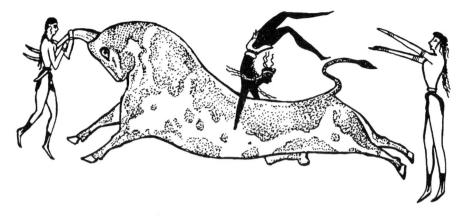

Figure 10.4 Bull-Leaping Fresco from Knossos

Plate 10.2 The trident of Poseidon was used as a mason's mark at Knossos

generations . . . until they made the building a marvel to behold for size and beauty' (*Crit.* 115C). This opens a range of issues about the Labyrinth. The blending, indeed confusion, of the ideas of 'palace' and 'temple', which seems to be present in the account Plato inherited is still a matter of keen discussion. Evans went to Knossos in 1895 with the idea fully formed in his mind that the

140

site was that of a bronze age palace. He had met Schliemann, who is known to have seen Knossos as a 'prehistoric palace' after excavating palace-citadels at Mycenae and Tiryns. Evans was therefore predisposed to interpret what he found at Knossos as evidence of a secular administrative centre, and that predisposition coloured his interpretation.[6] Even when he found overwhelming evidence that room after room had been equipped and used for religious cult activity, he clung to the palace interpretation, inventing a priest-king to explain why the building was dominated by religious observances. So persuasive and evocative were his accounts of the excavation that the palace interpretation has been accepted as the norm by succeeding generations of scholars.

Sinclair Hood is representative of Evans' disciples. A distinguished scholar with significant archaeological experience at Knossos itself, Hood commands universal respect. The common sense that pervades his writing gives his work an unusual authority. After the publication of my book *The Knossos Labyrinth* in 1989, Hood was kind enough to correspond with me. In the end, perhaps inevitably, I was unable to convince him that the thrust of the evidence from the Labyrinth at Knossos is not towards the authority of a dynasty of Minoan kings but instead towards the authority of an elite of priestesses. He went as far as agreeing that there is no archaeological proof of a king at Knossos, but argued that there must have been a king there because kings were the norm in the eastern Mediterranean region. There are two separate issues here: first, whether there was a king based somewhere in the city of Knossos, which was a state capital, and second whether the large building named by Evans 'the Palace of Minos' was a palace or a temple. The arguments for the Labyrinth as a temple have been offered by Paul Faure and at greater length by myself.[7] Hood's reply reaffirms the Evans idea of a building inhabited by gods and men.[8] He nevertheless makes concessions towards the temple interpretation, acknowledging that extensive areas of the temple-palace (his choice of term), in five different locations, were devoted to religious cult. Hood is right to point to Egyptian, Middle Eastern and Anatolian precursors of the Knossos Labyrinth, and it is useful to see how those 'foreign' temples functioned. He offers evidence that, in the east, monarchs lived in vast temple complexes. There are nevertheless difficulties in arguing too much from parallels. It would, for instance, have been possible for Cretans to import an architectural idea from Anatolia whilst adapting its function to different social, religious and political circumstances prevailing in Crete. Hood's argument encounters further problems when he looks closely at the Near Eastern labyrinths. He finds that by the time the first labyrinth was built at Knossos it was becoming unusual for kings to inhabit the same buildings as gods and goddesses. For a variety of reasons it was inconvenient to live with gods. A document from Mari records the anxiety of the king of Aleppo, at the time his daughter became engaged to marry Zimri-Lim, king of Mari: evidently the queen would be obliged to leave the temple of Mari whenever she menstruated.[9] By the time the first temple was built at Knossos, it was normal in the Near East to build separate temples for the gods.[10] Hood's

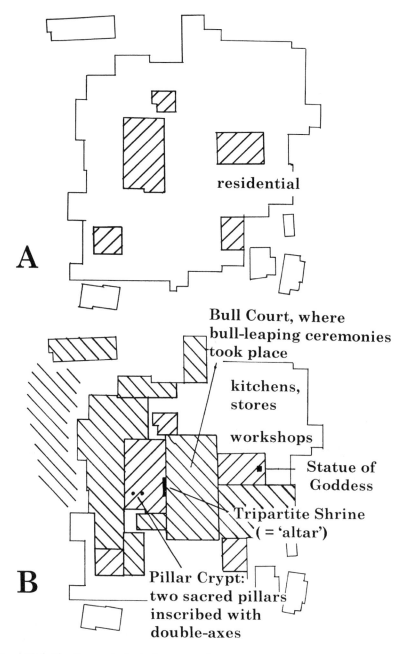

A

residential

Bull Court, where
bull-leaping ceremonies
took place

kitchens,
stores

workshops

Statue of
Goddess

Tripartite Shrine
(= 'altar')

Pillar Crypt:
two sacred pillars
inscribed with
double-axes

B

Figure 10.5 The Knossos Labyrinth as a temple
Note: A: areas conceded by Hood (1994) as being reserved for religious cult activity
(shaded); B: additional areas dedicated to religious cult activity according to Castleden
(1989)

evidence can therefore be turned against him, and used to support the idea that the huge building was exclusively a temple-complex. Hood's (and Evans's) assumption that its East Wing was a residential quarter stands unsupported; Cameron's reconstruction of the Grand Staircase fresco authenticates the East Wing as yet another area dedicated to religious cult activity, probably male initiation ceremonies.

Other scholars seem close to accepting the temple interpretation. In 1994 MacGillivray commented that when the site was cleared for the building of the 'palace' everything was removed except the Monolithic Pillar Basement; since this had a cult use, its preservation implies that the new building was to have a religious dedication. Describing the western half of the building, MacGillivray says its uses were 'very much as one might expect in a temple', and of the eastern half that its suites with pier-and-door partitions seemed 'suited to ritual'.[11] It has been generally overlooked that the Cretan peak sanctuaries were built at the same time as the first urban temples, but this strongly implies that a religious movement was key to the legitimization of the temple elite (Cherry 1986); the power of those responsible for the building and maintenance of the temples was religious in origin.

When, in the seventeenth century BC, the city of Knossos reached its zenith in population and extent, the Labyrinth too reached its fullest development. Then, as Niemeier noted in 1994, a ring of special 'urban villas' was built round the Labyrinth to house the high-status priests and priestesses who served in the

Plate 10.3 The Knossos Labyrinth as restored by Evans: the East Wing at the top, revetment walls supporting the tell to the right

temple; the two great tombs built at this time, the Isopata and Temple Tombs, may be royal – or high-priestly. In the first century AD, Pliny (*Historia Naturalis* XXXVI, 19. 85–90) described the Knossos Labyrinth as a standing ruin. Its corridors did not merely turn back on themselves like the mazes on Roman mosaics: their walls had doors in them to add to the confusion. Daedalus built Knossos on the model of the Egyptian labyrinth at Hawara. Pliny described the Egyptian labyrinth at some length, with its columns and images of gods, explicitly calling it a temple and adding, 'What has been said applies equally to the Cretan labyrinth', so Pliny clearly thought of the Knossos Labyrinth as a temple.

Another idea embedded in Plato's comment, 'At the very beginning they built the palace in the habitation of the god and of their ancestors', is the long ancestry of the Knossos site. It was the location of a very early settlement, the earliest known village in Crete, in 6100 BC. The mud-brick houses disintegrated and were rebuilt repeatedly, so that by the end of the neolithic the village, its outline plan almost matching that of the later temple, stood on a tell 6 metres high. Though the settlement grew outwards in all directions, it was the historic nucleus that was chosen as the site for the temple in 1930 BC. It too was repeatedly rebuilt, and the later work has to a great extent destroyed the remains of the earlier, but it is clear that the builders 'continued to ornament [the Labyrinth] in successive generations' and the final version of the building was 'a marvel to behold for size and beauty'.

> There were in the interior of the temple other images which had been dedicated by private persons . . . and there were many other great offerings of kings and private persons, coming both from the city itself and from the foreign cities over which they held sway.
>
> (*Crit.* 116E)

A statue of the goddess, larger than life, is known to have stood in the Great Goddess Sanctuary, and it may be that other statues have been destroyed or removed by thieves.[12] On the walls were paintings, perhaps sponsored by wealthy donors, of entire life-sized processions of people. Offerings of every kind flowed into the temple: a huge area of store rooms was reserved for them, and administrators recorded them on clay tablets. One reads:

> In the month of Deukios; to Diktaian Zeus, one measure of oil; to the Daidalaion, two measures of oil; to Pa-de, one measure of oil; to – , one measure of oil; to Therasia, one measure of oil; . . . to the Priestess of the Winds, four measures of oil.[13]

Plato mentions 'many temples built and dedicated to many gods' and the worship of many gods is amply proved by the clay tablets. The fact that the Laby-rinth was built as a collection of separate suites of rooms with interconnecting doors strongly suggests that the Labyrinth was like a cathedral with side chapels dedicated to a variety of saints; this need not interfere with the temple having an overall dedication to one or two deities.

'The order of precedence among [the Atlantean kings and their subjects] and their mutual relations were regulated by the command of Poseidon. These were inscribed by the first kings on a pillar situated in the middle of the island, at the temple of Poseidon' (*Crit.* 119C–D). The fresco evidence from Thera shows that in the Minoan world there was differentiation not only by caste or family but by age-group. Doubtless this stratification was supported by the priesthood, and fresco evidence from both Thera and Knossos shows that these were theocratic societies, so socio-political regulation by a deity is exactly what was happening in the bronze age. Inscription on pillars is also to be seen at Knossos. There are two pillar crypts in the West Wing covered in double-axe carvings. The double-axe symbolizes the goddess, which implies that the carvings confirm the dedication of the West Wing, at least, to the worship of the goddess. The temple's overall plan revolves round the large rectangle of the central Bull Court. The layout of the West Wing is to an extent related geometrically to the Bull Court. For instance, the Tripartite Shrine,[14] itself uncompromisingly symmetrical, was built in the centre of the Bull Court's west side, evidently as its ritual focus. The south wall of the East Pillar Crypt (the larger and more important of the two) is in line with the southern end of the Tripartite Shrine. The crypt's north wall is in line with the midpoint of the Bull Court. The east face of the square pillar, the face you see as you enter the crypt, coincides with the Snake Goddess Sanctuary's north–south axis.[15] Although these geometrical features could be coincidental, it is more likely that they are not, that at least the final version the West Wing was meticulously designed in relation to the existing open space of the Bull Court, and its interior plan revolved round the East Crypt pillar. The pillar's ritual importance is proved by the provision of a libation pit on each side of it.

Plato emphasizes the elaborate ritual nature of the meetings of the ten kings of Atlantis, evidently a federation of some kind, and this accords well with the archaeological evidence from Thera, Kea, Melos and Knossos:

> They consulted about their common interests, enquired if anyone had transgressed in any matter and passed judgement . . . There were bulls who had the range of the temple of Poseidon. The ten kings, being left alone in the temple, after offering prayers to the god that they might capture the victim which was acceptable to him, hunted the bulls without weapons, but with staves and nooses, and the bull which they caught they led up to the pillar and cut its throat over the top of it so that the blood fell upon the sacred inscription. After slaying the bull, they proceeded to burn its limbs. They filled a bowl with wine and cast in a clot of blood for each of them . . . They drew from the bowl in golden cups and poured a libation.

They offered up prayers and dedicated their cups to the temple.

Plate 10.4 The pillar in the East Pillar Crypt at Knossos. The double-axe carvings are associated with Potnia, the Lady of the Labyrinth, and mark the pillar as a structure of great sanctity

Here we come to the most distinctive Minoan practices, the rituals of the bull cult. From the evidence of figurines and frescoes at Knossos itself, it is possible to reconstruct the capture and sacrifice of bulls, and the bull-leaping ritual.[16] Bulls were released into the Bull Court as into a bullring. A team of bull-leapers, grapplers and acrobats performed extraordinary feats in a dance that was both a sport, watched by a large mixed audience, and a religious observance, hosted by the priestesses. The bulls were captured in weaponless hunts and no weapons were used in the bull dance either. At the end of the bull dance the bull may have been sacrificed and its blood poured as a libation over pillars and sacral horns. The double-axe pillars were accessible just behind the Tripartite Shrine, and the Shrine itself was embellished with sacral horns; we know from the painting at Akrotiri that blood was splashed over sacral horns. The ceremonial meal Plato mentions may have taken place in the refectory, a large chamber that stood on the first floor above the Pillar Hall.

From all this we can see that the Labyrinth as it existed in 1600–1400 BC was very similar to the Temple of Poseidon at the centre of the Atlantean capital. Late Minoan Knossos overwhelmingly dominated the rest of Crete, and it is reasonable to assume that Knossos' ruling elite to a great extent controlled what happened in Crete and co-ordinated the network of trading links across the Aegean and beyond. This was the heart of Atlantis, or at least of that part of Atlantis authentically originating in the bronze age.

PLATO AND TRUTH

A point scholars often contemptuously sweep aside is that Plato insisted he was telling the truth. 'Extraordinary though [the story] is, it is certainly true' (*Tim.* 20D); 'Solon vouched for its truth' (*Tim.* 20E); 'not mere legend, but an actual fact' (*Tim.* 21A); 'authentic achievement of our city' (*Tim.* 21A); 'true and worthy of the goddess' (*Tim.* 21A); 'a veritable tradition' (*Tim.* 21D); 'the story which Solon told you as true' (*Tim.* 21E); 'real' (*Tim.* 26D); 'a fact not a fiction' (*Tim.* 26E). He even claimed that his narrator Critias held documentary evidence, the account Solon brought back from Egypt: 'These very writings were in the possession of my grandfather and are actually now in mine, and when I was a child I learnt them all by heart.'

It is important to establish what Plato meant by the word 'true'. Would Plato, transported to a modern courtroom, be able to swear that the evidence he was giving was the truth, the whole truth? Certainly he understood the concept of lying or untruth, believing that governments had the right to lie if that produced the right response in their citizens. He even argued that it was possible through education for a government to propagate any doctrine and have it believed by the entire population within one generation.[17] This brand of untruth was the 'royal lie', a falsehood deliberately promoted for the good of the state.

But what Plato understood by 'truth' is less straightforward. In his doctrine of ideas,[18] he proposed that although there may be many manifestations of an object there is only one idea for that object. Various individual beds are unreal, mere copies of the bed idea, which is the one real bed. This puts Plato's thinking some distance from our own, in that most of us would say that the bed we sleep on and daily remake is real and the ideal bed of the imagination is not. In the *Menexenus*, we witness a conversation between Socrates and Pericles' mistress Aspasia, two historically real people, who discuss the Corinthian War; but the war did not begin until several years after Socrates' death. Though factually reported, this discussion cannot have taken place.

Another exotic feature of Plato's thought is that he imagined that opposites could be true.[19] The number 6 is greater than 4 but less than 12, so it is both great and small. This seemed a puzzle to Plato, whereas the idea of relative values would present no problem for modern people. This opens a window on the Atlantis controversy, in that Plato may have felt driven to insist that the story was entirely true, since the only alternative was that it was entirely false. This is supported by a passage in the *Theaetetus*,[20] where Socrates says, 'if all things are either known or unknown, there can be no opinion which is not comprehended under this alternative'. Theaetetus answers cryptically, 'Most true'.

One difficulty is that we cannot know what Plato really believed. In the *Gorgias*, he put an account of the judgement of the dead by Zeus into the mouth of Socrates. Socrates may have believed in its literal truth; Plato may have believed in it: he certainly believed in its poetic truth. 'This is what I have heard, Callicles, and I believe it to be true.' As a vision of the future likely to turn people away from wrongdoing it was good, and therefore in Plato's eyes true. Later, he implies a belief in relative truth: 'There would be nothing strange in despising it if our searches could discover a better and truer account.'[21]

Plato's contemporary Isocrates remained silent on the question of Atlantis in the *Panathenaius*, and other ancient scholars seem to have accepted the story, yet in modern times there has been no shortage of forthright scholars prepared to cast doubt on Plato's truthfulness. Daniel Dombrowski fairly represents modern scholars who see the story as 'a powerful literary device invented by Plato'.[22] But the account was not repudiated in Plato's time; it aroused a lot of interest, and there were plenty of Greeks living in Sais who could have checked whether he was telling the truth. Others later accused Plato of deception or plagiarism: he was accused of lifting material for the *Timaeus* from a work by Philolaus of Croton which he bought in Syracuse,[23] though this must refer to the cosmology section, since Philolaus is known to have made advances in astronomical theory.

Although the relationship between the Atlantis story and the cosmology of the *Timaeus* remains unclear, the fact that Plato paired them tells us that a connection exists. Much of Plato's cosmology is obscure to modern readers, but it includes some remarkably forward-looking scientific ideas. The earth is a sphere millions of years old floating in space, rotating on its axis like the other

Plate 10.5 Plato. A first-century AD Roman copy in marble of the bronze portrait by Silanion, which was probably made during Plato's lifetime

planets; the moon is lit by the sun; the heavenly bodies appear small but are actually immense; the sun is much larger than the earth; the planets follow circular orbits. Plato's science is far from fanciful: it is a serious attempt to reach the objective truth, and we should accept the Atlantis account that precedes his fullest cosmological statement as equally serious in intention.

If Plato was telling the literal truth about Atlantis, how do we account for the battery of discrepancies between his account and the events of the Aegean bronze age as archaeologists and geologists now reconstruct them? Fredericks compiled a list of the discrepancies,[24] which deserves answering:

1   Thera was far too small to be Atlantis.
2   Thera was the wrong side of the Pillars of Heracles (as was Crete).
3   Thera's topography is/was not geometrical enough.
4   The Thera eruption was too late.
5   Thera remains unsubmerged.
6   There is no mention in Plato's account of a volcanic eruption.

Several of the apparent inconsistencies have already been clarified. Thera alone was not Atlantis: it was one of the islands in the Atlantis group. Plato makes it clear that there was one large island, for which Crete is the obvious candidate, but also many smaller islands of which Thera could easily have been one. Thera is the wrong side of the Pillars of Heracles if they are defined as the Rock of Gibraltar and Monte del Hacko, but it was only in late antiquity that they acquired a fixed location there. Since an earlier alternative location was the two southernmost headlands of the Greek mainland, Thera and Crete could truly be said to be outside the pillars.

It is true that Thera is not and never was laid out in concentric circles, though before the bronze age eruption it did have an overall circular shape and the South Bay was also probably rounded in form; the rigidly geometric layout Plato describes has to be an invention, whether of Plato's, Solon's or the Egyptians' devising. The altering of the dates by an order of magnitude can be explained as a scribal error. The proto-Greek Linear B 'thousand' is a circle with four short rays, 'hundred' a circle without rays;[25] reading '9,000 years' as '900 years' brings the fall of Atlantis to 1500 BC, very close to the likely date of the Thera eruption, although that does imply that the story of Atlantis was preserved at Sais in Linear B, which is hard to explain. Thera may still be visible, but the centre of the island did subside at the climax of the eruption taking a large area of the island to the bottom of the sea. The main part of the Atlantean sea empire consisted of a network of shipping routes and, for a time after the eruption, these went out of use: the Minoan economic enterprise figuratively sank without trace, as if sent to the seabed.

Answering Fredericks' sixth point, there is no mention of a volcanic eruption, and we cannot know whether it would have been included in the *Critias* account. At first sight it may seem odd that one of the most spectacular elements

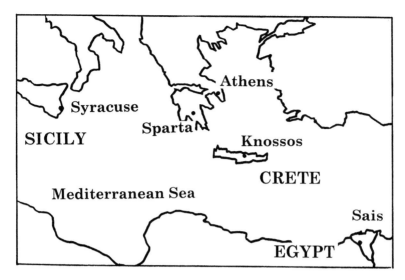

Figure 10.6 Plato's world

in the catastrophe should have been missed out: the subsidence and the earth-quakes are there. The answer is simple; that earthquakes centred on Thera were experienced over a large area in the Aegean and therefore could be reported and remembered by those who survived on the other islands; that it would have been obvious to those sailing past the island after the catastrophe that its centre had vanished: there may even have been some down-faulted blocks still remaining round the caldera walls to indicate how the island had fallen in. But no witnesses of the eruption itself can have lived to tell the tale. We can infer the progress of the eruption sequence in detail using modern techniques of archaeology and geology, but no-one could have done that in the bronze age, or indeed in Plato's day.

What emerges is that many of the problems that have been seen as stumbling blocks to accepting Plato's account of the destruction of Atlantis as fundamentally true and relating to the Aegean are not major problems at all. Nevertheless, Plato has evidently embellished the truth.

Plato was ambivalent about truth in myth. In the *Laws*, an Athenian, a Spartan and a Cretan discuss the constitution needed for the new Knossian colony. The Cretan says that glorious as the truth is, it is often hard to convince people of it.[26] The Athenian responds with a question about the improbable fable of teeth sown in the ground and germinating into armed men. He thinks the tale false, 'yet the example is striking proof for a law-giver that the youthful mind will be persuaded of anything, if one will take the trouble to persuade it'.[27] The Athenian thinks only the gullible would believe the fable. More directly in the third book of the *Laws* the Athenian asks, 'What view do you take of the ancient legends? Have they any truth behind them? ... those which tell of

151

repeated destructions of mankind by flood, pestilence, and from various other causes, which leave only a handful of survivors?'[28] This is a direct reference back to the story of the destruction of Atlantis in the *Critias*, and it looks as if Plato changed his mind about writing a trilogy consisting of the *Timaeus*, *Critias* and *Hermocrates*, leaving the *Critias* unfinished and abandoning the *Hermocrates* altogether; the *Laws* was written instead of the *Hermocrates* and it deployed some of the material Plato intended for it. The opening of the *Critias*, the second dialogue, shows that Hermocrates is to speak third: 'Hermocrates, you who are posted last and have another in front of you' (*Crit.* 108C).[29] The Cretan thinks the ancient legends perfectly credible. Ultimately, Plato was more interested in the effect of what he wrote than its literal truth. Plato says of his fictional tale of Er, 'it could save us if we believe it'.

To understand Plato's attitude towards myth we must bear in mind that before, during and after Plato's time, the Greeks conventionally used myth as a frame for a story or as a starting-point for political satire. A small number of writers, notably Hesiod, were prepared to record myths straight, but most adapted and developed them. Plato was concerned that the stories he used showed the gods in a good light; those showing them in a scandalous or immoral light were bad examples to hold before the young or weak, and therefore 'untrue'.[30] Plato was aware that myths could be developed, that it was possible to fashion myths by gathering and systematizing ancient traditions.[31] In the *Lysis*, Ctesippus says that Hippothales 'gave in a poem the whole account of the entertainment of Heracles, how his [Hippothales'] ancestor received the hero into his house on the strength of his relationship . . . such are old wives' tales.' Both Ctesippus and through him Plato were able to see that myths could be invented, and that once invented those myths could be useful socially and in other ways to their inventor. Plato was not averse to inventing tales himself. In the *Phaedrus* he has Socrates telling the Egyptian myth of Theuth and Thamus. Phaedrus says, 'It is easy for you, Socrates [= Plato], to make up tales about Egypt or anywhere else you fancy.'[32] In the *Republic* he develops the idea of the 'noble fiction'.[33] It is permissible for a ruler to lie 'for the good of the city'.[34] If the fiction is beneficial, its literal untruth becomes a poetic truth. The noble fiction 'is useful because of our ignorance of what truly happened of old. We then make the fiction as like the truth as we can, and so make the lie or untruth useful.'[35]

Plato knew that colourful stories made his parables more palatable. In the *Protagoras*, Protagoras says, 'Now shall I put my explanation in the form of a story, or give it as a reasoned argument? I think it will be pleasanter to tell you a story.'[36] Plato used myth in four different ways. First, there are brief allusions to mythic events, such as the references to Alcestis, Orpheus and Achilles in the *Symposium* or to Oedipus and Hippolytus in the *Laws*. Second, there are fuller accounts of myths that are recognizably based on genuine ancient traditions, like the judgement of the dead which occurs in the *Gorgias* and again in the *Phaedo*. It is the thrust of this book that the Atlantis story is of this type. Third, there is the mythic story that has the full form and texture of a genuine ancient tradition and contains some traditional elements but is mainly an invention of Plato's, like the judgement myth known as the tale of Er,[37] or the myth of the flood,[38] in which he incorporates the flood and the sack of Troy but also a Platonic framework and message. Fourth, there is the mythic story that is Plato's own invention from start to finish. Plato says poets made people believe his Phoenician tale,[39] but it would take a great deal of persuasion to have it believed in Athens. Clearly there is more than one level of deception at work here.

In the *Politicus*, the Stranger tells Socrates about Zeus altering the movements of the heavenly bodies, introducing the idea of alternating cycles of divine control and withdrawal. When God is at the helm the universe rotates one way, when not, the other; at the moments of reversal there are geological upheavals, with earthquakes causing widespread destruction.[40] When God is in control, good prevails. When not, humanity drifts from godly ways. This was what Plato had in mind when he wrote of the Atlanteans having once been close to Poseidon, but losing touch with the gods and moving into a state of sin; in this Plato seems to misrepresent the Minoan theocracy. The Atlantis story also gives a graphic account of the destructive end of one of the cosmic cycles. This does not mean the Atlantis catastrophe was not a historical event; it is rather that the description of the destruction of Atlantis in Solon's notes, familiar to Plato since childhood, shaped his ideas about geological catastrophes punctuating human history. The doctrine of periodic catastrophes leaving few survivors was in any case part of the 'science' of Plato's time.[41]

There is another ingredient of the Atlantis story which Plato used elsewhere. In the *Symposium*, Plato gives us a sequence of after-dinner speeches at a gathering hosted by Agathon. Instead of telling the story as straight reportage or fiction, Plato sets the scene by having Apollodorus tell the story to a friend many years after the event; Apollodorus got the story from Aristodemus, who had actually attended the supper party. The way the story's antecedents and credentials are built up is useful in building dramatic tension and raising the listener's expectations. Plato uses the same technique in the Atlantis tale, although there the scene-setting is more elaborate, partly, I suspect, because the events are much further back in time, partly because he really did have the story from Solon as he claimed. Plato was claiming to hold the key to the earliest known history, and therefore needed to go to some lengths to substantiate it.

Plato saw myth as a useful vehicle for presenting his ideas. It was emotive, entertaining and persuasive. It offered 'another road to truth'.[42] For him literal truth was subordinate to poetic truth. From his asides and preambles it is evident that he enjoyed cloaking his ideas behind myths. The constantly deployed device of ventriloquizing through the dead Socrates was part of the same play-acting. As we have seen, his 'myths' are of more than one kind. I believe the Atlantis myth to be a myth of the second kind (based mainly on genuine ancient traditions), though I am aware that many scholars believe it to be a myth of the third kind (using some traditional elements but mainly a Platonic invention) or even fourth kind (entirely a Platonic invention).[43]

Plato's insistence that he was telling the truth is seen by some as playful irony. He is teasing us. The more he insists, the more doubts he raises, as with Mark Antony's insistence that Brutus was an honourable man. But to how many other writers would we apply this kind of stricture? He must be lying because he says he is telling the truth? Perhaps Plato insisted on the truth of his story because he knew that unlike many of his other stories it was true twice over, poetically and literally, in that he knew his account of the provenance of the story was accurate. If, in addition, he believed that the events described actually happened, the story acquired a third layer of truth, but he was more interested still in making the story speak – truly – of issues that were nearer his own time.

PLATO AND SICILY

Not all of the Atlantis account is about Thera, Crete or the Aegean in the sixteenth century. Plato grafted on references to more contemporary events. He came to write the *Timaeus* and *Critias* in about 355 BC, and in order to understand what was in his mind it is necessary to look at his earlier experiences.

Plato was born in 427 BC into a distinguished Athenian family. When he was 12, a two-year war broke out between Athens and its colonies in Sicily. In 409 BC, Plato reached the age of 18 and probably went into military service, perhaps fighting against the Spartans in the Peloponnesian War, which must have been a major formative influence in his life. In the same year, the Carthaginian Wars broke out. Four years later, when the Carthaginian Wars ended in defeat for the Sicilian city-states, the Syracusan general Dionysius was elected tyrant of Syracuse. A year later, in 404 BC, the Peloponnesian War ended in defeat for Athens. Plato must have shared the bitterness and despair of all Athenians at the violation of their city. He was disgusted by the regime of the Thirty Tyrants set up in Athens at the instigation of Sparta, with its year-long persecution of democrats: in 403 BC democracy was restored, but both Plato and his teacher Socrates had been disillusioned by public life, turning from politics to philosophy:

> My feelings were not surprising for a young man: I thought [the Thirty Tyrants] were going to lead the city from an unjust to a just way of life, so I observed with deep interest. And I saw how, in a short time, these men made the old regime look like a golden age.
>
> (*Epistle* VII, 325)

The twenty-seven-year-long Peloponnesian War was a period of major development in the technology of warfare and defence. The war developed into one of city sieges and fortress building.[44] The threat from Carthage forced Sicilian commanders to review their defensive works. The result was that the Greeks both in Sicily and the Peloponnese developed fully fledged defensive stone towers with roofs and internal rooms. Existing city walls were fitted with new low walls in front of them, making them harder to reach with siege engines; new manuals were written, laying out construction details. The catapult was invented at Syracuse in 399 BC by Dionysius' team of engineers.

Dionysius started strengthening his position in Syracuse, building a defensive wall round the island of Ortygia, then a 5-kilometre-wall along the northern edge of the Epipolai plateau;[45] this secured the city from a land attack from the north-west. Dionysius may not at first have intended it to be a circuit wall, but he went on to add a new wall along the southern edge of the plateau to defend the city from attack from the Anapos valley, giving Syracuse the longest circuit wall of any Greek city.[46]

In 399 BC came the third major formative influence on Plato, the execution of Socrates, 'the most upright man then living'.[47] Plato was apparently not well enough to attend Socrates' execution. This did not prevent him from writing the most detailed and moving account of his teacher's death,[48] presumably based on interviews with those present. Socrates' students felt themselves to be at risk and Plato withdrew from Athens to take refuge at Megara, later travelling extensively outside Greece.

Dionysius fought another war against Carthage, by the end of which he had achieved overlordship of most of Sicily. Plato visited the philosopher and political leader Archytas of Taras in southern Italy, and was persuaded to cross to Sicily. It is not certain whether he went primarily to see Etna's lava flows[49] or was invited by Dion for political reasons. Plutarch's explanation is credible,[50] that Plato was invited to Dionysius' court at the instigation of the tyrant's brother-in-law, Dion, who was keen to moderate the harshness of Dionysius' absolutism.[51] Plato went and did his best to teach Dionysius, who regularly won second and third prizes in the Athenian poetry competitions which he continually entered.[52] Plato failed with Dionysius but made an influential friend in Dion and when Dionysius died in 367 BC, of over-excitement at winning a poetry competition, Dion worked hard to get Plato to return and educate his young successor, Dionysius II. Plato did return and was welcomed handsomely, conveyed from the harbour in the chariot of state, accompanied by Dionysius II on a mule. But again the educational project was a failure, and Plato went back to Athens. He risked a third visit in 361 BC in an attempt to have the exiled Dion recalled, but this intervention was unwelcome and he had difficulty in getting safely back to Athens, where he stayed for the rest of his life.[53]

In 357 BC, with a small force of five merchant ships, Dion led an attack on Syracuse and expelled Dionysius, a major achievement in the face of Dionysius' fleet of 400 warships, but Dion was assassinated by his own political enemies three years later, at about the time when Plato wrote his Atlantis story. Curiously, it was one of Plato's Academicians, Callipus, who organized the murder.

For all his political theorizing, Plato was unable to influence events in Sicily constructively, though he was able to observe the extraordinary war machine

Figure 10.7 Syracuse

Dionysius I had built up, and the longest circuit walls in the known world. The first wall towers in Syracuse were the Ortygia towers. Rising in three stages, they looked like little temples on three-stepped podia. Later came the five Euryalos towers, which were smaller and built of white Syracuse marble. The towers of Syracuse were the wonder of the age, and Plato must have been impressed by the craftsmanship, strategy and wealth invested in them. Diodorus refers to the walls as 'expensive and having high towers at close intervals'.[54] Round the island of Ortygia, only two towers survive, but they are very close together; if all the towers were this close together round the high wall, the visual effect would have been overwhelmingly impressive.

The fortifications found their way into Plato's description of the capital of Atlantis, albeit in disguised form. Plato described three walls enclosing concentric circles, whereas the walls of Syracuse enclose three adjacent irregular areas. The smallest area was Ortygia (where the original settlement was founded in 734 BC), the medium-sized area was the adjacent mainland area of Achradina, and the largest was the Epipolai plateau to the west. Plato gilded the lily when he coated the walls with orichalchum, tin and brass (*Crit.* 116B); this nevertheless enshrined a poetic truth, that the walls were impregnable and magnificent.

It may be that Plato imported the idea of metal-coated walls from Homer's description of the lavish royal palace of king Alcinous of the Phaeacians at Scheria.[55] Spanuth lists an impressive twenty-five parallels between Homer's Phaeacia and the Atlantis of Plato and Diodorus.[56] Among the most telling are the economic foci of the culture; the Phaeacian men are skilled seafarers, while the women are expert weavers.[57] An often overlooked but telling detail of Homer's description of the island-kingdom is that it 'looked like a shield laid on the misty sea';[58] the Minoan shield was sometimes a figure-of-eight shape but more often, as shown in the Theran frescoes, a long narrow rectangle – the shape of Crete. Many writers[59] have suggested that Plato drew extensively on Homer for his description of Atlantis, but this is another of the curious literary loops we keep encountering. It may be, as has been suggested more than once, that Homer's Phaeacians, who lived on an island at the edge of the world, were actually the Minoans. Scheria, according to Woudhuizen,[60] was the name of the town beside the Minoan temple of Ayia Triadha. So, even if Plato did borrow from Homer's description of the Phaeacian palace for his Atlantean palace, he may still have been describing the architecture of Minoan Crete; the two accounts may alternatively represent parallel but separate traditions concerning the pre-Helladic Aegean.

Ortygia's design is particularly interesting; Dionysius turned it into a royal citadel with a double circuit wall and built an inner fort within them, so Ortygia itself had Plato's three concentric ring-walls. Like the Royal City of Atlantis, Ortygia had several springs and temples. There were large temples dedicated to Apollo and Athena (rather than Poseidon and Cleito). The Athena temple was ornate, with doors of gold and ivory: the Atlantean temple of Poseidon and Cleito was richly adorned with gold and ivory. Other elements of the capital of Atlantis were also drawn from fourth-century Syracuse. Plato describes a canal 100 metres wide which linked the sea to a harbour, 'leaving an opening sufficient to let the largest vessel in' and 'they bridged the zones of sea which surrounded the ancient metropolis, making a road to the royal palace' (*Crit.* 115B–C). This describes the bridged channel dug across the isthmus connecting Ortygia to the mainland, and the link it made between the Little Harbour and the Grand Harbour. Plato also mentions 'a stone wall on every side, placing towers and gates on the bridges where the sea passed in' (*Crit.* 116A). The surviving Dionysian Towers on Ortygia show that the circuit wall bristling with towers passed right in front of the bridge to the mainland, and Plato may have developed what he saw here, on his memorable chariot ride to the royal palace, into *many* bridges with defensive towers and *many* artificially cut zones of sea.

The structure of Dionysian Syracuse was similar to that of Plato's Atlantean metropolis, except that Plato separated his four urban zones from one another by rings of water. There was an innermost zone, the citadel with its royal palace, temple, grove and springs; then there was a zone with temples and gardens; the third was more complex, with temples, gardens, a stadium and gymnasia; the fourth, outermost, zone was the busy mercantile quarter. From descriptions in Diodorus and Cicero, Syracuse was seen in antiquity as having four quarters: it was a 'tetrapolis', consisting of Ortygia as the innermost zone, Achradina as the second zone, Tycha, with its temples and athletics grounds as well as much housing, and finally mercantile Neapolis.

Like Aristotle,[61] Plato will have felt the importance of fortifications for a city's strength and well-being, not least because he had seen that the fortifications of Athens were of no avail against Sparta and the result had been defeat and humiliation. Seeing the walls and towers of Syracuse will have reawakened memories of another humiliation for Athens, the disastrous Sicilian Expedition of 413 BC. Plato was 14 at the time, an impressionable age.

Behind the fifth- and fourth-century BC obsession with Sicily lay the westward thrust from Persia, which seemed to oblige the Athenians to look to the west for colonial expansion.[62] In 480 BC Themistocles had spoken of the possibility of an Athenian migration towards Italy.[63] In 416 BC, the writings of Thucydides brought the idea of Sicily to the forefront of this line of thought. There was a new generation of Athenians, full of hope, enterprise, dreams of conquest. The conquest of Sicily was justified as a means of subduing Carthage, but the truth was that Sicily was big enough, far enough away and little enough known to give free rein to the Athenian New World dream. Sicily stood out in the Greek imagination as an incredibly large island. By comparison with the compact world of their Peloponnesian city-states, it was huge. Ten times bigger than Plato's Attica, it seemed (like Crete) to approach continental size. Like Gibraltar and Salamis, it also lay due west of Athens. Other features of Sicily parallel the description of Atlantis. Plato made a point of ascending Etna, and would have been well aware of the geological instability of Syracuse, its proneness to earthquakes. The 'large fertile plain' of Atlantis found its Sicilian counterpart in the Plain of Catania.

The First Athenian Expedition was triggered by the arrival in Athens in 416 BC of envoys from the Sicilian town of Segasta, asking for military help against Syracuse. In 415 BC the Segastan envoys were in Athens again, with silver enough to pay the crews of 60 triremes for a month. Opinion in Athens was divided, Socrates being among those who opposed the expedition, but a war fever was whipped up and an Athenian fleet set sail with crews totalling 25,580 men. The Athenians miscalculated badly, in that the Sicilian cities did not rally to the Athenian cause, siding instead with Syracuse. The Athenians laid siege to Syracuse, building siege walls and cutting off the water supply. The Syracusans responded by building three counter-siege walls.

The Second Expedition was launched in 413 BC after a vote in the Athenian assembly that demonstrated the ineffective working of the democratic process. Nicias was entrusted with the command, even though he had failed on the First Expedition. There was a sea battle in the harbours of Syracuse, where the Athenian ships were trapped and rammed by heavy-beaked Syracusan warships.

The Athenians retreated along the coast before surrendering. Demosthenes attempted suicide but was prevented by the Syracusans, then Nicias surrendered: Nicias' shield long hung on display in a temple in Syracuse. Seven thousand of the Athenians were imprisoned in stone quarries, many of them 'rescued' by Syracusans and enslaved. A few escaped. Those who managed to get back to Athens could not make the Athenians believe what had happened.[64]

The failure of the Sicilian Expeditions was a terrible blow to Athens. Sicily had embodied the Athenians' colonial dreams. The clash between the two great military machines may have been an ingredient in Plato's Atlantis account. The story was 'improved', made more truthful poetically, by bringing the Athenians out on top. The moral charges made against the Atlanteans fit Plato's likely views of the Sicilian ruling elite. The Athenians needed the Syracusans to be strong enough to keep Carthage at bay, but not so strong as to resist the will of Athens; there was an ambivalence which is carried over into Plato's description of the Atlanteans, who are both admirable and hostile ('they possessed great spirits': *Crit.* 120E). The expedition was led by Athens, but her allies took part, and it is clear that Syracuse was supported by other Sicilian city-states, the situation exactly noted by Plato in the war between Atlantis and Athens (*Crit.* 108E): 'The city of Athens was reported to have been the leader and to have fought out the war; the combatants on the other side were commanded by the kings of Atlantis.' The Atlanteans' slide from grace and virtue is described at length (*Crit.* 120E–121B), until 'human nature got the upper hand . . . they then behaved unseemly . . . tainted with unrighteous ambition and power' (*Crit.* 121B). During Plato's last visit to Sicily, Dionysius II had become envious and suspicious of the philosopher's friendship with Dion. His (well-founded) distrust of Dion led him to confiscate Dion's property; he also forced Dion's wife to divorce him and remarry a man called Timocrates, and led her young son into vice. Plato observed the tyrant's descent into depravity at close quarters, and there can be little doubt that the passages in the Atlantis story referring to moral decline were drawn from Plato's Sicilian experience and were intended to be read in that way by his readers.

What Plato was doing was converting and adapting the story which, though containing genuine bronze age traditions, was made to serve the needs of his own time. He was alerting the Athenians of 355 BC to the dangers inherent in slack government: the tyrants of Syracuse were a warning of what could happen in any city-state if matters were not properly regulated. Plato was also consciously reminding Athenians of the horrors of the Sicilian adventure, perhaps partly in order to make it clear that it *was* the Sicilians he was alluding to. We have shifted from a view of Plato as a pseudo-historian to an idea of him as a political satirist. He is using picture-language, parables and past events that contain parallels, in order to warn his contemporaries of imminent dangers. Reference back to the Sicilian Expeditions would have made Athenians shudder, and awakened the memory that the enterprise was a democratically approved military fiasco. Athens could become Atlantis.

After the fiasco, the Athenians lashed out in anger at the politicians who had argued for the expedition. 15,000 men had died in Sicily. At the same time plague had wiped out one-third of Athens, so that by 413 BC Athens could muster only 9,000 hoplites and 11,000 thetes (rowers and marines), a stunning and crippling reduction in Athens' fighting capacity. At least 216 triremes had been lost. Their most experienced generals were lost: Demosthenes, Nicias, Lamachas and Eurymedon. Alcibiades was in exile in Sparta. There was a political vacuum.[65] These were sour memories to reawaken, so the pill had to be sugared. It is Athens that is portrayed as virtuous and triumphant, and Sicily, the 'American dream' of the fifth and fourth centuries BC, that is turned into an imploding nightmare.

PLATO AND SPARTA

The relevance of the Atlantis parable to the Athenians of 355 BC was emphasized by another humiliation bitter in the Athenian memory, the spectacular defeat of their city at the end of the Peloponnesian War in April 404 BC. The traumatic memory of Spartans overrunning the city was still alive when Plato was writing; he himself had been about 23 at the time. His attitude was ambivalent. Sparta was Athens' rival and enemy, yet he admired many of its customs and qualities. His description of Atlantis is similarly ambivalent. Atlantis is great-spirited, magnificent – and wrong-headed.

Plato's view may have been idealized. He saw Sparta as a state where all citizens were equal, or at any rate more equal than under the Athenian democracy. He admired the way the young were trained to be obedient servants of the state, and the general suppression of individualism. He liked the lack of ostentatious luxury and the 'geometry' of the state organization.

The power struggle between Athens and Sparta lasted from 431 until 404 BC. After the Sicilian Expedition, the Athenians feared that their allies would fall away as the victorious Syracusans sailed to support the Peloponnesians. In September 405 BC, Lysander, the Spartan commander-in-chief, waited until most of the Athenian ships at Aegospotami were unmanned. There was no battle. Lysander simply took the Athenian fleet. Twenty ships escaped under general Conon, who sent a few ships with the news to Athens and, unable to face the wrath of the Athenians, fled. Lysander rounded up all the Athenians at Aegospotami, 3,000 of them, massacred them and advanced on Athens. The consternation in Athens was unparalleled, as it was feared that everyone would be butchered. When Lysander arrived in Piraeus with 150 triremes, negotiations began. The Athenians were forced to agree to destroy the Long Walls between Piraeus and Athens, give up all claims to the cities of their empire, surrender all but twelve triremes and become Sparta's ally. Some of Sparta's existing allies, Corinth included, pressed for Athens to be destroyed, which would have meant killing the men and selling the women and children into slavery, but Sparta

Figure 10.8 The states of the Peloponnese in the fifth and fourth centuries BC

refused to go this far, fearing that with Athens off the map Corinth might aspire to supremacy.[66]

This was the Sparta Plato knew Athens should fear. It was a secretive state; it allowed outsiders to understand that its institutions were totalitarian but hid their true nature from the world. It is difficult to know whether fifth-century BC Sparta really was unique: certainly its neighbours believed it to be. Thucydides was unable to give a detailed account of Spartan military organization because the facts were kept secret.[67] Ironically, Strabo declined to describe the Spartan constitution for the opposite reason, that it was, by that time, too well known.[68] In the third century BC there was a spate of *Spartan Constitutions* by various authors,[69] so it seems that Plato, two generations earlier, was at the beginning of the fashion for admiring Sparta.

Some later Spartan inscriptions give details that may represent survivals from the earlier institutions. The information we have for the third century BC is quite full. Spartan boys were taken from their parents at 7, organized into 'herds' under the leadership of older boys. For the 10–13-year-olds there were contests in music and gymnastics, after which the victors dedicated sickles to Artemis. The 14–20-year-olds were *epheboi*, and some were proud to boast in later life that they had been leaders of herds. The *epheboi* were grouped into four local associations, staging violent mock battles as part of their training. When they reached 19, they were known as *melleirenes*: when they were 21 they were *eirenes*. There was a scourging ordeal, which may have been the final rite of passage for the oldest boys. The ephebic organization as a whole was ancient, and similar to that practised in Crete in the fourth century BC.[70] It was probably imported from Crete at some stage; the Spartans referred to their traditional music as 'Cretan'.

Those fourth-century BC Cretan customs in turn were in part inherited from Minoan customs of centuries before. It may be that the scene shown on a fourteenth-century BC vase from Ayia Triadha shows a herd leader inspecting a group of younger boys displaying their herd status by wearing animal skins. The Theran wall-paintings show even more clearly that age groups in boys and girls were sharply differentiated in the Minoan world. What we are seeing here is another inadvertent loop in Plato's Atlantis account. The starting-point, the ancient reality underpinning the main story, is the destruction of a bronze age civilization, which is identifiable as the Late Minoan culture of Crete and the closely related Late Cycladic culture of the islands of the south Aegean. The contemporary reality which Plato wanted the story to illuminate included a society that had kept alive some inherited relics of those older cultures. Plato cannot have known that – the Cretan nature of Sparta is a coincidence – but it adds a layer of irony to our enjoyment of the myth.

State affairs in Sparta were directed by the Gerusia, a body of elders elected for life from among the aristocracy. The Gerusia too had its exact counterpart in earlier Crete. The elders were assisted by a college of five *ephors* (magistrates) who supervised citizens' daily lives. They read the constitution aloud to assemblies of *epheboi*. Their control was absolute, even to the enforcement of traditional dress.

How ancient the Spartan way of life was is not known. The region was overrun by Dorians in about 1150 BC, and it may be that Sparta only diverged significantly from other Peloponnesian states from about 600 BC, only then turning into a barracks. But even the beliefs concerning kingship were rooted in Crete. Every nine years Sparta held a ceremony of watching the night sky to see if a new king was needed; this is close to the tradition of Cretan kings ascending mountains to confer with Zeus every nine years.[71]

Plato admired the law code used by the Spartans, not least for its great antiquity. The original Lycurgan code is thought to date from as early as 800 BC: no other legal system had endured for so long or was so well designed to allow development within a stable framework.[72] The Lycurgan code was celebrated every 81 years; it was celebrated in 401 BC, when Plato was 21, and at an unsettled time he may have been ready to be impressed by the antiquity and strength of Sparta's institutions. He credits Atlantis with these qualities. Admiration for Sparta, often mixed with criticism, is displayed in many of Plato's works. Aristocrats in Athens were beginning to idealize Sparta, partly as an ideological weapon against opponents; Plato praised Spartan moderation, prudence, endurance, courage, discipline, military skill, uniform care of children, education, stability.[73] But he also criticized Sparta for its overreaching ambition, narrow education programme, lack of emphasis on moral and intellectual values and indifference to science.[74]

Many of these themes appear in early dialogues, then reappear in more systematic and mature form in the *Republic* and the *Laws*. Plato thought the Spartan polity of his youth was the best of existing governments, and he explicitly drew elements from it to construct his ideal state.[75] Plato approved of timocracy, the characteristic elements of which were courage and the desire for honour. The fictionalized version of Sparta in the *Republic* contains some genuinely Spartan traits: warriors prohibited from engaging in crafts, state education, endless military exercises. The state has undeniably unsatisfactory elements, in that citizens have no private property, the state is perpetually on a war footing, and a large proportion of the population is reduced to slavery. This stage, the timocracy that develops out of the aristocracy, is founded on the Sparta that overwhelmed Athens when Plato was young.[76] A further stage in the evolution of the state in the *Republic* is the development of the oligarchy, in which a ruling clique consisting of a few wealthy citizens excludes all others from power. This is what happened to Sparta between 400 and 375 BC. The problem is the competitive acquisition of private property and hoarding. When a few become very wealthy, there is competition among them to become even wealthier and the state splits into two – rich and poor.[77]

During his lifetime, Plato observed Sparta's moral, economic and military decline, and here is a second fourth-century BC theme that he wove into the Atlantis story: the fall from grace of an ancient and distinguished race, and the development of a vain, overreaching and destructive ambition. The Atlantis story made a good vehicle for his views on Sparta. It has been convincingly argued that it is the Proto-Athens in the myth that is Sparta, that Plato intended Atlantis to be the contemporary Athens, and wanted to draw attention to the change in Athens' standing as a state.[78] If that is so, Plato was using double irony in his allegory. The *Timaeus* was written as a sequel to the *Republic*; Socrates requests a story to illustrate the ideal state in action, and gets the Atlantis story, with Proto-Athens, Plato's idealized view of rural Sparta, pitting its simple virtues against the sophistication and aggression of Atlantis, contemporary Athens.

Plato offers a clue that he wanted people to see that Atlantis might be Athens in his 'ten kings of Atlantis'. In Mycenean Attica there were around twelve city-states, but in more recent times, as late as the sixth century BC, there had been four Ionian tribes. They were replaced by Cleisthenes with *ten* new tribes named after Attic heroes. Each tribe consisted of separate coastal, inland and city demes, each sending representatives to Cleisthenes' Council of Five Hundred in Athens, where they drew lots to find the President for each day. The gatherings of the *ten* Atlantean kings may thus refer to an Athenian polity.

THE SOURCE OF THE ATLANTIS STORY

Plato's detractors have accused him of inventing the Atlantis myth in its entirety, but a book called *Atlantis* was written a century before. Unfortunately, only a fragment of Hellanicus' *Atlantis* survives, including the line, 'Poseidon mated with Celaeno, and their son Lycus was settled by his father in the Isles of the Blest and made immortal'.[79] This bears similarities with Plato's account, where Poseidon mates with Cleito and their son Atlas becomes ruler of a marvellous island. Plato may have borrowed from the earlier book, taking its title as the name for his lost land, while Hellanicus in his turn may have taken the story from a still earlier Atlantis epic;[80] alternatively, both may have drawn on Solon's story, which may have had a wider currency in the sixth century than we now realize. The Isles of the Blest were often thought of as being far to the west; Strabo (1. 1. 5) specifically located them to the west of Morocco, possibly thinking of the Canaries. Slightly in conflict with this, from the Greek viewpoint, is the fact that Crete, to the south-east, was also sometimes called 'the Blessed Isle',[81] but it does nevertheless confirm the identification of Crete as a part of Atlantis, while Diodorus follows another tradition using 'Isles of the Blest' for the Aegean islands along the Anatolian coast from Lesbos to Rhodes.[82] In fact both usages are consistent with an early Greek view of the islands of the far *east* and *south* of the Aegean as being at the world's end.

The probability that Plato was able to draw upon an existing written tradition is increased by descriptions like those in Hesiod's *Theogony* (c. 750 BC), where there is a battle between Zeus and Typhon that sounds startlingly like the Thera eruption:

> The heat and blaze from both of them was on the dark-faced sea,
> From the thunder and lightning of Zeus and the flame of the monster,
> From his blazing bolts and the scorch and breath of his storm winds,
> And all the ground and the sky and the sea boiled, and towering
> Waves were tossing and beating up and down the promontories
> In the wind of these immortals, and a great shaking of the earth came
> on.[83]

Plato says he got his story from Solon. 'Extraordinary though it is', he makes Critias say,

> it is absolutely true, having been attested by Solon . . . a relative and dear friend of my great-grandfather Dropides, as he himself says in his poems; and he told the story to Critias, my grandfather, who remembered and repeated it to us.
>
> (*Tim.* 20)

Before approaching the matter of Solon's acquisition of the story, we must check whether Plato can be telling us the literal truth so far, especially since some scholars have written off the elaborate preamble as part of Plato's romancing.

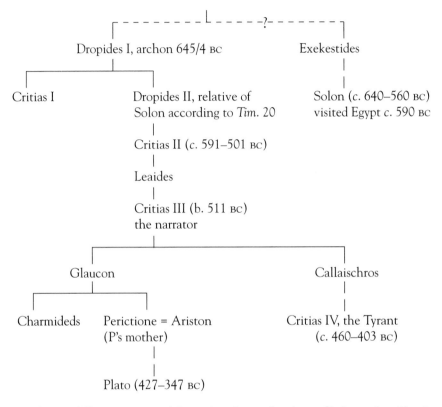

The carefully reconstructed Dropides–Critias family tree[84] shows that Plato's narrator, Critias III, was Plato's great-grandfather. This means that the story could have arrived in Plato's hands in much the same way that he describes; it could have been told to him in childhood by his father or grandfather, or he could have inherited the writings themselves. If Critias II was born in 591 and lived to be 90, he could have told a 10-year-old Critias III the story in 501 (*Tim.* 21A). These dates fit the documented facts and they corroborate Plato's account. Solon's Poem 39 is addressed to Critias, son of Dropides, so it is possible that other poems, now lost, were addressed to Dropides himself, as Plato says. There is no reason to doubt what has been said so far.

Plato tells us that as boys Critias III and his friends recited Solon's poetry to Critias II. The old man said, 'If only Solon had made poetry the business of his life, and completed the tale which he brought with him from Egypt, he would have been as famous as Homer' (*Tim.* 21C–D). Solon had visited the city of Sais in the Nile delta, and asked the priests there about antiquity (*Tim.* 21E–22A).

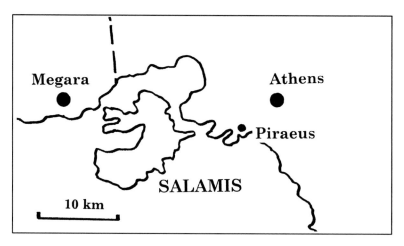

Figure 10.9 Salamis

Solon was a soldier, statesman and reformer who turned his skill in writing poetry to practical use.[85] His political poems brought him into prominence during the struggle with the city of Megara over the island of Salamis, which became a matter of Athenian national prestige. Solon's interest in Salamis may have been partly personal in origin; according to tradition he was born there. He wrote an elegiac poem called *Salamis*, which made a great impact in Athens. The closing lines survive:

> Now let us go to Salamis to fight for the longed-for island,
> And drive from ourselves the stain of foul disgrace.

The events according to Plutarch are as follows. The Athenians chose him by acclamation as commander-in-chief to take Salamis. Solon's tactic was to decoy the Megarians into attacking what looked like aristocratic Athenian women engaged in a festival to Demeter, but were really fully armed Athenian boys in disguise. The attackers were all killed, and the Athenians sailed swiftly to Salamis and captured it. Some scholars are sceptical,[86] but there is no reason to doubt Plutarch's account. Solon's behaviour on taking Salamis was extraordinary. He used archaeology to prove Athens' right to the island; he had a grave excavated and showed that the corpse had been buried Athenian-style, single burial facing west, not Megarian-style, multiple burial facing east. The use of Athenian burial customs showed an enduring link with Athens, not Megara. This archaeological perspective is entirely consistent with Solon's behaviour in Egypt, where Plato tells us his instinct was to probe into prehistory.

It is an indication of the strength of academic prejudice against Atlantis that Professor Jowett, the leading translator of Plato in the late nineteenth century, felt it necessary to insist that Solon's visit to Egypt to collect the story of Atlantis was legendary.[87] Even that was rejected, yet there is evidence that

166

Solon did visit Egypt. Luce believes Solon travelled there in about 590 BC, after completing his controversial programme of economic and political reform in Athens. Solon may wisely have withdrawn while his measures were implemented. Plato does not say when Solon went to Egypt; he does not actually say Amasis (569–525 BC) was pharaoh at the time, but implies it by mentioning him by name. Herodotus, writing little more than a century after Solon's visit, is definite that it took place in the reign of Amasis.[88] If so, Solon would then have been at least 71. Herodotus adds that Solon was away from home for ten years. Diogenes Laertius takes a similar view.[89]

One line of Solon's poetry referring to Egypt survives because Plutarch quoted it:[90] 'At the outpouring of the Nile, close to the Canopic shore . . . ' This may belong to a description of Sais. Plato tells us Solon was well received in Egypt, which is likely under the pharaoh Amasis, a philhellene. Amasis gave major concessions to the Greek 'treaty port' of Naucratis, and there is archaeological evidence that at the time of Solon's visit there were many Greeks living in Egypt;[91] Naucratis was the natural disembarkation point for them, and for Solon too. A natural next step would have been for Solon to travel to Sais, the delta's administrative capital, 16 kilometres away.

Egyptians at this time took a serious interest in their past, so Solon's visit would have come as no surprise to the priests; they were the curators of the 'house of books', a normal adjunct of Egyptian temples. If a reach backwards of 900 years into the past seems unlikely, we can point to Thucydides who, in the fifth century BC, discussed archaeological evidence (Carian graves on Delos) for events several centuries earlier.[92] We also have good evidence that the Egyptians were in contact with the Minoans in 1530–1520 BC, when Ahmose commissioned Minoan artists to decorate his palace at Avaris with bull-leaping scenes.[93]

Proclus, a Neoplatonist writing in the fifth century AD, noted that Crantor, a pupil of Plato's, supported the literal truth of the Atlantis story and went to Egypt to verify it. If true, this would demonstrate that Athenians in 300 BC wanted proof that Plato had told the literal truth, and considered it worth proving. Peter James has recently thrown doubt on the Crantor story, on the strength of an alleged ambiguity in Proclus:

> With respect to the whole of the narration about the Atlanteans, some say it is straightforward history; this was the opinion of *Crantor*, the first interpreter of Plato, *who* says that Plato was derided by those of his time for not being the inventor of the Republic, but transcribing what the Egyptians had written on the subject; and that *he* so far regards what is said by these deriders as to refer to the Egyptians this history about the Athenians and Atlanteans, and to believe that the Athenians lived conformably to this polity. Crantor adds that this is testified to by the prophets of the Egyptians, who assert that the particulars are written on pillars which are still preserved.

James makes much of the fact that in the original the last sentence opens with 'he', not 'Crantor', proposing that 'he' stands for 'Plato'.[94] It is nevertheless evident from the admittedly long and opaque previous sentence that it is 'Crantor' who is referred to in the italicized 'who' and 'he'. 'He' in the second sentence must mean 'Crantor' too.

We could play devil's advocate and argue that since Plato also visited Egypt he would have been able to supply this local colour from his own experience. There is nevertheless no internal inconsistency in the account as it stands; Solon could have acquired the story in the way Plato describes. There is no reason to disbelieve Plato. The priests of Sais could have held documents about the destruction of Thera in 1520 BC, the subsequent decline of the Minoan civilization and the earthquake in Athens in 1225 BC. There are, after all, documents surviving today in Egypt which refer to the Keftiu (Cretans) and 'the isles in the midst of the Great Green' (the Cyclades): the Egyptians knew about Atlantis. The phrase 'isles of the Great Green' only occurs between 1470 and 1150 BC, in the period when the Myceneans took over the Minoan trading empire, and it may have been used to refer implicitly to the Mycenean civilization.[95] The priests may have talked Solon through documents such as the carved pillars Proclus mentions. If Solon asked about Keftiu, he would have been told that it was far to the west: to the Egyptians Crete was a legendary distance away. The Ipuwer papyrus uses the expression 'as far away as Keftiu'.[96] They probably knew of Crete's influence over the isles of the Great Green, and of Crete's disappearance from long-distance trade around 1500 or 1400 BC – 900 years before. Whether they knew anything of the Thera catastrophe is conjectural: they may have recorded second- or third-hand reports. Even so, it is clear that an outline of the Atlantis story was drawn in.

Whether Solon understood that the Egyptians had described Crete and the Cyclades is not clear. He may have taken the very long distances to mean that Atlantis was beyond the western end of the Mediterranean. A location there for a mysterious lost land would have been possible, in that the Straits of Gibraltar were controlled by the Carthaginians, who intercepted and turned back all foreign vessels trying to reach the Atlantic.[97] Pindar wrote of the forbidden ocean, 'What lies beyond the Straits is forbidden ground to wise men and unwise alike'.[98] Solon may, on the other hand, by translating the place names and names of deities, have realized that he was hearing about the ancient history of a region much closer to home – the Aegean. If so, it may have been Solon who added the phrases that have caused so much trouble, those dealing with the geographical location of Atlantis in relation to the pillars of Heracles. A connection between Atlas, who held up the sky just as the pillars did, and the name Atlantis has been suggested by Luce,[99] but this is unnecessary. There was a regional name in Linear B that referred to at least the centre and east of Crete – Atlunus (ta-ru-nu) – which is so close to the name 'Atlantis' that it suggests that the Egyptians knew this was the name of the region disabled by ashfall.[100]

Solon could not read the Egyptian script; he 'enquired into the meaning of names, found that the early Egyptians in writing them down had translated them into their own language, recovered the meaning of the names and when copying them out again translated them into our language' (*Crit.* 113A). This has been mocked by some scholars,[101] but it is exactly what Egyptian scribes did when converting Minoan names into hieroglyphs. A writing exercise from 1500 BC is entitled 'How to make the names of the Keftiu'; Solon was carrying out the same exercise as Egyptian schoolboys 900 years earlier. It has been suggested that this was when the 'order of magnitude' error occurred. Galanopoulos and Luce proposed that the numbers were exaggerated by a factor of ten either when they were translated into Greek from hieroglyphs, or centuries earlier when they were translated from Linear B into hieroglyphs by Egyptian scribes.[102] At first this sounds reasonable enough, but it is hard to see how hieroglyphic numbers could have been misread. The symbol for '100' is a coiled rope, whereas that for '1,000' is a lotus flower, so dissimilar they might have been chosen to prevent this kind of mistake. The priests cannot have misread a hieroglyphic number and, if the mistake was Solon's, he will have made so many other mistakes that the resulting translation will have been meaningless. Mavor saw the flaw in Galanopoulos's reasoning, proposing that the mistake was made earlier, when Egyptian scribes were translating an Aegean account.[103] This looks more promising, in that the Linear A and B symbols for '100' and '1,000' are very similar: a circle and a circle with a short tick at each of the four compass points.[104] James rightly rejects this explanation of the error in the dates on the grounds that survivors of the bronze age disaster could not have known whether they were living 9,000 or 900 years before Solon: the concept is nonsensical.[105] Aegean scribes could have written accounts that included distances that were meaningful at the time of writing, and these could have been mistranslated in Egypt, explaining the exaggeration of the linear measurements. This nevertheless leaves us without a credible explanation for the exaggeration of the dates, unless the story was kept in Linear B until shortly before Solon's arrival.

An alternative not considered before is that although the original account may have been carved in hieroglyphs on a pillar, or a pair of pillars as Proclus tells us was described by the third-century BC Egyptian historian Manetho, the priests may have copied it onto papyrus for scholars to read in the house of books. During the period between the Thera eruption and Solon's visit, hieroglyphs continued to be used for carved inscriptions, but a more relaxed script, hieratic, had become the norm for written documents; this changed rapidly, becoming less pictorial, more cursive, more difficult to read accurately. In the seventh century a third script, demotic, evolved. We therefore have several new possibilities. The priests may have copied the text they showed Solon more than once, and made mistakes in copying older forms of hieratic into newer, or in copying hieratic into demotic. The informality and speed with which the later scripts were written makes mistakes in writing or reading far likelier.[106]

The Egyptians liked, out of pride, to exaggerate the antiquity of their culture. Herodotus was told by Egyptian priests that king Menes, the first Egyptian king, ruled 11,340 years before the Assyrian invasion (701 BC). It would have been in character for the Saite priests to try to impress Solon by claiming that their city had been founded 8,000 years before. Given that the priests, or Solon or Plato, wanted to establish the great antiquity of Atlantis, its date would have to be still earlier; so the exaggeration introduced by the priests turned into an auction. The problem with this line of reasoning is that while it may explain why both dates offered are too ancient it does not explain how the date for the destruction of Atlantis came to be exactly ten times too old, just as many of the distances are exactly ten times too great. Can that be a mere coincidence? In the end, I suspect that the crucial facts needed to resolve the problem have been lost. We might speculate, for example, that a refugee community of Cretans or Therans settled in the delta after 1500 BC, keeping its own records in its own language. Possibly some subsequent copy of the account, still in Linear B, had 'before present' dates added, and it was this that was later mistranslated and developed by the priests not long before Solon's visit. An alternative possibility is that the Egyptians were counting in lunar months, not solar years. Diodorus mentions that 'in early times it was customary to reckon the year by the lunar cycle'.[107] A contemporary of Plato's, Eudoxus of Cnidos, gave the same explanation: 'The Egyptians reckon a month as a year.' Given 12.3 lunar cycles per year, the interval '9,000 years' might have been intended to mean 730 years. This would bring the fall of Atlantis to 1330 BC, i.e., to the steep decline of the Minoan civilization following the fall of the Knossos Labyrinth.

James has been too quick to ridicule the date the Egyptians apparently claim for themselves.[108] He is right to point out that reducing the 'text' date for the loss of Atlantis to 1500 BC necessitates reducing the date for the Egyptian foundation to 1400 BC. He dismisses this as absurd, because the date is far too late for the building of the pyramids, but Plato does not claim that. What he says is: 'She founded your city [Athens] a thousand years before ours, of which the constitution is recorded . . . to be 8,000 years old' (*Tim.* 23E). In other words, it is not Egyptian civilization but the *city of Sais* that dates from 1400 BC. When Sais was founded is not known. Although it had high status as the delta capital in 590 BC, it emerged from obscurity only 200 years earlier. The priests might credibly have estimated an 'antiquity' for Sais stretching 600 years earlier still.

Solon would have been interested in the Atlantis story for its own sake, but he would also have been interested in it as a vehicle 'for his poem', because it gave him a framework for his ideas about Athens and what was wrong with it. Plutarch says Solon tried to compose a poem using the Atlantis material because he was intrigued by the special connection it had with the early history of Athens.[109] An early poem of Solon's, *Eunomia*, gives guidelines for the ordering of society, opening with a statement of faith in the power of the gods, especially Athena, the city's protectress. But divine protection would be of no avail if the citizens 'in their folly are willing to destroy a great city'. Solon saw Athens as progressively corroded by greed, strife and the unreasonable demands of its citizens; unless a cure was imposed – a fair system of laws properly obeyed – Zeus would bring down destruction.

> Riches the immortal gods bestow upon men.
> Ruin, however, also appears for them, when Zeus
> Sends her to bring redress.

Like Plato, Solon had a sense of cosmic justice attending all our endeavours. To link human and divinely controlled physical worlds was fashionable,[110] and maybe he, not Plato, added the moral dimension to the story of Atlantis. It would have seemed as natural to Solon as to Plato for Atlantis to sink because it was humanly unsound. Solon was possibly intending to write a poem about Athens and its relationship with Salamis, in which case the Atlantis story would have made a marvellous political parable. Salamis was an island west of Athens; like Atlantis it came into conflict with Athens; like Atlantis it was defeated by Athens; like the Atlanteans the Megarians were annihilated by a morally superior people. Since Solon was responsible for engineering the conquest of Salamis, giving the tale of conquest this cosmological status would have appealed to his ego.

How much progress Solon made with his poem is not known. Possibly he introduced some of the stylistic devices. The use of dramatic monologue, as in the long section of the *Critias* 113A–121C, was earlier used by Solon. He did not invent it, but borrowed it from Archilochus. Solon also used the Platonic device of appearing as someone else and addressing the reader through the voice of a persona. His poem *Salamis* opens with the lines:

> I am a herald from longed-for Salamis and I bring you
> Instead of a speech a fine collection of verses.

Obviously Plato could have devised these techniques for himself or borrowed them from another poet, but the possibility is there that Solon did in fact draft an unfinished Atlantis poem, including several of the features familiar to us from the *Timaeus* and *Critias*.

Solon had a reputation for honesty and straightforwardness. From the evidence available, he was not given to gratuitous mystification. According to Plutarch, Solon reproved Thespis for including 'lies' in his plays: 'If [even in plays] we allow ourselves to honour make-believe, the next thing will be to find it creeping into our serious business.' If Solon returned to Greece with a story that was false, the only possibility left is that the Egyptians were mistaken. It will nevertheless be clear from what has been said that the story has fairly sound credentials back to Egypt in around 590 BC.

11

DECONSTRUCTION OF ATLANTIS

THE OLD ATLANTIS

When dismantled, Plato's story is seen to have a foundation of proto-history. Events that happened on the threshold of history were remembered with imperfect accuracy and later recorded with less – yet they are still recognizable. The earliest of these proto-historic elements are those describing the bronze age Aegean civilization that reached its zenith in the sixteenth century BC.

This was a non-Helladic, pre-Athenian civilization in contact and often in conflict with the peoples of mainland Greece, and it was in existence in around 1500 BC.[1] Crete, the cradle of the Minoan civilization, is large, by far the largest island in the region, far to the west of Egypt, with its western tip in front of the Gulf of Laconia, the ancient mouth of the pillars of Heracles.[2] To bronze age sailors, voyaging eastwards along the interminable north coast of Crete would have seemed more like following the north coast of Africa than sailing round any island in the Aegean: Crete must have been perceived as near-continental in scale. The power that held sway in Crete, over many of the smaller islands of the Aegean, and over some colonies on the Anatolian coast, was the economic and political power of the Minoan civilization, which organized and controlled an extensive trading operation bringing raw materials and goods in from far and wide,[3] and even included ostrich eggs and elephant tusks from Africa.[4] The maritime nature of this civilization is beautifully illustrated by the frescoes at Akrotiri.

The development of the Mycenean settlements on the Greek mainland was stifled by this oppressive trading system, and the mainlanders would have felt threatened, suffocated, enslaved and resentful. The legend of Minos exacting tribute-children from Athens may crystallize a memory of the way the Cretans intimidated mainland coastal communities.[5] Proto-Athens, Mycenean Athens, forms part of the early material Plato used. This Athens had an orderly, stratified society, and led an 'Attic league' of a dozen cities.[6] Its warrior elite based on the Acropolis lived in simple, modest accommodation in part on the north side of a massive citadel wall. The Mycenean Athenians drove a well deep into the rock just inside the perimeter wall to ensure their water supply, though it collapsed in an earthquake later in antiquity, around 1225 BC.[7]

The bronze age civilization the Mycenean cities of the mainland were pitted against was more ancient still. It was an urban society, with towns at Knossos, Phaistos and a dozen other sites on Crete by 2000 BC, possibly each boasting its own king. By the fifteenth century Knossos had become so much more powerful than all the others that it is tempting to see its leader as an over-king in a confederation of kingdoms; there is, on the other hand, no direct evidence yet that there was a king of Knossos.[8] There were also towns on the larger islands of the Cyclades, usually one on each island, such as Phylakopi on Melos, Ayia Irini on Kea and Akrotiri on Thera. These towns were repaired and rebuilt several times over, often on the sites of early villages. Kea was occupied as early as 3900 BC, Akrotiri by 4500 BC, and the Knossos Labyrinth was built on the site of the earliest known settlement in Crete, occupied in 6100 BC.[9] The Cycladic–Minoan civilization evolved over a long period, and its fully fledged cities were big by the standards of their day and very densely developed.[10] Akrotiri may have been 1 kilometre across, as big as Cretan Palaikastro, and Knossos between 1 and 2 kilometres across. Some Minoan towns were defended by partial circuit walls: Phylakopi had fortifications and, to judge from the fresco evidence, Akrotiri had a circuit wall and at least one tower-like gate; a seal impression shows a similar tower-gate at Khania in Crete.[11]

Akrotiri, probably then known as Therassos, functioned as a major entrepreneurial centre for the Aegean trading operation. It was located centrally in the southern Aegean, on a small round island with a round bay inside, where inhospitable cliffs rose sheer out of the sea.[12] Actively volcanic, it was earthquake-prone and may have had hot springs.[13] The lava landscape supplied white, red and black rock for building, and the selection of different coloured stones for dado panels was an architectural feature of the town.[14] Perhaps the most striking feature was the wall-paintings, which emphasize the importance of religion. The Theran and Knossian frescoes speak of communities closely in touch with their deities. Therasia, the Theran goddess, seems to have adopted the Therans as her children.[15]

In the Knossos Labyrinth, plumbed,[16] barbaric,[17] bristling with sacral horns,[18] the fresco evidence is less complete. There were many sanctuaries in the Labyrinth;[19] it is not certain who the dedicatees were, though the huge investment in terms of human commitment and wealth is evident.[20] The goddess who regularly manifests in fresco, seal and figurine is probably the one referred to in the archive tablets recording offerings as The Lady of the Labyrinth.[21] The god was not represented there in human form but manifested as a bull, and the bull-leaping ritual, in which bulls were released into the Bull Court in the Labyrinth and vaulted over by weaponless acrobats, represented a homage to Poseidon. Bulls were also sacrificed to Poseidon, and their blood may have been splashed over the sacral horns on the elaborate Triple Shrine in the Bull Court.[22] The dedication of the Knossos Labyrinth was thus jointly to Poseidon and 'The Lady'.[23] The huge investment in this and the other Cretan temples suggests a

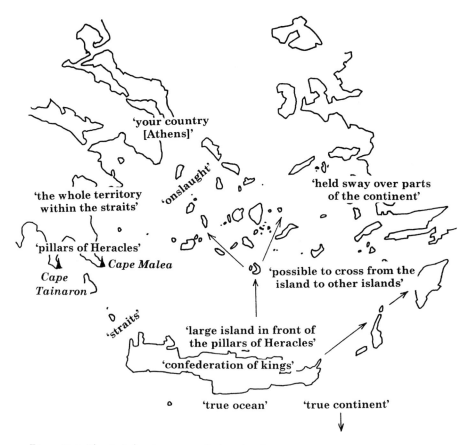

'your country
[Athens]'

'onslaught'

'the whole territory
within the straits'

'held sway over parts
of the continent'

'pillars of Heracles'

Cape Malea

Cape
Tainaron

'possible to cross from the
island to other islands'

'straits'

'large island in front of
the pillars of Heracles'

'confederation of kings'

'true ocean'   'true continent'

Figure 11.1 Plato's Atlantis story applied to the Aegean

theocracy, a society in which gods and goddesses ruled; the high status of the Knossian priestesses bears this out.[24]

In the heart of the Knossos Labyrinth, indeed the temple may have been designed round it, was a stone pillar inscribed with double-axes,[25] and there were two libation pits at its foot.[26] In the temple repositories nearby were found intricately made models of the ceremonial dresses offered either to the priestesses or to statues[27] of the goddess to wear.[28] In the East Wing were wall-paintings of dancing priestesses and dolphins,[29] and frescoes in the Procession Corridor showed lines of priestesses and worshippers of noble bearing.[30] Many of the walls, pillars and floors were painted red.[31]

Well to the south of Knossos, beyond a high ridge giving shelter from cold north winds, and which possibly supplied cedar wood for temple-building,[32] is the huge rectangular Plain of Mesara, the fertile, well-watered food-basket of Crete. Its Mediterranean climate has wet winters and hot dry summers, and it offers views of the high mountains of Ida and Dikte to the north, and access to the sea to the south.[33]

There are over seventy parallels between Plato's account of Atlantis and the Minoan world. His account includes a further twelve references to the ending of that world, starting with the destruction of Thera in 1520 BC.[34] Much of Thera sank in a series of violent earthquakes[35] that was part of an eruption sequence as the low central volcano[36] became active. The details Plato gives are few, but enough to give a broad-brush picture of a geological catastrophe on the grandest scale, involving not only earthquakes but major earth movements taking land areas down to the bottom of the sea.[37] The archaeology and geology of Thera show that there were large earthquakes and a massive caldera eruption culminating in the centre of the island's rapid collapse into the empty magma chamber.[38] The eruption of huge volumes of ash coated what remained of the island, and the sea round Thera was clogged with mudbanks for decades afterwards.[39] Earthquakes vibrating the seabed generated tsunamis, which caused widespread flooding of coastal settlements on all Thera-facing shores in the Aegean.[40] Many Minoan warships and merchant vessels will have been lost, along with harbour installations.

There was tsunami flood damage in ports on the north coast of Crete such as Amnisos, as well as a coating of ash covering the eastern half of Crete. The Minoan trading operation probably ceased altogether for a short time, resumed, then contracted progressively during the fifteenth century as Mycenean traders exploited Crete's weakened state.[41] The Myceneans took the Minoans' empire piecemeal, beginning in around 1520 BC; Kea and Melos fell in about 1450 BC and the job was completed by about 1380 BC, when the Knossos Labyrinth fell. After 1380 BC there was Mycenean supremacy in the Aegean.

The bronze age component of the Atlantis story was somehow collated in Egypt, perhaps in part from the reports of merchants travelling between Egypt and the Aegean, perhaps in part from negative information. Minoan merchants and envoys had been seen regularly in Egypt; it may be that, after about 1520 BC or so, they did not visit any more. From this the Egyptians inferred that Crete had disappeared. Reports of the Thera disaster reached Egypt and the priests compressed and combined the separate though related events: the sudden disappearance of Thera and the more gradual disappearance of the Minoan trading empire. The priests told Solon their city had not been founded until 1400 BC, which suggests that the story may not have been recorded in Egypt until then. It was conserved in some way, perhaps in a wall-painting or carving, perhaps on a stone stele. That it cannot be seen today should not arouse suspicion: virtually nothing of ancient Sais has survived.

Nine hundred years later Solon arrived in Sais to translate and copy the bronze age component. He intended to use the material as a vehicle for a parable-poem, probably with a political message about the Athens of the sixth century, by showing how Athenians had behaved in the remoter past. More specifically, the poem was probably to have been about Athens and Salamis.

Whether Solon introduced any changes to the bronze age material at this stage, any importations that would make the story more recognizably refer to his conquest of Salamis, for instance, cannot be inferred. A difficulty here is that what Solon intended to do was very similar to what Plato eventually did. It is unclear whether Solon got as far as writing some lines of an Atlantis poem. Plato says that Critias' 'grandfather [Critias II] had the original writing, which is still in my possession', but it is not clear whether the writing is the notes Solon made in Sais, or a polished, edited account he wrote later, or a draft of the unfinished poem. Because Solon's and Plato's methods and intentions were similar, we cannot be sure whether the monologue sections, dialogue sections and persona-adoption were introduced by Solon or Plato; since the Solon poem, if written, was later lost, we cannot examine it.

The bronze age component, perhaps now with importations relating to Salamis or Solon's view of Athens and perhaps in verse, passed down through the family of Dropides II. Critias II told his grandson Critias III the story in around 501 BC and apparently left him the written account as well. It is not likely that Critias III would have lived long enough to pass the story direct to Plato. If Critias III died aged 90, Plato would then have been 6. Critias is likely to have left the story to his son Glaucon, who may have given it either to his daughter Perictione, Plato's mother, or to his son Charmides, Plato's uncle. Plato could therefore have inherited the story, either as a written document or as a piece of story-telling, from any of these relatives; given that he was the scholar of the family it is likely that he would have received the document if it survived. There is no suggestion that he ever produced it as evidence, which may be taken to indicate his 'guilt', but nor is there any suggestion that in his few remaining years he was challenged to produce it, so we have to presume his 'innocence'.

Plato complicated matters significantly by adding ideas concerning the geomorphological development of Attica. His description and explanation of the processes of denudation and soil erosion in the Athens area (*Crit.* 112A) are amazingly perceptive and accurate. Unfortunately, they are also anachronistic, matching his literal time-scale (reaching back to 10,000 BC) though not that of the bronze age city of Athens. So, even here, Plato was putting together two identifiable but separate strands of Athenian prehistory.

Plato then set to work, putting the Solonized bronze age story to use. Some important changes in geographical perception had taken place between 1500 and 350 BC and we need to be aware of them. To the Egyptians of 1500 BC, any land as far away as Crete was indeterminate and incalculably distant. Their reference to the Aegean islands under the Myceneans as the 'Isles of the Great Green' shows typical imprecision. By Solon's time, the world had expanded considerably. The pharaoh Necho II (610–595 BC) caused Phoenician vessels to venture out into the Atlantic and along the coast of Morocco, so the Atlantic was a contemporary concept of the Far West.[42] The priest reading the hieroglyphs for Solon may have added this expansion of the text for him.

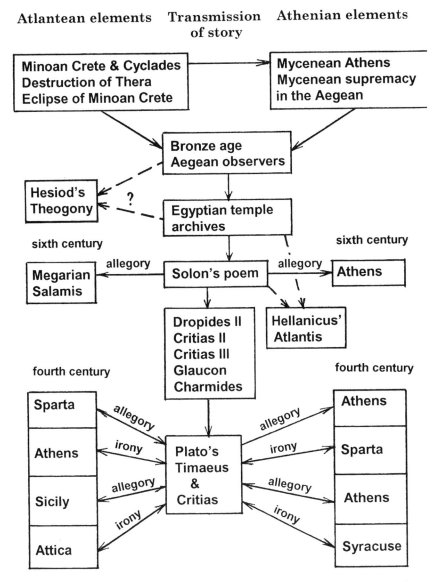

Figure 11.2 Evolution of the Atlantis story in antiquity. Double-ended arrow = bronze-age story applied allegorically to a contemporary issue, dtails of which were grafted into the story.

There are clues in the *Timaeus* (24D) that this occurred: '[the Atlantean army] came forth out of the Atlantic Ocean, for in those days the Atlantic was navigable'. This implies that the Atlantic was *not* considered navigable at the time of writing, that Necho's sailors had gone out beyond Gibraltar and been appalled at the sea conditions, terrified perhaps by the size of the waves; it would have been in their professional interest to return saying that the Atlantic was not navigable. The huge mysterious ocean nevertheless existed as a new horizon for the imagination, a new place to put monsters and lost lands. Plato realized he had to alter the passage immediately following to fit the Atlantic location. The reference to Atlantis lying midway between Africa and Anatolia made no sense if Atlantis was out in the Atlantic, so it was changed – by Plato – into a statement about the size of Atlantis: 'larger than Libya and Asia put together'. Plato must have added part of the Egyptian priest's lecture to Solon as well (*Tim.* 22C–23C). These lines develop the idea of cyclically recurring destructions leaving few survivors, an idea that belongs to Plato's Athens rather than to Sonchis's Sais, and an idea to which Plato frequently returns.

Clearly entertainment was part of Plato's purpose: he tells the story well, with more circumstantial detail than is necessary to make his moral and philosophical points. He nevertheless frankly wanted it as a vehicle for a parable:

> I am ready to tell the story as I heard it. We will transfer the imaginary citizens and city you described yesterday [in the *Republic*] to the real world, and say that your city is the city of my story and your citizens the historical ancestors of ours whom the priest described . . . Tell us, Socrates, do you think this story will suit our purpose?
>
> (*Tim.* 26D)

And Plato had more than a notional ideal in mind: he wanted an allegory for an Athens in need of reform. During Plato's lifetime, three nightmares hung over Athens, tarnished its glory. In 399 BC, Athens had executed the teacher he so greatly respected, an event that may have launched him towards designing a better state. In 404 BC Athens had been defeated, violated and humiliated by Sparta. After that, along with many other Athenians, he had developed an ambivalent admiration for Sparta; but now, towards the end of his life, he saw Sparta as an unworthy ideal and wanted to hold up a mirror to both Sparta and Athens. In the defeat of the Sicilian Expedition in 413 BC, he saw the need for another warning. Athens was not invincible, her colonial strategy was ill-founded, and the way political decisions were made was suspect. He had also been closely involved in trying, and failing, to rehabilitate two successive tyrants of Syracuse, and may have wished partly out of frustration to show how dangerous the Syracusan rulers were.

The Atlantis story as it stood did very well as a commentary on Sparta. The idea of a mighty host threatening and blockading Athens, backed by an alliance of Peloponnesian kingdoms, was already there, as was the threat of slavery. The only two additional passages that were needed were the slide from moral grace[43] and the massive gearing-up for war, a distinctively Spartan characteristic.[44] Plato's story does not, of course, end with the Athenians defeated and in shame, dismantling the Long Walls as a condition of surrender. It could not, and Plato did not make that decision simply because he knew the story described some other, older event. Plato was less concerned with historical truth than with poetic truth, with the effect his story would have, and an Athens defeating the overreaching Spartans/Atlanteans would be more inspirational, more likely to produce the right behaviour in his listeners. Another Spartan reading of the tale is, as suggested earlier, to turn it on its head and, for 'Atlantis' read fifth- and fourth-century Athens, for 'Athens' read fifth-century Sparta. In this way, the allegory becomes an indictment of the aggression, greed and over-ambition of Plato's own city.

Sicily was a large earthquake-prone island remote from Athens,[45] with a fertile plain, the Plain of Catania, supporting wealthy villages and surrounded by mountains.[46] In the west there were the famous hot springs of Selinus.[47] The main city, Syracuse, had seen a revolution in its defensive works, with the building of unparalleled lengths of circuit walls punctuated by numerous bastions and towers,[48] displaying the city-state's power and wealth.[49] The three major districts of the city, Ortygia, Achradina and Tycha, were surrounded by three separate circuit walls; Ortygia itself had three concentric walls, a double wall round the edge and an inner citadel.[50] The Syracusans had brilliant engineers, not only designing new kinds of tower and inventing the catapult, but building aqueducts to ensure the city's water supply.[51]

The innermost, most inaccessible part of Syracuse was the small walled island of Ortygia that contained the royal citadel and, among other temples, grandiose temples to Apollo and Athena.[52] The royal palace was built on the site of the earliest colony at Syracuse.[53] Ortygia itself was an artificial island, separated from the mainland by a bridged canal that connected the city's two harbours: there were docks near the southern end of the cut.[54] Dionysius dominated the kings of the other Sicilian city-states.[55] The power of the tyrant of Syracuse and his ruling elite was such that he came to control most of Sicily, the Lipari Islands and parts of the European mainland as far away as Ancona.[56] Athenians saw Dionysius' power as a threat to the Greek hegemony: Sicily might sever its already loose ties with Athens and become an independent power as dangerous as Carthage.[57]

There are forty-five parallels between the Platonic account and fourth-century Sicily, enough to show that Plato must have been conscious that what he was writing would be read as a commentary on contemporary Sicily. That conclusion is inescapable. Some might go further and argue that Plato used first-hand knowledge of Sicily to write an entirely new myth developed on Sicily alone, but the much larger number of parallels between the account and the Aegean bronze age makes that unlikely. Plato himself argues strenuously for the antiquity of the tradition, claiming that the events happened '9,000 years' before Solon and taking care to give the story's long pedigree in detail. He simply selected and emphasized features of 'Atlantis' that would ring a Sicilian bell in the memories of his listeners and readers. He needed just enough of Sicily in the parable to make people think that Atlantis was Sicily in disguise, and we can be sure that that is what they thought. Plato added two more clues, in calling one of the characters in the dialogues Hermocrates, the name of a well-known Syracusan general, and another Timaeus, an astronomer from southernmost Italy.

Nevertheless, if we regard 'Atlantis' as a satire on Sicily, there are peculiarities that need to be explained. The Syracusans were certainly geared up for war, but principally because they were menaced by Carthage, not because they wished to invade and enslave Athens.[58] It was the *Athenians* who launched two unprovoked expeditions against Syracuse,[59] and the *Athenians* who were defeated.[60] This is a conspicuous example of Plato's noble fiction. His motive in juggling with historical reality was that in the end the reader, whether Athenian or Syracusan, would see Athens as a rock of moral rectitude. He is also, I suspect, exhibiting the playful irony of the political satirist, fictionally turning people and situations into what they are not. The effect can be arresting and thought-provoking. The image of Syracuse making unprovoked attacks on innocent Athens was the blackest of black humour. Whether it occurred to Plato that in the royal court of Syracuse his parable would be inverted – for 'Athens' read 'Syracuse', for 'Atlantis' read 'Attica' – to take a different and more subversive meaning is uncertain.

Plato was haunted by his vision of an ideal state, one in which there was perfect civic harmony, no greed, no class war and no injustice; to achieve it, private aspirations would need to be subordinated to the common good: hence his fascination with Sparta. But none of the city-states he saw matched his ideal. The Athens that judicially murdered Socrates was imperfect, and he looked elsewhere. Only Syracuse seemed to rise to it. Plato hoped to turn two of its rulers into ideal philosopher-kings, was doubly disappointed when he failed. As Bertrand Russell wrote, the problem of finding suitably wise men to whom you can entrust government is insoluble.[61] 'Atlantis' was a desperate last throw at reforming Syracuse from afar. It was a Parthian shot, all that an old man in Athens could offer.

There are several reasons why there have been so many misunderstandings about the nature of Atlantis and its location in space and time:

1   Plato left the various elements in the story's evolution visible and undigested. Although he altered it, he did not do so thoroughly and the result is that Atlantis as described cannot have existed at all. That has led some commentators to claim mistakenly that the story is fiction from start to finish, and thus to overlook the proto-historical content.

2   The Egyptians who acquired the story in 1520 BC or shortly afterwards had a very different geographical sense from the Greeks of Plato's or Solon's time. To the sixteenth-century Egyptians, the Aegean was a long way to the

west. When the story was passed to Solon, the known world was expanding rapidly, and either Solon or the priest may have assumed that Atlantis was out in the newly visited Atlantic Ocean. This mistake may actually have led to the ocean being named after the lost land, rather than the other way round as most people have assumed.

3   The geographical mistake was compounded by a misreading of Linear A or B numerals, or a misreading of hieratic or demotic copies of the story made in Sais by Egyptian scribes, in the fifteenth century or later. This led to a tenfold exaggeration of many of the distance measurements, and a hundredfold exaggeration of area, so that the Plain of Mesara, instead of being small enough to fit into central Crete, was inflated to the size of the southern Aegean. The land areas involved became too big to fit into the Mediterranean: another reason for removing Atlantis to the outer ocean.

4   A similar mistranslation of numerals led to an exaggeration of the 900 years elapsing between Thera's destruction and Solon's Egyptian visit to 9,000 years. The idea of an advanced bronze age culture with cities, kings, palaces and temples existing in 9600 BC has always been unacceptable to pre-historians, and that has helped to push Atlantis to the outer fringes of academic study.

5   The hypothesis revived repeatedly in the twentieth century – that Minoan Crete was Atlantis – has proved inadequate to the case and has rightly been rejected. The parallel hypothesis, based on more recent archaeological evidence, that Cycladic Thera was Atlantis is also in itself inadequate. Because these hypotheses can be rejected separately, many have rejected the idea that Atlantis might have existed in the south Aegean, understandably overlooking the possibility that if the two hypotheses are *combined* they *do* meet the needs of Plato's description.

6   By Plato's time the pillars of Heracles had become fixed at the western end of the Mediterranean. It is clear when he mentions them that he expects them to be understood as a known reference point. The description of Atlantis as an island just beyond the pillars thus seems to confirm its position in the North Atlantic. But here too there was a shift in perception. The pillars were located at or near the borders of the known world. In Solon's time and earlier, the world as perceived by both Greeks and Egyptians was smaller, and a location for the pillars on the two southern-most headlands of Greece significantly changes the specifications for the location of Atlantis.

7   It is possible that contemporary allegorical readings of the tale were intended to be implicitly ironic, and that in relation to Sparta and Syracuse Plato intended Athens to be Atlantis. From the execution of Socrates, Plato learned the value of circumspection and may have chosen, for safety's sake, not to say directly what he meant.

The shifts in perception, meaning and understanding nevertheless add layers of mystery which to some are as irresistibly alluring as the dance of the seven veils.

THE NEW ATLANTIS

Like the sixteenth–eighteenth century search for Terra Australis, the rumoured southern continent, the search for Atlantis continues apace. Many locations have been proposed; the Gulf of Syrtis, the Tyrrhenian Sea, the Sea of Azov, the eastern Mediterranean off Israel, the western Mediterranean off Almeria, the North Sea near Heligoland, Antarctica, the Celtic sea off Cornwall and the eastern Irish Sea.[62] A surprisingly large number of the proposed locations are on dry land; Morocco, Cadiz, Palestine, Malta, Belgium, Catalonia, southern Sweden, the Caucasus, the Massif Central, the Ahaggar Plateau in the Sahara and of course Crete and Thera.[63] There is no shortage of candidates and ingenious explanations. It says much for the power of Plato's tale that it has fired so many imaginations in so many different directions. Many of these quests are rationally based searches for the Old Atlantis, Plato's lost kingdom. It is important to recognize that a significant proportion of what has been written in the twentieth century has not been about Plato's Atlantis at all, but a New Atlantis, one that has really existed as an idea only since 1882.

Plato's account took on a new lease of life after America was discovered. Several people, such as Gomara in 1553 and Guillaume de Postel in 1561, assumed that America was Atlantis. Postel anticipated Ignatius Donnelly in drawing attention to the native name for Mexico, Aztlan. Sir Francis Bacon more light-heartedly identified America as Atlantis in his philosophical romance, Nova Atlantis; it was not the first time a philosopher had looked westward across the sea to a New World where there was a chance that an ideal state might be established. The first map known to have shown Atlantis was drawn by Athanasius Kircher in 1644. It shows a pear-shaped landmass in the middle of the Atlantic directly opposite Gibraltar, with two smaller islands on the American side, a gesture towards the West Indies.

The New Atlantis as a literary phenomenon is nevertheless scarcely more than a century old, the virtually single-handed creation of Ignatius Donnelly. It is possible that the description of Captain Nemo's visit to the lost capital on the seabed in Jules Verne's Twenty Thousand Leagues Under the Sea, published in 1870, inspired Donnelly to explore the idea further. Donnelly's book The Antediluvian World (1882) set out the grandiose hypothesis that the continent of Atlantis really existed out in the Atlantic in prehistory and was the cradle of all civilization, the heartland of an empire extending from the Mississippi and Amazon in the west to the Eurasian steppes and India in the east. He added a strong mythic element. Atlantis was 'the Garden of Eden; the Garden of the Hesperides; the Elysian Fields; the Gardens of Alcinous; the Mesomphalos;

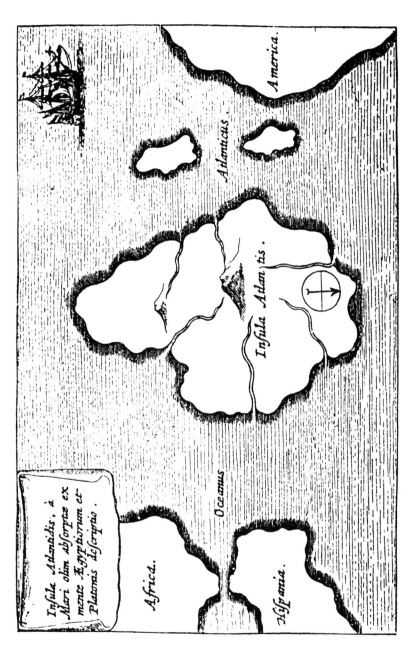

The map content (as labeled within the figure):

America.

Atlanticus.

Insula Atlantis.

Africa.

Oceanus.

Hispania.

Insula Atlantidis, à
Mari olim absorpta ex
mente Ægyptiorum et
Platonis descriptio.

Figure 11.3 The first known map of Atlantis, published by Athanasius Kircher in 1665

the Olympos; the Asgard of the traditions of the ancient nations'. Donnelly admitted Eden was a problem,[64] because it was supposed to be to the *east* of Palestine. The gods and goddesses of Greece, Scandinavia and India were really the kings, queens and heroes of Atlantis.

Donnelly's arguments depended on the diffusionist theory of culture. If pyramids were found in Egypt and Latin America and the decimal system of counting was found among Peruvians and Anglo-Saxons, people must have travelled from one area to another, taking the concepts and techniques needed for pyramid-building and decimal counting with them. Placing a landmass in the Atlantic Ocean would make this diffusion easier by shortening the sea journeys involved. Once the heartland sank under the waves, the colonies developed separately, but still displaying vestiges of the original culture.

The physical remains of Donnelly's Atlantis are the Azores, Madeira and the Canaries, once mountains on the old continent. Donnelly's book was published shortly after the first major oceanographic survey of the North Atlantic, which revealed the existence of the Mid-Atlantic Ridge, an underwater mountain range equal in scale to the Rockies and Andes. The ocean floor was spattered with seamounts, extinct volcanoes, down to depths of 1,000 metres or more. Donnelly seized on the new information as evidence that there had once been land in mid-Atlantic. But the ridge was narrow and left wide seas for his Atlanteans to cross, so he proposed connecting ridges, causeways by which people, animals and plants could migrate between New and Old Worlds.

Donnelly's case rests on four lines of evidence: the newly discovered mid-ocean ridge, parallel ecological developments on opposite sides of the Atlantic, parallel cultural developments, and the assumption that diffusion is the cause of all similarities. The diffusionist approach has subsequently been countered by an evolutionist approach, which holds that pyramids might be invented independently in different places by different communities without reference to one another. In the end, Donnelly's idea depends on an assumption that civilization is homogeneous, which it clearly is not. Even the pyramids, often quoted by Donnelly's supporters, are not at all similar. Donnelly's idea gained immediate and widespread popularity, the more so since many scholars were ready to denounce the Old Atlantis as pure fiction; it is an early example of the appeal of conspiracy theory.[65] The scepticism of the scholars intensified when in 1912 a young man claiming to be Schliemann's grandson – a claim at that time calculated to *increase* his credibility – said his grandfather had found at Troy a vase with the inscription 'From King Kronos of Atlantis'.[66] This hoax did nothing for the cause of either Atlantis.

Donnelly's vision was flawed, and not just because of his diffusionist approach. The seabed features he seized on as proof of a vertically sunken land area have, since 1960, been explained by geologists in a very different way. The Mid-Atlantic Ridge is a line of weakness in the earth's crust where lateral tension opens fissures tens or hundreds of metres long, releasing lava. The floor of the western Atlantic inches westwards: that of the eastern Atlantic inches east-

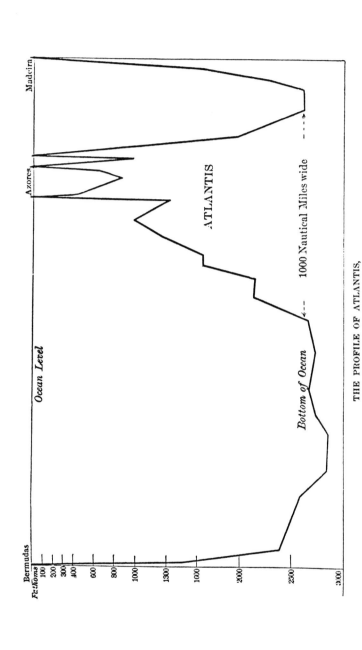

Figure 11.4 Profile of the Mid-Atlantic Ridge, as portrayed by Donnelly (1882)

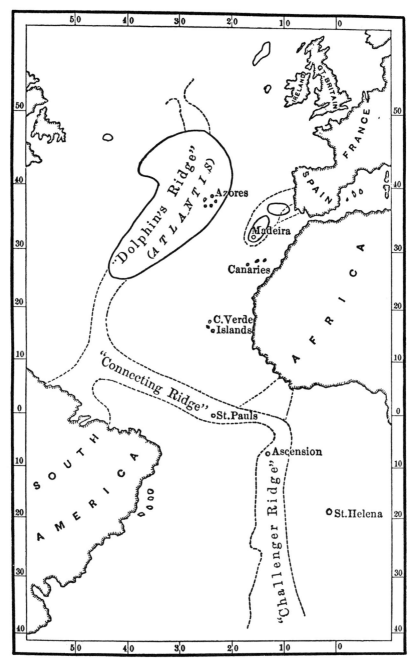

MAP OF ATLANTIS, WITH ITS ISLANDS AND CONNECTING RIDGES, FROM DEEP-SEA
SOUNDINGS.

Figure 11.5 Ignatius Donnelly's map of Atlantis (1882)

186

wards.[67] Long-lived upward-moving plumes of material in the mantle push the mid-ocean ridge up so that in places it breaks the surface of the ocean. Volcanoes that are active while located over the plumes move gradually sideways and down into the ocean basins, as on slow-moving conveyor belts: they become extinct as they leave the crest of the ridge. There is no sudden submergence: the processes are gradual and slow. Inspection of the ocean floor shows that Donnelly's connecting ridges do not exist, at any depth.

Some supporters of the New Atlantis have attempted to use the results of post-1950 research into the environmental changes of the Pleistocene Ice Age, seeing sea level change as the key to the problem. During a cold stage, such as the Devensian (80,000–10,000 years ago), a great deal of water was trapped on the land in middle and high latitudes in mantles of snow and slow-moving ice sheets, while evaporation from the ocean surface continued apace in the tropics. This produced a global lowering of sea level of 110–150 metres, exposing large areas of shallow water as dry land:[68] the seabed of the English Channel, for instance, was exposed. Glaciation in earlier cold stages is thought by climatologists and geomorphologists to have caused the sea to drop to approximately the same level. Relatively small areas adjacent to present-day Atlantic islands would have become dry land under these conditions: nearly all the Mid-Atlantic Ridge is deeper than 200 metres. Even if sea level dropped 200 metres, it would still not be enough to create the mini-Atlantis in the Azores that some have proposed. The physicist Peter Warlow wrote in 1982, 'If the sea level were to be lowered or the land raised by a matter of some 200m, then the present Azores archipelago would become the mountainous region of a substantial island.'[69] But the contours of the seabed show that this is simply not true: the Azores would remain separate islands.

One interesting feature, however, is that the most recent change from cold to warm conditions occurred around 9,600 years ago, the date given by Plato for the subsidence of Atlantis, and this would have resulted in geologically rapid sea level rise,[70] but still only at 1 or 2 centimetres per year, which could not cause a continent to vanish overnight. Henri Martin, a disbeliever in Atlantis, commented as early as 1841 that it would simply not be possible for a continent-sized island in the Atlantic to submerge suddenly – whatever the cause – and leave the geography of southern Europe unchanged.[71]

The New Atlantis has gone rapidly through many transformations, some dizzily overlapping with the world of the occult. Charles Berlitz proposed that Atlantis still exists on the seabed below the Bermuda Triangle, and that the disappearance of ships and planes in the area is due to the malign activities of the Atlanteans below.[72] Other writers have tried to retain the spectacle of a continent foundering in the Atlantic without recourse to the supernatural. Immanuel Velikovsky proposed that a collision between the earth and a comet in about 1500 BC caused an array of disasters;[73] the result is some exciting science fiction writing, which was anticipated in outline as early as 1788, when G. R. Carli proposed that Atlantis had been swamped by a comet.[74]

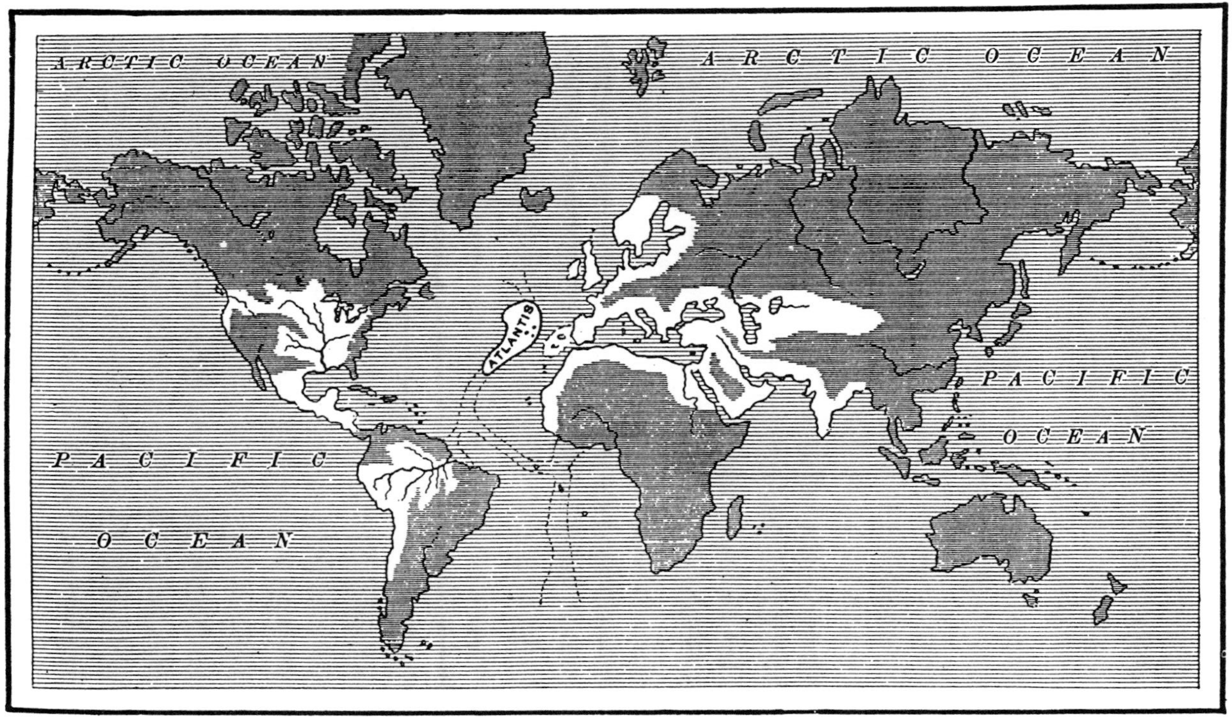

THE EMPIRE OF ATLANTIS.

Figure 11.6 The empire of Atlantis

But much of the New Atlantis literature does not attempt to argue on rational grounds at all. The mediation of academic research is not necessary, as everything hinges on subjective insight.[75] In some ways it is like the Pelagian heresy that threatened to disrupt Christianity in the sixth century by proposing that an individual relationship with God without the mediation of priests was possible. In some ways it returns to Plato's world, where historical and geographical truth are subordinated to poetic truth. Rudolf Steiner used intuition to set the destruction of Atlantis 80,000 years ago and to assert that the Atlanteans used organic energy to make their vehicles 'float a short distance above the ground'.[76] Assertions like these are, by their very nature, entirely impregnable, and we should waste no time in trying to refute them. There is also Ron Fletcher's interpretation of the Roman mosaic at Woodchester in Gloucestershire as a map of Atlantis. Its central roundel does indeed consist of concentric zones, but Fletcher is not content with this: he sees the mosaic as a star map as well; as a bonus, he claims the Woodchester Mosaic as King Arthur's Round Table, with the associated villa as Camelot.[77] Once the floodgate of personal revelation is open, the ideas flow thick and fast.

Devotees of the New Atlantis genuinely intend to promote better human behaviour by what they write, and it is indeed possible that better behaviour might result from the belief that all the people of the world are bonded by being the legatees of a great and ancient civilization. The New Age approach to Atlantis merges seamlessly with the worlds of ley lines, UFO-logy, alien abduction, astrology, dowsing, oriental mysticism and magic. The wanderings of David Childress, representative of this approach, lead with dizzying lack of logical connection from the loss of Atlantis by way of Sauniere and the Priory of Sion to crop circles and Stonehenge.[78] Indeed Atlantis has come to symbolize the blurring of boundaries, not just of disciplines, but between objective reality and personal fantasy, thought and feeling, reason and unreason, analysis and intuition, nature and supernature. It is because it is a totem for intellectual anarchy that most academics throw up their hands in despair at the mention of the name.[79]

The New Atlantis has become associated in some minds with the beginning of the Age of Aquarius. It is not clear how this link with astrology has come about, but it has something to do with the pseudo-religious significance some people attach to it. For Donnelly, Atlantis was the Garden of Eden; now for some it is not only Eden before the Fall but the promised Kingdom of Heaven too. *There is a happy land, far, far away.* While Christians may hope for a second coming at the millennium, as they hoped at the last, so New Agers may look towards the New Atlantis. At the beginning of the Age of Pisces, in the first century AD, Ignatius of Antioch felt the surging spirit of the age shattering tyrants, destroying the power of the old magicians. John Michell evidently hopes for the same again: for science to give way to what he calls revelation.[80]

We all share, if not a common ancestral 'Atlantean' culture, a common yearning for a better world. For many this desire once found expression within

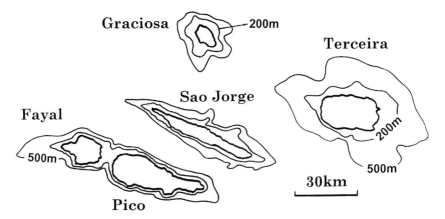

Figure 11.7 The Azores; present knowledge of the shape of the seabed shows that falls in sea level of 150 or even 200 metres during the Pleistocene will *not* have produced a large land area in the middle of the Atlantic Ocean

formal religion, but in the nineteenth and twentieth centuries, particularly in the West, increasing numbers drifted away from the traditional faiths and were either content to do without religion altogether or sought refuge in religion-substitutes, especially pseudo-religions that made few behavioural demands. Nineteenth-century humanists hoped that science, in its broadest sense, would replace religion but, whereas religion proved too demanding morally, science proved too demanding intellectually. People were left with neither formal religion nor true science. Donnelly's thesis is just one of the weeds colonizing this clearing. The assertions of the New Age frequently fly in the face of the research findings of academics in many branches of the sciences and humanities; they cock a snook at university professors, and therefore appeal to those who feel disempowered and disadvantaged.

The New Atlantis concocted during the last hundred years by Ignatius Donnelly and his successors scarcely survives the process of deconstruction. Like a mirage, it dissolves and shimmers away into nothingness while you are in the act of scrutinizing it. But the Old Atlantis, the Atlantis of the *Timaeus* and the *Critias*, fares better. It is, as Plato insisted nine times over, true. It is a true tradition, in the sense of being truly ancient, and contains at its core some fragments of historically true Aegean bronze age prehistory. It is possible to trace the alterations that were made to those fragments, some mistakenly as a result of mistranslation, some deliberately to make the tale into an allegory of the forces that threatened Athens, from within and without, in the fourth, fifth and sixth centuries BC. Even then, even in Plato's treatment, the story was 'improved' in the interests of making the world a better place.

APPENDIX:
DATING THE THERA ERUPTION

A major controversy

The traditional date around 1500 BC was first proposed in the 1930s by Marinatos. It has recently been challenged by a controversial new date of 1628 BC, dividing prehistorians into two camps and generating heated debate.[1]

A search for acidity peaks in ice cores taken from the Greenland ice sheet failed to produce anything perceptible for 1500 BC, but revealed an acidity peak for 1645 BC, which some eagerly identified as evidence of an early date for the Thera eruption.[2] Major eruptions produce enormous volumes of ash and sulphuric acid aerosols which reduce atmospheric temperatures and may be detected in tree rings as years of slow growth. Rings in bristlecone pines show inhibited growth in 42, 1626 and 2035 BC: of these, only 1626 BC could correspond to the Thera eruption. An independent study of Irish bog oaks revealed that 1628–1626 BC were very poor growth years. Since narrow rings for 1153 BC, 207 BC and AD 540 were known to correspond with large-scale eruptions, it seemed natural to connect the 1626 BC hardship ring with an eruption too.

From Thera itself comes a different kind of evidence. Three Egyptian juglets in the Thera Museum came from the collection of Dr Nomikos and may have been found by him during the excavations on the south coast of Therasia, though their provenance is unknown. Their style suggests a date between 1650 and 1550 BC so, if they were found in the Late Cycladic buildings excavated by Fouqué, they support the earlier date for the eruption.[3]

Some radiocarbon dates for the destruction level on Thera are too old for the traditional eruption date. Charcoal from a Minoan hearth discovered in the Athinios quarry in 1979 was dated to 1800 BC; fava beans found in a jug in Building 4 produced a date of 1700 BC. It has been claimed that increasing numbers of radiocarbon dates favour the older date, but the claimed mean date of 1670 BC does not match either 1645 BC (ice cores) or 1628 BC (tree rings). In fact, the average of over twenty radiocarbon dates from Akrotiri is 3200 bp, which calibrates to 1500 BC.

In spite of the strenuous lobbying in favour of a seventeenth-century BC date, the evidence in its favour is inconclusive.[4] To begin with, eruptions are not the only cause of narrow tree rings: weather patterns vary for a great many reasons.

Nor was Thera the only volcano in the world to erupt in the bronze age, so neither the 1645 acidity peak nor the 1628 hardship rings can be tied to Thera. It is more likely that a high-latitude volcano in Iceland or Alaska – and most likely the Aniakchak caldera in Alaska – would produce an acidity peak in Greenland and poor tree growth in northern Europe. Another problem is that exponents of the seventeenth-century date claim extreme accuracy for their dating methods, yet the two dates cited, 1645 BC and 1626 BC, are significantly at variance with one another.

The lack of evidence in ice and tree rings for a 1500 BC eruption begs another question. Why do they show no evidence of the far bigger eruption at about that time of Rabaul in Melanesia? Some large-scale eruptions in the historic period show very poorly if at all in ice cores or tree rings. There was, coincidentally, an eruption of Etna in about 1500 BC, which could disguise any impact Thera had. The earlier date also happens to be very close to the best current estimate for a major eruption of Vesuvius, the so-called Avellino eruption, which happened in 1650 BC. There is thus no particular reason to connect Thera with the events of 1650–1620 BC that show in the ice core and tree-ring records, and no particular reason either to deny the occurrence of an eruption around 1500 BC.

Estimates for the Minoan eruption of Thera suggest that it released 3–5 megatonnes of sulphuric acid into the atmosphere, substantially lower quantities than are needed to produce acidity spikes in Greenland. That being so, the 1645 BC spike is unlikely to be anything to do with Thera. Close examination of the history of volcanic activity also shows that as many as three eruptions in every decade are big enough to contribute to the stratospheric sulphuric acid inventory, effectively making it impossible to pin any of the acidity peaks on Thera.

Given that the mean of the Akrotiri dates, when calibrated, is so close to 1500 BC, it would be sensible to retain the traditional date for the time being. The charred seeds found in Building 4 were radiocarbon dated more than once. The first set of dates produced a wide scatter with a mean of 1500 BC, and two further sets of dates from the same material produced a similar end result, though with varying scatter. The wide scatter presented by the radiocarbon dates may have been produced statistically, by a wave in the calibration curve used to convert raw radiocarbon dates to calendar dates. In the period 1700–1500 BC, the curve is fairly flat with a few wiggles. Because of this ripple, some dates can be made to convert either to dates around 1550–1520 BC or to dates a century earlier. The wiggles make the dates ambiguous, and it may be that the calibrated dates of 1640–1620 BC are not real at all, but result from a statistical distortion; it could be that all the samples at Akrotiri date from around 1520 BC.

An extraordinary atmospheric event accompanied by flooding was witnessed in Egypt in the reign of Ahmose. If the Tempest Stele recording the event dates from the last years of Ahmose's reign, around 1520 BC, it supports Peter Warren's modification of the chronology. The trend of the evidence seems to me to be towards a volcanic destruction of Thera in 1520 BC; at the time of writing, support for this later date for the eruption has begun to gather again.[5]

NOTES

1 ALL THE ISLAND AND MANY OTHER ISLANDS ALSO

1 e.g. Chapman 1931; Fite 1934; Crossman 1939; Popper 1945.
2 Rauschning 1939.
3 Frost 1909.
4 Taylor 1929, pp. 1–6.
5 Galanopoulos and Bacon 1969; Vitaliano 1978.
6 Davis and Cherry 1990 list the thirteen sites.
7 Doumas 1983, pp. 106–7 shows the earthquake-scarred village of Oia.
8 *Crit.* 113C: 'Poseidon took for his allotment the island of Atlantis and settled on it the children whom he had begotten of a mortal woman.'
9 Papadopoulos 1990.
10 Marinatos 1939.
11 Papadopoulos 1990.
12 Huijsmans and Barton 1990.

2 PRELUDES TO DISCOVERY

1 *Histories* IV, 147.
2 *Histories* V, 58.
3 See Chapter 10.
4 If so, some Therans did survive the catastrophe after all; see Chapter 9.
5 Page 1970; Fouqué 1869 and 1879.
6 Page 1970.
7 Davis and Cherry 1990.
8 Page 1970; Mamet 1874.
9 In September 1966 the team led by James Mavor searched for the ruins explored by the French a century earlier but found nothing. In 1967, Spyridon Marinatos spent six weeks looking for them and found nothing. When I looked for them in 1990, I could find nothing either.
10 Page 1970.
11 Barber 1987, pp. 67–8.
12 Renfrew 1978a; 1981, pp. 67–80; Burn and Burn 1986, pp. 21–3.
13 Barber 1987, p. 181.
14 ibid., pp. 32, 42, 236–7.
15 Sotirakopoulou 1990.

16 Barber 1987, p. 26.
17 *Annual Report of the British School at Athens*, 1985–6.
18 Branigan 1981.
19 Barber 1987, p. 138.
20 ibid., p. 139.
21 Vaughan 1990.
22 Around 1700 BC the settlement at Akrotiri emerged as a town, evolving out of the earlier settlements on the same site.
23 Doumas 1990.
24 Marthari 1990.
25 Warren, in Marthari 1990 discussion.
26 Papazachos in discussion in Betancourt *et al*. 1990.
27 The text assumes the traditional date throughout. The evidence for the controversial revised date 100 years earlier is reviewed in the Appendix.
28 Pashley 1835; Castleden 1989, p. 20.
29 Castleden 1989, pp. 31, 33–5, 43–5.
30 Frost 1909, 1913; Baikie 1910; Forsyth 1980, p. 112.
31 *Odyssey* 19.
32 Castleden 1989, p. 143.
33 Marinatos 1971a.
34 Platon 1968, p. 198.
35 Cottrell 1963, p. 183.
36 Broneer 1948, 1949, 1956.
37 Zangger 1992.
38 Parry 1997. The Ulu Burun wreck, on the seabed near Kas, southern Turkey, has been dated to 1316 BC.

3   THERA: THE SECOND REDISCOVERY

1 Barber 1987, p. 224.
2 Burn and Burn 1986, pp. 78–80.
3 Barber 1987, p. 178.
4 ibid., pp. 185–6.
5 Burn and Burn 1986, p. 80.
6 Barber 1987, p. 187.
7 Much of this section is based on Mavor's vivid and entertaining book.
8 Galanopoulos and Bacon 1969.
9 Barber 1987, p. 202.
10 Marinatos 1968, *Excavations at Thera I–VII*.
11 Mavor is exact about the moment: 3.07 pm on 25 May.
12 The excavation is still confined to the Akrotiri ravine.
13 Marinatos 1969, *Excavations at Thera I–VII*.
14 ibid.

4   THE BRONZE AGE CITY OF THERA EMERGES

1 Marinatos 1970, *Excavations at Thera I–VII*.
2 Marinatos 1971a, p. 11.
3 A simpler numbering system is proposed; see Figure 13.
4 Marinatos 1971a, p. 30.

5 Marinatos 1971a.
6 Marinatos 1972, *Excavations at Thera I–VII*.
7 Marinatos 1976, *Excavations at Thera I–VII*.
8 Doumas 1983, pp. 13–14.
9 ibid., p. 45.
10 ibid., pp. 13, 55.
11 ibid., p. 50.
12 Marinatos 1970, *Excavations at Thera I–VII*.
13 Castleden 1989, pp. 91–2, 63; 1990, pp. 72–3.
14 The first flushing water closet was invented by John Harington in 1589 at his house at Kelston near Bath.
15 Dickinson 1994, pp. 149–51.
16 Graham 1987, pp. 224–9.
17 Doumas 1983, p. 52.
18 Cadogan 1990.
19 Sali-Axioti 1990.
20 Palyvou 1984.
21 Asimenos 1980.
22 Cameron 1980.
23 Hockmann 1980.
24 Building 4 contains a succession of three floors, together with earlier rock-cut hollows containing Middle Cycladic vases (*Annual Report of the British School at Athens*, 1984–5). In 1987, Doumas proved the existence of *two* earlier buildings before the ruined building that we now see (*Annual Report of British School at Athens*, 1987–8).
25 Seward and Wagner 1980.
26 Shaw 1990.
27 ibid.

5 ATLANTEAN ARTS AND CRAFTS

1 Katsa-Tomara 1990.
2 Papagiannopoulou 1990.
3 Wiener 1990.
4 Kilikoglou *et al.* 1990.
5 Marthari, Marketou and Jones 1990.
6 Doumas 1983, pp. 110–12.
7 Devetzi 1990.
8 Warren 1980.
9 Barber 1987, p. 192; Doumas 1983, pp. 115–16.
10 Barber 1987, p. 193.
11 Michailidou 1990.
12 Stos-Gale and Gale 1990.
13 Doumas 1983, p. 116.
14 ibid., p. 117.
15 Tzachili 1990.
16 Morgan 1988, pp. 90, 97.
17 Tzachili 1990.
18 ibid.
19 Morgan 1988, p. 95.
20 ibid., pp. 98–9.

21 Castleden 1990, pp. 140–1.
22 Its absence from Cretan art is explained by the difference in wall-painting technique, and the relative incompleteness of the fresco record.
23 See Castleden 1989, pp. 70, 116, 120–1, 190; seal impressions showing dresses carried as offerings and miniature dresses have been found at Knossos.
24 A replica is displayed in the National Archaeological Museum in Athens.
25 *Annual Report of the British School at Athens*, 1993–4, p. 69.
26 Plato has his Atlantean kings sitting on the ground, but that may have been in a ritual context only. He says nothing of Atlantean furniture.

6 THERAN FOOD AND TRADE

1 Doumas 1983, p. 129.
2 Gamble 1980.
3 Fouqué 1879, p. 122; Vickery 1936, pp. 61, 72.
4 Marinatos 1969, *Excavations at Thera I–VII.*
5 Morgan 1988, p. 17.
6 The one thing Plato is specific about in Atlantean agriculture is that there were two crops per year (*Crit.* 118E).
7 Marinatos 1975, *Excavations at Thera I–VII,* p. 24.
8 Morgan 1988, p. 18.
9 Friedrich *et al.* 1990.
10 Doumas 1983, pp. 118–19.
11 Pliny, *Natural History* XXI, 17. 31–2.
12 Barber 1987, p. 170.
13 Dickinson 1994, p. 25.
14 Thucydides, *The Peloponnesian War* I, 4.
15 ibid., I, 8.
16 Lambrou-Phillipson 1990.
17 Marinatos 1976, *Excavations at Thera I–VII,* p. 30.
18 Buchholz 1980.
19 Sakellerakis 1990.
20 Warren in Sakellarakis 1990 discussion.
21 Buchholz 1980.
22 Stos-Gale and Gale 1990.
23 Cadogan 1990.
24 ibid.
25 Poursat 1990.
26 Wiener 1990.
27 Branigan 1981.
28 Doumas 1983, p. 126.
29 Herodotus *Histories* I, 171; III, 122.
30 Doumas 1983, pp. 127–8.
31 Branigan 1981.
32 Doumas 1983, p. 127.
33 Caskey 1970; Chadwick 1976, pp. 102–5.
34 Vermeule 1975.
35 Doumas 1983, p. 132.
36 ibid., p. 132; Iakovides 1979. To an extent the interpretation reflects the politics of the prehistorian. Marinatos preferred the Mycenean military takeover at Akrotiri: a similar military takeover in Athens had led to his own promotion.

37 Doumas 1983, pp. 132–3.
38 e.g. Palanquin Fresco and terracotta model from Knossos (Castleden 1990, p. 177).
39 Brown 1980.
40 Book XI.
41 Sakellariou 1980.
42 Compare Mochlos in Crete.
43 Brown 1980.
44 ibid.
45 Negbi 1978.

7   WRITING AND WALL-PAINTING

1 Castleden 1989, pp. 89–90.
2 Castleden 1990, pp. 100–2.
3 Castleden 1989, p. 182; 1990, pp. 124, 129.
4 Evans, *Palace of Minos* III, p. 89.
5 ibid., p. 314.
6 Hiller 1990.
7 ibid.
8 Castleden 1990, p. 178.
9 Abbate 1972.
10 Doumas 1982, p. 19.
11 Laffineur 1990.
12 ibid.
13 see Castleden 1989.
14 Marinatos 1984, pp. 31–2.
15 Warren, in Doumas 1982, p. 13.
16 Marinatos 1984, p. 96.
17 ibid., p. 94.
18 Doumas 1982, p. 34.
19 Marinatos 1984, p. 97.
20 ibid., pp. 99–105.
21 Morgan in Hardy and Renfrew 1990, p. 259
22 Boulotis 1987.
23 Marinatos 1984, p. 116.
24 Doumas 1992, p. 110.
25 Marinatos 1984, p. 106.
26 ibid., p. 109.
27 Rackham 1980.

8   ART, RELIGION AND SOCIETY

1 Doumas 1992, p. 47.
2 Marinatos 1984, p. 37.
3 Televantou 1990.
4 Televantou (1990) has added several pieces to the fresco and argues convincingly for as many as nine vessels.
5 Marinatos 1984, p. 38.
6 The remains of Minoan shipsheds have been identified at Kommos and Mallia on

Crete (see Shaw 1990). It is likely there were shipsheds along the waterfront at Akrotiri, not far west of the archaeological excavation.

7 Marinatos 1984, pp. 38–40.
8 Morgan 1988, pp. 82–3.
9 This account closely follows that of Morgan 1988, pp. 156–60.
10 Televantou 1990, pp. 316–17.
11 The east wall frieze is only 1.8 metres long: the northern half has been destroyed.
12 Televantou 1990.
13 Morgan 1988, pp. 146–9.
14 ibid., p. 149.
15 Televantou (1990, p. 320) calls this Town 3.
16 see Chapter 4.
17 Morgan 1988, p. 18.
18 Morgan (1988, p. 38) is wrong to describe this as a delta. The two rivers are clearly shown flowing right to left from the mountainous skyline as they reach the sea.
19 Dickinson 1994, p. 65.
20 Wiener 1990.
21 Davis and Cherry 1990.
22 McGillivray 1990.
23 ibid.
24 Morgan 1988, p. 162.
25 Televantou 1990.
26 Marinatos 1984, pp. 45–9.
27 Saflund 1987.
28 Nanno Marinatos (1984) has made much of the possible use of pier-and-door partitions in relation to the wall-paintings. There is every likelihood that the doors were used in this way, deliberately opened to reveal selected images and closed to conceal others as the ceremony progressed.
29 Castleden 1990, pp. 170–1.
30 Cameron 1987.
31 ibid.
32 *Annual Report of the British School at Athens*, 1993–4, p. 69; 1994–5, p. 57.
33 Dickinson 1994, pp. 89–99.
34 ibid., p. 88.
35 Presumably in reality the two stood for four, one at each corner.
36 See Marinatos 1990, p. 374 for examples.
37 As in tablet Fp(1) + 31, see Chadwick et al. 1986.
38 Hiller 1990.
39 Taylor 1820, Book 1, p. 148.
40 Diodorus III, 56. 2–4.
41 Castleden 1989, pp. 115–18; 1990, pp. 175–7.
42 Wiener 1990.

9   THE LAST DAYS OF AKROTIRI

1 The dates given here are designed to fit in with an interpretation of the evidence, including radiocarbon dates, for a final destruction by volcanic eruption in 1520 BC. See Appendix for a discussion of the evidence for a date one hundred years earlier.
2 Doumas 1990; Limbrey 1990.
3 Doumas 1990.
4 Blong 1980.

5 Doumas 1990.
6 29 kilometres according to Wilson (1980), 35 kilometres according to Keller, Rehren and Stadlbaurer 1990, 36 kilometres according to Sparks and Wilson 1990.
7 Thorarinsson 1970.
8 Wilson 1980.
9 Pichler and Friedrich 1980.
10 Sali-Axioti 1990.
11 From my own fieldwork. Readers are advised against exploring the Phira Quarry. Only an experienced geologist or geomorphologist will be able to make anything of the exposures. They do not exhibit any Minoan ruins or prehistoric finds at present. When the wind is strong the dust stings your skin, irritates your eyes, makes breathing difficult and induces despair. A place to avoid.
12 Estimates of the duration of the eruption vary enormously. Some believe the whole sequence could have occurred within a few hours, others that it took several years.
13 Doumas 1990.
14 Wilson 1980.
15 Baillie 1989.
16 Sparks and Wilson 1990.
17 Hedervari 1980.
18 Heiken and McCoy 1990.
19 This was agreed at the conclusion of the 1980 Thera Conference, and no evidence has subsequently emerged to revise it.
20 Renfrew 1980.
21 Hedervari (1971) calculated the total energy released in the eruption sequence as 4.45×10^{27} ergs, which makes it the most violent in the world in the last 4,000 years. It scored an estimated 6.9 on the volcanic explosivity index, which makes it the second most violent in the last 4,000 years: only Tambora in 1815 exceeded it (Renfrew's closing remarks in Hardy and Renfrew 1990).
22 Marinatos 1939; 1950; 1971a; Luce 1969, pp. 60–72.
23 Yokoyama 1980.
24 Time lapse is from ibid.
25 Marinos and Melidonis 1971.
26 Keller 1971.
27 Francaviglia 1990.
28 These figures are after settlement and compaction, and represent original falls that were twice as thick: Page 1970.
29 McCoy 1980.
30 The Minoan ash covered the ash footprint of the 23,000 BC eruption, also oriented WNW–ESE, but covered a smaller area. Interestingly the huge prehistoric eruption of Vesuvius and Ischia also produced ash plumes trailing east-south-eastwards across the Eastern Mediterranean. Coincidentally, a WNW wind was blowing at the time of each of these four great eruptions.
31 Page 1970.
32 Krakatoa (1883) reduced global temperatures by half a degree Celsius; Tambora (1815) and Pinatubo (1991) the same, and with much greater effects locally, temperatures in North America falling 3 degrees.
33 Fragments of the Tempest Stele were found in the third pylon of the temple of Karnak in 1947–51.
34 Medinet Habu inscriptions 37, 46, 80, 102, 109; Spanuth 1979, p. 175; Crit. 115B.
35 Vitaliano 1978, cross-section on p. 145.
36 Zhirov (1970, p. 25) mentions an eruption in Iceland in 1783 smothering the sea for 200 kilometres in all directions with ash and pumice, making navigation impossible for a time.

37 Euripides, *Hippolytus*, ll. 734–47.
38 Galanopoulos and Bacon 1969, p. 120.
39 Sigurdsson *et al.* 1990, discussion.
40 Marinatos 1971a.
41 ibid.; Pindar *Ode* IV, ll. 37–41.
42 Marketou 1990.
43 Barber 1987, p. 224
44 Renfrew 1990.
45 Soles and Davaras 1990.
46 Doumas 1990.
47 Marketou 1990.
48 Barber 1987, p. 223.
49 Castleden 1990, pp. 158–78.
50 Furumark 1980.

10   ATLANTIS DESTROYED

1 Andrews 1967.
2 Plato, *Laws* I, 625.
3 ibid., I, 624.
4 ibid., IV, 706.
5 Graham 1987, pp. 73–83; Castleden 1989, pp. 130–9, 1990, pp. 145–8.
6 Castleden 1989, pp. 27–37, 43–58.
7 Fauré 1973, pp. 184–203; Castleden 1989, pp. 70–104.
8 Hood 1995.
9 Durand 1987, pp. 89–102.
10 Hood 1995, pp. 403–4.
11 MacGillivray 1994, pp. 51, 53.
12 The Boston Goddess was stolen from the site at the time of the Evans dig, and probably represents a large number of objects removed from the site over a long period.
13 *Knossos Corpus*, Tablet Fp (1)1.
14 The Tripartite Shrine at Knossos is a natural candidate for the 'altar which in size and workmanship corresponded to this magnificence' (*Crit.* 116E). See Castleden 1989, p. 82 for a reconstruction of the shrine.
15 Based in part on Presiozi 1983.
16 For detail see Castleden 1989, pp. 30–9, 1990, pp. 146–8.
17 Russell 1946, pp. 133–4.
18 Plato, *Republic* last book.
19 *Theaetetus*, quoted in Russell 1946, pp. 171–2.
20 Jowett 1892, p. 543.
21 *Gorgias* 527.
22 Dombrowski 1981. Several modern writers, apparently bent on discrediting Plato, have alleged that Aristotle did not believe Plato's Atlantis story, but we have only a third-hand report, which contains an oblique reference, and Aristotle's name is not actually mentioned.
23 Diogenes Laertius VIII, 85.
24 Fredericks 1978.
25 Chadwick 1976, p. 13.
26 Plato, *Laws* II, 663.
27 ibid., II, 663–4.
28 ibid., III, 677.

29 Taylor (1929, p. 6) disagrees with the view that Plato intended a third dialogue led by Hermocrates, arguing that the suggestion that Hermocrates might be nervous when it came to his turn is just a joke. Taylor also argues that there would be nothing left to discuss. These arguments are thin and unconvincing, since the material used in the *Laws* could have filled the *Hermocrates*. Cornford (1937, pp. 7–8) argues that Plato found he had *too much* material to fit into his *Timaeus* trilogy, and broke off the Critias in order to set this out in an entirely new book. The ideas in the *Laws* continue where the *Critias* would have ended, with the regeneration of the human race after the Atlantis catastrophe. The view that a third dialogue was intended has much to recommend it.
30 *Republic* II, 377; *Laws* X, 886.
31 Luce 1978.
32 *Phaedrus* 275.
33 *Republic* III, 414.
34 ibid. III, 389.
35 ibid. II, 382.
36 *Protagoras* 320.
37 *Republic* X, 614–21.
38 *Laws* III.
39 *Republic* III, 414.
40 *Politicus* 270.
41 Stewart 1904.
42 *Politicus* 268.
43 e.g. Taylor 1929; Cornford 1937, p. 37, n.1.
44 Karlsson 1992.
45 Diodorus XIV, xviii, 1–8.
46 ibid. XV, xiii, 5.
47 Plato *Epistle* VII, 324B–325D.
48 *Phaedo*.
49 See Hegesandros in *Athen.* XI, 507.
50 Plutarch, *Dion* 5.
51 Freeman 1892, p. 195.
52 ibid.
53 Plutarch, *Dion* 19, 20.
54 Diod. XIV, vii, 2.
55 Homer *Odyssey* VII, ll. 84 ff.
56 e.g. Spanuth 1979, pp. 218–21.
57 *Odyssey* VI, 270 ff; VII, 105 ff.
58 *Odyssey* V, 280–2.
59 From von Rudbek 1675.
60 1992, pp. 44–7.
61 *Politics* 1331a. 8–13. Plato did not entirely despair of creating wise philosopher-kings; he thought he had found one in Archytas of Taras.
62 Meiggs 1972.
63 Plutarch, *Themistocles*, 32.
64 Kagan 1987.
65 ibid.
66 Based on Xenophon, *Hellenica* II, 2.
67 Thucydides, V, 68.
68 Strabo VIII, 365.
69 e.g. Hippasus, Pausanias and Nicocles.
70 Chrimes 1949, pp. 205–47.
71 cf Homer: *Odyssey*, XIX, 179.

72 Chrimes 1949.
73 David 1981.
74 Plato: *Alcib.* I. 120E–121C, 122C–E; *Hipp. Mai.* 283A–285A, 285C; *Laches* 182E–183A; *Prot.* 342B; *Symp.* 209D.
75 Xenophon *Resp.* 544C, 545A; Aristotle *Pol.* 1316A, 18–25.
76 David 1981, pp. 59–67.
77 *Rep.* 552D.
78 Gill 1977; 1980.
79 Ganz 1993, p. 216.
80 Robert (1917) identifies an older fragment of the Atlantis epic in Oxyrhynchus Papyrus 11, 1359. These shreds of a pre-Platonic Atlantis legend go a long way towards vindicating Plato's insistence that the tradition he was offering was true.
81 e.g. Pliny *Nat. Hist.* IV, 58.
82 Diod. V, 81, 7.
83 Hesiod *Theogony* ll. 844–9.
84 by Davies 1971. Diogenes Laertius gives Exekestides as Solon's father. I add the suggestion that Dropides I and Exekestides were brothers; Solon and Dropides II were not brothers, or Plato would have said so. They were 'relatives and dear friends' which could have meant they were cousins.
85 Murray 1898, p. 82.
86 e.g. Podlecki 1984.
87 Jowett 1892, III, p. 431.
88 Herodotus I, 29–30. Herodotus himself consulted the priests of Sais less than 150 years after Solon, in about 454 BC.
89 Diogenes Laertius I, 50.
90 Plutarch, *Solon* 31.
91 Boardman 1964, pp. 133–50.
92 Lambrou-Phillipson 1990.
93 Bietak 1992.
94 James 1995, pp. 172–3; Cameron 1983.
95 Luce 1969, pp. 38–9.
96 Gardiner 1909.
97 Cary 1949, p. 240.
98 Pindar *Olympia* III, 76–8; *Nemea* III, 35–6.
99 Luce 1969, p. 42.
100 Woudhuizen 1992, pp. 78–9.
101 'Farcical' according to Taylor 1929, pp. 103–4.
102 Galanopoulos 1969, p. 134; Luce 1969, p. 181.
103 Mavor 1969, pp. 33–4.
104 Evans *Palace of Minos* I, p. 642.
105 James 1995, p. 75.
106 Friedrich 1957, pp. 5–7.
107 Diod. I, 26.
108 James 1995, p. 77.
109 Plutarch, *Solon* 31.
110 Podlecki 1984, p. 130.

11   DECONSTRUCTION OF ATLANTIS

1 *Tim.* 23C, 23E; *Crit.* 108E.
2 *Tim.* 24E; *Crit.* 108E.

3 *Tim.* 24E, 25A; *Crit.* 114E, 117E.
4 *Crit.* 114E.
5 *Tim.* 24E, 25B; *Crit.* 108E.
6 *Tim.* 24A–B.
7 *Crit.* 109–12.
8 *Tim.* 25A; *Crit.* 118C.
9 *Crit.* 113E, 116C, 117E.
10 *Crit.* 117E.
11 *Crit.* 116A.
12 *Crit.* 113D, 115D, 118D.
13 *Crit.* 113E, 117A.
14 *Crit.* 116B.
15 *Crit.* 113C.
16 *Crit.* 115C.
17 *Crit.* 116D.
18 *Crit.* 116D.
19 *Crit.* 117C.
20 *Crit.* 121A.
21 *Crit.* 120C.
22 *Crit.* 117A, 118E.
23 *Crit.* 116C, 118D, 118E.
24 *Crit.* 118C.
25 *Crit.* 118E.
26 *Crit.* 118E.
27 *Crit.* 116E.
28 *Crit.* 120B, 120C.
29 *Crit.* 116E.
30 *Crit.* 116E.
31 *Crit.* 116D.
32 *Crit.* 114E.
33 *Crit.* 113C, 114E, 118A, 118E.
34 *Tim.* 23E; *Crit.* 108E.
35 *Tim.* 25C; *Crit.* 108E.
36 *Crit.* 113C.
37 *Tim.* 24C; *Crit.* 108E.
38 *Tim.* 25C.
39 *Tim.* 25C; *Crit.* 108E.
40 *Tim.* 25C.
41 *Tim.* 25C.
42 Herodotus IV, 42.
43 *Crit.* 120E–121C.
44 *Crit.* 119A–B. The Atlantean army consisted of a chariot force of 10,000, four times larger than the largest known Egyptian force. This would appear to be another tenfold exaggeration.
45 *Tim.* 24A, 25C; *Crit.* 105E, 108E.
46 *Crit.* 113E, 118B, 118E.
47 *Crit.* 113E, 117A.
48 *Crit.* 116A.
49 *Crit.* 121A.
50 *Crit.* 113D, 116A, 116B.
51 *Crit.* 115C.
52 *Crit.* 115E, 116A, 117C.
53 *Crit.* 115C.

54 *Crit.* 115B, D, E, 117D.
55 *Crit.* 118C.
56 Fears 1978, p. 132; *Tim.* 25B; *Crit.* 114C, D, 120D.
57 *Tim.* 24E.
58 *Tim.* 25.
59 *Tim.* 24D.
60 *Tim.* 25C.
61 Russell 1946, p. 128.
62 Noroff 1854, Joleaud 1924, Butavand 1925, Russo 1930, Beaumont 1946, Rousseau-Liessens 1956, Spanuth 1956, Flem-Ath and Flem-Ath 1995; Dunbavin 1992 and many others.
63 Rudbeck 1675, Berlioux 1883, Rudbeck 1625, Galanopoulos 1960, among others. See de Camp 1970 for a comprehensive list.
64 Donnelly 1882, p. 267.
65 Forsyth 1980, pp. 5–6.
66 Hess 1962.
67 Van Andel 1989, 1990; Wright 1978, p. 164.
68 Chappell and Thom 1977; Castleden 1996, pp. 12–13, 24–6.
69 Warlow 1982, p. 129.
70 Emiliani 1975.
71 Martin 1841.
72 *The Mystery of Atlantis*; *The Bermuda Triangle*.
73 Velikovsky 1950.
74 Otto Muck (1976) also sank Atlantis by comet impact – in 8498 BC.
75 e.g. Edgar Cayce's revelations about Atlantis during trances (James 1995, p. 54).
76 Steiner 1928, p. 14.
77 Sullivan and Wilder (undated).
78 Childress 1996, e.g. pp. 295–301, 348–9.
79 Cornford (1937) gives only one page to Atlantis in his book on the *Timaeus*.
80 Michell 1969.

APPENDIX

1 e.g. at the 1989 Thera Congress. Most of what follows is simplified from papers in Hardy and Renfrew (eds) 1990, vol. 3. The evaluation is my own.
2 Scarre 1988.
3 Astrom 1971.
4 Scarre 1988.
5 Warren and Hankey 1989; Dickinson 1994, pp. 17–20.

BIBLIOGRAPHY

Abbate, F. (1972) *Egyptian Art*, London: Peerage Books.

Abramowitz, K. (1980) 'Frescoes from Ayia Irini, Keos', *Hesperia* 49, 57–85.

Andersen, H. (1949) 'Atlantean traces in the Cape Verde Islands', *Atlantean Research* 2: 1, 13.

Andrews, P. B. S. (1967) 'Larger than Africa and Asia?' *Greece and Rome* 14, 76–9.

Anhalt, E. K. (1993) *Solon the Singer: Politics and Poetics*, Lanham, Maryland: Rowman and Littlefield.

Ashe, G. (1992) *Atlantis: Lost Lands, Ancient Wisdom*, London: Thames and Hudson.

Asimenos, K. (1980) 'Technological observations on the Thera wall-paintings', in Doumas (ed.) 1, 571–8.

Aston, M. and Hardy, P. (1990) 'The pre-Minoan landscape of Thera: a preliminary statement', in Hardy and Renfrew (eds) 2, 348–60.

Astrom, P. (1971) 'Three Tell el Yahudiyeh juglets in the Thera Museum', in *Acta of the First Scientific Congress on the Volcano of Thera*, 415–21.

Atkinson, T. D. *et al.* (1904) *Excavations at Phylakopi in Melos*, London: Society for the Promotion of Hellenic Studies.

Babbit, F. C. (1936) *Plutarch's Moralia*, London: Heinemann.

Babcock, W. (1922) *Legendary Islands of the Atlantic*, New York: American Geographical Society.

Bacon, E. (ed.) (1963) *Vanished Civilizations*, London: Thames and Hudson.

Baikie, J. (1910) *The Sea Kings of Crete*, London: Black.

Baillie, M. (1989) 'Do Irish bog oaks date the Shang dynasty?', *Current Archaeology* 117, 310–13.

—— (1990) 'Irish tree rings and an event in 1628 BC', in Hardy and Renfrew (eds) 3, 160–5.

Barber, R. L. N. (1974) 'Phylakopi 1911 and the history of the later Cycladic Bronze Age', *Annual of the British School in Athens* 69, 1–53.

—— (1987) *The Cyclades in the Bronze Age*, London: Duckworth

Beaumont, C. (1946) *Riddle of Prehistoric Britain*, London.

Berlioux, E. F. (1883) *Les Atlantes: histoire de l'Atlantide et de l'Atlas primitif*, Lyon.

Berlitz, C. (1984) *Atlantis: The Lost Continent Revealed*, London: Macmillan.

Betancourt, P. (1990) 'High chronology or low chronology: the archaeological evidence', in Hardy and Renfrew (eds) 3, 19–23.

Betancourt, P., Goldberg, P., Hope Simpson, R. and Vitaliano, C. (1990) 'Excavations at Pseira: the evidence for the Theran eruption', in Hardy and Renfrew (eds) 3, 96–9.

Biddle, M. and Ralph, E. K. (1980) 'Radiocarbon dates from Akrotiri: problems and a strategy', in Doumas (ed.), 2, 247–52.

Bietak, M. (1992) 'Minoan wall-paintings unearthed at ancient Avaris', *Egyptian Archaeology: Bulletin of the Egypt Exploration Society* 2, 26–8.

Bjorkman, E. (1927) *The Search for Atlantis*, New York: Alfred Knopf.

Blong, R. J. (1980) 'The possible effects of Santorini tephra fall on Minoan Crete', in Doumas (ed.) 2, 217–26.

Boardman, J. (1964) *The Greeks Overseas*, Harmondsworth: Penguin.

Boneff, N. (1949) 'An asteroid as the possible cause of the Atlantis submersion', *Atlantean Research* 2: 4, 50–2.

—— (1950) 'The theory of the tides and the problem of Atlantis', *Atlantis* (London) 4, 36–7.

—— (1959) 'The problem of Atlantis', *Atlantis* (London) 12, 63.

Boulotis, C. (1987) 'Nochmals zum Prozessionsfresko von Knossos: Palast und Darbringung von Prestige-Objekten', in Hägg and Marinatos (eds) 145–56.

Bowra, C. M. (1969) *Pindar: The Odes*, Harmondsworth: Penguin.

Braghine, A. (1940) *The Shadow of Atlantis*, London: Dutton.

Braghine, A. (1952) *L'Enigme de l'Atlantide*, Paris.

Bramwell, J. (1974) *Lost Atlantis*, California: Newcastle.

Branigan, K. (1981) 'Minoan colonialism', *Annual of the British School in Athens* 76, 23–33.

—— (1984) 'Minoan community colonies in the Aegean', in Hägg and Marinatos (eds) 49–53.

Broneer, O. (1948) 'What happened at Athens?', *American Journal of Archaeology* (1948), 111–14.

—— (1949) 'Plato's description of early Athens, and the origin of Metageitnia', *Hesperia* Suppl. 8, 47–59.

—— (1956) 'Athens in the bronze age', *Antiquity* 30, 9–18.

Broodbank, C. (1992) 'The neolithic labyrinth: social change at Knossos before the bronze age', *Journal of Mediterranean Archaeology* 5, 39–75.

Brown, L. M. (1980) 'The ship procession in the miniature fresco', in Doumas (ed.).

Buchholz, H-G. (1980) 'Some observations concerning Thera's contacts overseas during the bronze age', in Doumas (ed.) 2, 227–40.

Buck, R. (1962) 'The Minoan thalassocracy re-examined', *Historia* 11, 129–37.

Burn, A. R. and Burn, M. (1986) *The Living Past of Greece*, New York: Schocken.

Bury, R. G. (trans) (1929) *Plato: Timaeus, Critias, Cleitophon, Menexenus, Epistles*, Cambridge, Massachusetts: Harvard University Press: Loeb Classical Library.

Butavandt, F. (1925) *La veritable histoire de l'Atlantide*, Paris.

Byrom, J. (1937) *Lost Atlantis*, London: Cobden-Sanderson.

Cadogan, G. (1982) 'A Minoan thalassocracy?' in Hägg and Marinatos (eds) 1984, 13–15.

—— (1990) 'Thera's eruption into our understanding of the Minoans', in Hardy and Renfrew (eds) 1, 93–7.

Cameron, A. (1983) 'Crantor and Poseidonius on Atlantis', *Classical Quarterly* 3: 1, 81–91.

Cameron, M. A. S. (1980) 'Theoretical interrelations among Theran, Cretan and main-land frescoes', in Doumas (ed.) 1, 579–92.

—— (1987) 'The "palatial" thematic system in the Knossos murals: last notes on Knossos frescoes', in Hägg and Marinatos (eds) 320–8.

Carli, G. R. (1788) *Lettre Americaine*, Paris.

Carpenter, R. (1966) *Beyond the Pillars of Heracles*, New York: Delacorte.

Cary, M. (1949) *The Geographic Background of Greek and Roman History*, Oxford: Clarendon Press.

Caskey, J. L. (1962) 'Excavations in Keos, 1960–1', *Hesperia* 31, 263–83.

—— (1966) Excavations in Keos, 1964–5', *Hesperia* 35, 363–76.

—— (1969) 'Crises in the Minoan–Mycenaean world', *Proceedings of the American Philosophical Society* 113, 433–49.

—— (1970) 'Inscriptions and potters' marks from Ayia Irini in Keos', *Kadmos* 9, 107–17.

Caskey, M. E. (1981) 'Ayia Irini, Kea: the terracotta statues and the cult in the Temple', in Hägg and Marinatos (eds) (1984) 127–35.

—— (1984) 'The Temple at Ayia Irini, Kea: evidence for the LH IIIC phases', in MacGillivray and Barber (eds).

Castleden, R. (1989) *The Knossos Labyrinth: A New View of the 'Palace of Minos' at Knossos*, London and New York: Routledge.

—— (1990) *Minoans: Life in Bronze Age Crete*, London and New York: Routledge.

—— (1993) *The Making of Stonehenge*, London and New York: Routledge.

—— (1996) *Classic Landforms of the Sussex Coast*, Sheffield: Geographical Association.

Cayce, H. L. (ed.) (1969) *Edgar Cayce on Atlantis*, London.

Chadwick, J. (1976) *The Mycenaean World*, Cambridge: Cambridge University Press.

Chadwick, J. et al. (1986) *Knossos Corpus*, vol. 1, Cambridge: Cambridge University Press.

Chapman, J. J. (1931) *Lucian, Plato and Greek Morals*, Boston: Houghton Mifflin.

Chappell, J. and Thom, B. (1977) 'Sea levels and coasts', pp. 275–91 in Allen, J. et al. (eds) *Sunda and Sahul*, New York: Academic Press.

Charroux, R. (1973) *Lost Worlds*, Glasgow: Collins.

Cherry, J. F. (1986) 'Polities and palaces: some problems in Minoan state formation', in Renfrew and Cherry (eds), 19–45.

Childress, D. H. (1996) *Lost Cities of Atlantis, Ancient Europe and the Mediterranean*, Stelle, Illinois: Adventures Unlimited Press.

Chrimes, K. (1949) *Ancient Sparta: A Re-examination of the Evidence*, Manchester: Manchester University Press.

Clausen, H. B., Friedrich, W. L. and Tauber, H. (1988) 'Dating of the Santorini eruption', *Nature* 332, 401.

Coldstream, J. N. (1969) 'The Thera eruption: some thoughts on the survivors', *Bulletin of the Institute of Classical Studies* 16, 150–2.

Coleman, J. E. (1974) 'The chronology and interconnections of the Cycladic islands in the Neolithic period and the early Bronze Age', *American Journal of Archaeology* 78, 333–444.

Cornford, F. M. (1937) *Plato's Cosmology*, London: Routledge and Kegan Paul.

Cottrell, L. (1963) *The Lion Gate*, London: Pan Books.

Crossman, R. H. S. (1939) *Plato Today*, Oxford: Oxford University Press.

David, E. (1981) *Sparta between Empire and Revolution (404–243 BC): Internal Problems and Their Impact on Contemporary Greek Consciousness*, New York: Arno Press.

Davies, J. K. (1971) *Athenian Propertied Families*, London.

Davies, N. de G. (1943) *The Tomb of Rekhmire at Thebes*, New York: Metropolitan Museum of Art Egyptian Expedition Publications.

Davis, E. (1990a) 'A storm in Egypt during the reign of Ahmose', in Hardy and Renfrew (eds) 3, 232–5.

—— (1990b) 'The Cycladic style of the Thera frescoes', in Hardy and Renfrew (eds) 1, 214–27.

Davis, J. L. (1980) 'Minoans and Minoanisation at Ayia Irini, Keos', in Doumas (ed.) 1, 257–60.

—— (1982) 'The earliest Minoans in the southeast Aegean: a reconsideration of the evidence', *Anatolian Studies* 32, 33–41.

—— (1984) 'Cultural innovation and the Minoan thalassocracy at Ayia Irini, Keos', in Hägg and Marinatos (eds) 159–66.

Davis, J. L. and Cherry, J. F. (1990) 'Spatial and temporal uniformitarianism in LCI: perspectives from Kea and Melos on the prehistory of Akrotiri', in Hardy and Renfrew (eds) 1, 185–200.

Dawkins, R. M. and Droop, J. P. (1911) 'The excavations at Phylakopi in Melos', *Annual of the British School at Athens* 17, 1–22.

de Camp, L. S. (1970) *Lost Continents*, New York: Dover.

Delibasis, N. *et al.* (1990) 'Surveillance of Thera volcano, Greece: microseismicity monitoring', in Hardy and Renfrew (eds) 2, 199–206.

Delibrias, G. and Guillier, M. T. (1971) 'The sea level on the Atlantic coast and the Channel for the last 10,000 years', *Quaternaria* 14, 131–5.

Devetzi, T. D. (1990) 'The stone industry at Akrotiri: a theoretical approach', in Hardy and Renfrew (eds) 1, 19–23.

Devigne, R. (1924) *Un continent disparu, l'Atlandide, sixieme part du monde*, Paris.

Dickinson, O. (1994) *The Aegean Bronze Age*, Cambridge: Cambridge University Press.

Diogenes Laertius (1964) *Lives of Philosophers*, Oxford: Clarendon Press.

Dombrowski, D. A. (1981) 'Atlantis and Plato's philosophy', *Apeiron* 15, 117–28.

Donnelly, I. (1882) *Atlantis: The Antediluvian World*, New York: Harper.

Doumas, C. (1974) 'The Minoan eruption of the Santorini volcano', *Antiquity* 48, 110–14.

—— (ed.) (1978, 1980) *Thera and the Aegean World: Papers Presented at the Second International Scientific Congress, Santorini, Greece, August 1978*, 2 vols., London: Thera Foundation.

—— (1982) 'The Minoan thalassocracy', *Archaologischer Anzeiger* 5–14.

—— (1983) *Thera: Pompeii of the Ancient Aegean*, London: Thames and Hudson.

—— (1990) 'Archaeological observations at Akrotiri relating to the volcanic destruction', in Hardy and Renfrew (eds) 3, 48–9.

Druitt, T. (1990) 'The pyroclastic stratigraphy and volcanology of Santorini', in Hardy and Renfrew (eds) 2, 27–8.

Druitt, T. and Francaviglia, V. (1990) 'An ancient caldera cliff line at Phira, and its significance for the topography and geology of pre-Minoan Santorini', in Hardy and Renfrew (eds) 2, 362–9.

Dunbavin, P. (1992) *The Atlantis Researches*, Nottingham: Third Millennium Publishing.

Durand, J-M. (1987) 'L'organisation de l'espace dans le palais de Mari', Levy (ed.) 39–110.

Ebon, M. (1977) *Atlantis: The New Evidence*, New York: New American Library.

Eisner, R. (1972) 'The Temple at Ayia Irini: mythology and archaeology', *Greek, Roman and Byzantine Studies* 13, 123–33.

Emiliani, C. (1975) 'Palaeoclimatological analysis of Late Quaternary cores from the north-eastern Gulf of Mexico', *Science* 189, 1083–8.

Eriksen, E., Friedrich, W., Buchardt, B., Tauber, H. and Thomsen, M. (1990) 'The Strongyle crater: geological, palaeontological and stable isotope evidence from C14 dated stromatolites from Santorini', in Hardy and Renfrew (eds) 2, 139–50.

Evans, A. (1921–36) *The Palace of Minos at Knossos*, 4 vols., London: Macmillan.

Evans, R. K. and Renfrew, C. (1984) 'The earlier bronze age at Phylakopi', in MacGillivray and Barber (eds) 63–9.

Evely, D., Hughes-Brock, H. and Momigliano, N. (eds) (1994) *Knossos: A Labyrinth of History*, Oxford: British School at Athens and Oxbow Books.

Fairbanks, R. G. (1989) 'A 17,000-year-old glacioeustatic sea level record', *Nature* 342, 637–42

Faure, P. (1973) *La vie quotidienne en Crete au temps de Minos*, Paris: Hachette.

Fears, J. R. (1978) 'Atlantis and the Minoan thalassocracy: a study in modern mythopoeism', in Ramage (ed.) 103–34.

Ferguson, J. (1975) *Utopias of the Classical World*, London: Thames and Hudson.

Ferro, R. and Grumley, M. (1970) *Atlantis: The Autobiography of a Search*, New York: Doubleday.

Figuier, L. (1872) *La terre et les mers*, Paris.

Fine, J. V. A. (1983) *The Ancient Greeks: A Critical History*, Cambridge, Massachusetts and London: Harvard University Press.

Fite, W. (1934) *The Platonic Legend*, New York: Scribner.

Flem-Ath, R. and Flem-Ath, R. (1995) *When the Sky Fell: In Search of Atlantis*, London: Weidenfeld and Nicolson.

Fouqué, F. (1869) 'Une Pompei antehistorique', *Revue des Deux Mondes* 1869, 39.

—— (1879) *Santorin et ses eruptions*, Paris: Maison et Cie.

Forsyth, P. Y. (1980) *Atlantis: The Making of Myth*, Montreal and London: McGill-Queen's University Press and Croom Helm.

Francaviglia, V. (1990) 'Sea-borne pumice deposits of archaeological interest on Aegean and east Mediterranean beaches', in Hardy and Renfrew (eds) 3, 127–34.

Fredericks, S. C. (1978) 'The mythological perspective', in Ramage (ed.) 81–99.

Freeman, E. A. (1892) *Sicily*, New York: Putnam's.

French, E. B. and Wardle, K. A. (eds) (1986) *Problems in Greek History*, Bristol Classical Press.

Friedrich, J. (1957) *Extinct Languages*, London: Peter Owen.

Friedrich, W. L., Wagner, P. and Tauber, H. (1990) 'Radiocarbon dated plant remains from the Akrotiri excavation on Santorini, Greece', in Hardy and Renfrew (eds) 3, 188–96.

Frost, K. T. (1909) 'The lost continent', *The Times*, 19 February 1909.

Frost, K. T. (1913) 'The *Critias* and Minoan Crete', *Journal of Hellenic Studies* 33, 189–206.

Furumark, A. (1980) 'The Thera catastrophe – consequence for European civilization', in Doumas (ed.) 1, 667–74.

Galanopoulos, A. G. (1960) 'Tsunamis observed on the coasts of Greece from antiquity to the present time', *Annali di Geofisica* 13, 3–4.

—— (1969) 'On the location and size of Atlantis', *Praktika Akad. Ath.* 35, 401–18.

Galanopoulos, A. G. and Bacon, E. (1969) *Atlantis: The Truth Behind the Legend*, London: Nelson.

Gamble, C. (1980) 'The bronze age animal economy from Akrotiri: a preliminary analysis', in Doumas (ed.) 1, 745–53.

Ganz, T. (1993) *Early Greek Myth*, Baltimore, Maryland: Johns Hopkins University Press.

Gardiner, A. H. (1909) *The Admonitions of an Egyptian Sage*, Leipzig.

Gattefosse, R-M. (1923) *La verite sur l'Atlantide*, Lyon: Legendre.

Gattefosse, J. and Roux, C. (1926) *Bibliographie de l'Atlandide et des questions connexes*, Cannes.

Germain, L. (1924) 'L'Atlantide', *Revue Scientifique* 62, 455–63; 481–91.

Gidon, F. (1935) *L'Atlantide*, Paris: Payot.

Gill, C. (1977) 'The genre of the Atlantis story', *Classical Philology* 72, 287–304.

—— (1980) *Plato: The Atlantis Story. Timaeus 17–27, Critias with Introduction, Notes and Vocabulary*, Bristol University: Bristol Classical Press.

Gillis, C. (1990) 'Akrotiri and its neighbours to the south: conical cups again', in Hardy and Renfrew (eds) 1, 98–116.

Giovanni, A. (1985) 'Peut-on demythifier l'Atlantide?', *Museum Helveticum* 42, 151–6.

Giroff, N. (1963) 'L'Atlandide comme une realite scientifique', *Le musée vivant* 27: 3, 425–9.

Graham, J. W. (1987) *The Palaces of Crete*, Princeton, New Jersey: Princeton University Press.

Hackforth, R. (1944) 'The story of Atlantis: its purpose and moral', *Classical Review* 58, 7–9.

Hägg, R. and Marinatos, N. (eds) (1982) *The Minoan Thalassocracy: Myth and Reality: Proceedings of the Third International Symposium at the Swedish Institute in Athens, 1982*, Stockholm.

—— (eds) (1984) *Sanctuaries and Cults in the Agean Bronze Age*, Stockholm: Swedish Institute in Athens.

—— (eds) (1987) *The Function of the Minoan Palaces: Proceedings of the Fourth International Symposium at the Swedish Institute in Athens, 10–16 July 1984*, Stockholm.

Hammer, C. U. and Clausen, H. B. (1990) 'The precision of ice-core dating', in Hardy and Renfrew (eds) 3, 174–8.

Hankey, V. (1993) 'A Theban "battle axe": Queen Aahotpe and the Minoans', *Minerva* 4: 3, 13–14.

Hapgood, C. (1970) *Maps of the Ancient Sea-kings*, Philadelphia: Chilton Publishers.

Hardie, W. F. R. (1936) *A Study in Plato*, Oxford: Clarendon Press.

Hardy, D. A. and Renfrew, A. C. (eds) (1990) *Thera and the Aegean World III. Proceedings of the Third International Congress, Santorini, Greece, 3–9 September 1989*, 3 vols, London: Thera Foundation.

Hedervari, P. (1968) 'Volcanophysical investigations on the energetics of the Minoan eruption of Volcano Santorin', *Bulletin volcanique* 32, 439–61.

—— (1971) 'Energetical calculations concerning the Minoan eruption of Santorini', in *Acta of the First Scientific Congress on the Volcano of Thera*, 257–76.

—— (1980) 'Geonomic notes on the bronze age eruption of Santorini', in Doumas (ed.) 1, 153–70.

Heezen, B. C., Tharp, M. and Ewing, M. (1959) 'The floors of the oceans: 1, the North Atlantic', *Geological Society of America*, Special Paper 65.

Heiken, G. and McCoy, F. (1990) 'Precursory activity to the Minoan eruption, Thera', in Hardy and Renfrew (eds) 2, 79–87.

Heiken, G., McCoy, F. and Sheridan, M. (1990) 'Palaeotopographic and palaeogeologic reconstruction of Minoan Thera', in Hardy and Renfrew (eds) 2, 370–6.

Hermann, A. (1927) 'Atlantis, Tartessos und die Saulen des Herakles', *Pettermanns Geographische Mitteilungen* 73, 288.

Hesiod (1953) *Theogony*, trans N. O. Brown, New York: Bobbs-Merrill.

Hess, J. (1962) 'History of ocean basins', pp. 599–620 in Engle, A. E. J. *et al.* (eds) *Petrologic Studies*, Colorado: Geological Society of America.

Hildreth, W. (1990) 'The Katmai eruption of 1912: a comparison', in Hardy and Renfrew (eds) 2, 455–62.

Hiller, S. (1980) 'Minoan *qe-ra-si-ja*: the religious impact of the Thera volcano on Minoan Crete', in Doumas (ed.) 1, 675–80.

—— (1990) 'The miniature frieze in the West House – evidence for Minoan poetry?', in Hardy and Renfrew (eds) 1, 229–34.

Hockmann, O. (1980) 'Theran Floral Style in relation to that of Crete', in Doumas (ed.), 1, 605–16.

Hoffmann, P. (1953) 'Snorre Sturlasson and Atlantis', *Atlantis* (London) 5, 102–4.

Homer (1946) *Odyssey*, trans E. V. Rieu, Harmondsworth: Penguin.

Hood, M. S. F. (1971) *The Minoans: Crete in the Bronze Age*, London: Thames and Hudson.

—— (1978) 'Traces of the eruption outside Thera', in Doumas (ed.) 1, 680–98.

—— (1984) 'A Minoan empire in the Aegean in the sixteenth and fifteenth centuries BC?' in Hägg and Marinatos (eds) 33–7.

—— (1990) 'The Cretan element on Thera in LMIA', in Hardy and Renfrew (eds) 1, 118–23.

—— (1995) 'The Minoan palace as residence of gods and men', *International Cretological Congress* A1, 393–407.

Hope, M. (1991) *Atlantis: Myth or Reality?* London: Arkana.

Hubberten, H-W., Bruns, M., Calamiotou, M., Apostolakis, C., Fillippakis, S. and Grimanis, A. (1990) 'Radiocarbon dates from the Akrotiri excavations', in Hardy and Renfrew (eds) 3, 179–87.

Huijsmans, J. and Barton, M. (1990) 'New stratigraphic data for the Megalo Vouno Complex', in Hardy and Renfrew (eds) 2, 422–3.

Hutchinson, R. W. (1962) *Prehistoric Crete*, Harmondsworth: Penguin.

Iakovides, S. (1979) 'Thera and Mycenaean Greece', *American Journal of Archaeology* 83, 101–2.

Immerwahr, S. A. (1977) 'Mycenaeans at Thera: some reflections on the paintings from the West House', in Kinzl, K. H. (ed.) *Greece and the Eastern Mediterranean in Ancient History and Prehistory*, 173–91. Berlin.

—— (1990) 'Swallows and dolphins at Akrotiri: some thoughts on the relationship of vase-painting to wall-painting', in Hardy and Renfrew (eds) 1, 237–44.

James, P. (1995) *The Sunken Kingdom: The Atlantis Mystery Solved*, London: Jonathan Cape.

Joleaud, L. (1924) 'L'histoire biogeographique de l'Amerique et la theorie de Wegener', *Journale de la Societé Americanistes de Paris*, 16.

Jowett, B. (1892) *The Dialogues of Plato*, Oxford: Clarendon Press.

Kagan, D. (1987) *The Fall of the Athenian Empire*, Ithaca, New York and London: Cornell University Press.

Kamienski, M. (1956) 'The date of the submersion of Poseidonia', *Atlantis* (London) 9, 43–8.

Karageorghis, V. (1990) 'Rites de passage at Thera: some oriental comparanda', in Hardy and Renfrew (eds) 1, 67–71.

Karlsson, L. (1992) *Fortification Towers and Masonry Techniques in the Hegemony of Syracuse, 405–211 BC*, Stockholm: Swedish Institute in Rome.

Katsa-Tomara, L. (1990) 'The pottery-producing system at Akrotiri: an index of exchange and social activity', in Hardy and Renfrew (eds) 1, 31–40.

Keller, J. (1971) 'The major volcanic events in recent Mediterranean volcanism and their bearing on the problem of Santorini ash layers', in *Acta of the First International Scientific Conference on the Volcano of Thera*, Athens: Archaeological Services of Greece.

—— (1980) 'Prehistoric pumice tephra on Aegean islands', in Doumas (ed.) 2, 49–56.

Keller, J., Rehren, T. and Stadlbaurer, E. (1990) 'Explosive volcanism in the Hellenic Arc: a summary and review', in Hardy and Renfrew (eds) 2, 13–26.

Kilikoglou, V., Doumas, C., Papagiannopoulou, A., Sayre, E. V., Maniatis, Y. and Grimanis, A. P. (1990) 'A study of Middle and Late Cycladic pottery from Akrotiri', in Hardy and Renfrew (eds) 1, 441–4.

Kuniholm, P. (1990) 'Overview and assessment of the evidence for the date of the eruption of Thera', in Hardy and Renfrew (eds) 3, 13–8.

Laffineur, R. (1990) 'Composition and perspective in Theran wall-paintings', in Hardy and Renfrew (eds) 1, 246–50.

Lambrou-Phillipson, C. (1990) 'Thera in the mythology of the classical tradition', in Hardy and Renfrew (eds) 1, 162–9.

Lee, H. D. P. (trans) (1971) *Plato: Timaeus and Critias*, Harmondsworth: Penguin.

Levinson, R. B. (1953) *In Defense of Plato*, Cambridge, Massachusetts: Harvard University Press.

Levy, E. (ed.) (1987) *Le systeme palatial en Orient, en Grece et a Rome: Actes du Colloque de Strasbourg 19–22 juin 1985*, Strasbourg.

Limbrey, S. (1990) 'Soil studies at Akrotiri', in Hardy and Renfrew (eds) 2, 377–90.

Linforth, I. (1919) *Solon the Athenian*, Berkeley and Los Angeles: University of California Press.

Luce, J. V. (1969) *The End of Atlantis*, London: Thames and Hudson.

—— (1976) 'Thera and the devastation of Minoan Crete: a new interpretation of the evidence', *American Journal of Archaeology* 80, 9–16.

—— (1978) 'The sources and literary form of Plato's Atlantis narrative', in Ramage (ed.) 1978, 49–78.

McCoy, F. (1980) 'The upper Thera (Minoan) ash in deep-sea sediment: distribution and comparison with other ash layers', in Doumas (ed.) 2, 57–78.

—— (1992) 'Site unseen: with ground-probing radar, archaeologists can find buried ruins without lifting a shovel', *Earthwatch* March/April, 6–7.

MacGillivray, J. A. (1990) 'The Therans and Dikta', in Hardy and Renfrew (eds) 1, 363–9.

—— (1994) 'The early history of the palace at Knossos', in Evely *et al.* (eds) 45–55.

MacGillivray, J. A. and Barber R. L. N. (eds) (1984) *The Prehistoric Cyclades*, Edinburgh: Edinburgh University Press.

McKenzie, D. P. (1970) 'Plate tectonics of the Mediterranean region', *Nature* 226, 242.

McKusick, M. and Shinn, E. A. (1980) 'Bahamian Atlantis reconsidered', *Nature* 287, 11–2.

Mage, S. (1981) 'Plato and the catastrophist tradition', *Kronos* VI: 2, 33–46.

Malaise, R. (1949) 'The possibility of the Egyptian and Atlantean cultures having been contemporary', *Atlantean Research* 2: 4, 58–60.

Mamet, H. (1874) *De insula Thera*, Lille: Ernest Thorin.

Manning, S. (1988) 'The bronze age eruption of Thera: absolute dating, Aegean chronology and Mediterranean cultural interrelations', *Journal of Mediterranean Archaeology* 1, 17–82.

Marinatos, N. (1984) *Art and Religion in Thera: Reconstructing a Bronze Age Society*, Athens: Mathioulakis.

—— (1990) 'Minoan–Cycladic syncretism', in Hardy and Renfrew (eds) 1, 370–6.

Marinatos, S. (1939) 'The volcanic destruction of Minoan Crete', *Antiquity* 13, 425–39.

—— (1950) 'On the Atlantis legend', *Cretica Chronica* 4, 195–213.

—— (1968) 'The volcano of Thera and the states of the Aegean', *Acta of the Second Cretological Congress, 1967*, 1, 198–216.

—— (1968–76) *Excavations at Thera, I–VII*, Athens.

—— (1971a) *Some Words About the Legend of Atlantis*, Athens: Archaiologicon Deltion, 12.

—— (1971b) 'On the chronological sequence of Thera's catastrophes', in *Acta of the First Scientific Congress on the Volcano of Thera*, 403–6.

Marinos, G. and Melidonis, N. (1971) 'On the strength of seaqualles (*tsumanis*) during the prehistoric eruptions of Santorini' in *Acta of the First International Scientific Congress on the Volcano of Thera*, Athens: Archaeological Services of Greece.

Marketou, T. (1990) 'Santorini tephra from Rhodes and Kos: some chronological remarks based on the stratigraphy', in Hardy and Renfrew (eds) 3, 100–13.

Marthari, M. (1984) 'The destruction of the town at Akrotiri, Thera, at the beginning of LCI: definition and chronology', in MacGillivray and Barber (eds) 1984, 119–33.

—— (1990) 'The chronology of the last phases of occupation at Akrotiri in the light of the evidence from the West House pottery groups', in Hardy and Renfrew (eds) 3, 57–70.

Marthari, M., Marketou, T. and Jones, R. E. (1990) 'LBI ceramic connections between Thera and Kos', in Hardy and Renfrew (eds) 1, 171–84.

Martin, T. H. (1841) *Etudes sur la Timee*, vol. 1, 272. Paris.

Martina, A. (1968) *Solon: Testimonianze sulla Vita e L'opera*, Roma: Edizioni dell'Ateneo.

Matsas, D. (1991) 'Samothrace and the north-eastern Aegean: the Minoan connection', *Studia Troica* 1, 159–79.

Mavor, J. W. (1969) *Voyage to Atlantis*, London: Souvenir Press.

Meiggs, R. (1972) *The Athenian Empire*, Oxford: Clarendon Press.

Melas, E. M. (1988) 'Minoans overseas: alternative models of interpretation', *Aegeum* 2, 47–70.

Mertz, H. (1976) *Atlantis, Dwelling Place of the Gods*, Chicago: Swallow Press.

Michailidou, A. (1990) 'The lead weights from Akrotiri: the archaeological record', in Hardy and Renfrew (eds) 1, 407–19.

Michell, J. (1969) *The View over Atlantis*, London: Sago Press.

Morgan, L. (1988) *The Miniature Wall-Paintings of Thera: A Study in Aegean Culture and Iconography*, Cambridge: Cambridge University Press.

Morkot, R. (1996) *The Penguin Historical Atlas of Ancient Greece*, Harmondsworth: Penguin.

Morrow, G. R. (1960) *Plato's Cretan City*, Princeton, New Jersey: Princeton University Press.

Muck, O. (1976) *The Secret of Atlantis*, London: William Collins.

Muhly, J. (1991) 'Egypt, the Aegean and late bronze age chronology in the eastern Mediterranean: a review article', *Journal of Mediterranean Archaeology* 4, 235–47.

Murray, G. (1898) *A History of Ancient Greek Literature*, London: Heinemann.

Negbi, O. (1978) 'The miniature fresco from Thera and the emergence of Mycenaean art', in Doumas (ed.) 1, 645–56.

Nelson, D. E., Vogel, J. S. and Southon, J. R. (1990) 'Another suite of confusing radio-carbon dates for the destruction of Akrotiri', in Hardy and Renfrew (eds) 3, 197–205.

Niemeier, W-D. (1990) 'Mycenaean elements in the miniature fresco from Thera?' in Hardy and Renfrew (eds) 1, 267–82.

—— (1994) 'Knossos in the New Palace Period', in Evely et al. (eds) 71–88.

Ninkovich, D. and Heezen, B. C. (1965) 'Santorini tephra', in Submarine Geology and Geophysics, Colston Papers 17, 413–53.

Noroff, A. S. (1854) Die Atlantis nach Griechischen und Arabischen Quelles, St Petersburg.

Page, D. L. (1970) The Santorini Volcano and the Desolation of Minoan Crete, London: Society for the Promotion of Hellenic Studies.

Palyvou, C. (1984) 'The destruction of the town at Akrotiri, Thera at the beginning of LCI: rebuilding activities', in MacGillivray and Barber (eds) 1984, 134–47.

—— (1986) 'Notes on the town plan of LC Akrotiri, Thera', Annual of the British School at Athens 81, 179–94.

—— (1990) 'Architecural design at Late Cycladic Akrotiri', in Hardy and Renfrew (eds), 1, 44–56.

Papadopoulos, G. (1990) 'Deterministic and stochastic models of the seismic and volcanic events in the Santorini volcano', in Hardy and Renfrew (eds) 2, 151–9.

Papagiannopoulou, A. (1990) 'Some changes in the bronze age pottery production at Akrotiri and their possible implications', in Hardy and Renfrew (eds) 1, 57–66.

Parry, R. L. (1997) 'Exact date for the Ulu Burun wreck', Minerva 8: 1, 4.

Pashley, R. (1835) Travels in Crete.

Pegues, l'Abbe (1842) Histoire de Santorin ou Thera, Paris.

Pellegrino, C. (1991) Unearthing Atlantis, New York: Vintage.

Pendlebury, J. D. S. (1939) The Archaeology of Crete, London.

Pennick, N. (1987) Lost Lands and Sunken Cities, London: Fortean Tomes.

Perissoratis, C. (1990) 'Marine geological research on Santorini: preliminary results', in Hardy and Renfrew (eds) 2, 305–11.

Petruso, K. M. (1980) 'Lead weights from Akrotiri: preliminary observations', in Doumas (ed.) 1, 547–54.

Phelan, W. P. (1903) Our Story of Atlantis, San Francisco: Hermetic Brotherhood.

Phillips, E. D. (1968) 'Historical elements in the myth of Atlantis', Euphrosyne 2, 3–38.

Pichler, H. and Friedrich, W. L. (1980) 'Mechanism of the Minoan eruption of Santorini', in Doumas (ed.) 2, 15–30.

Pichler, H. and Schiering, W. (1977) 'The Thera eruption and Late Minoan IB destruc-tions on Crete', Nature 267, 819–22.

Platon, N. (1968) Crete, Geneva: Nagel.

—— (1971) Zakros: The Discovery of a Lost Palace of Ancient Crete, New York: Scribner's.

Podlecki, A. J. (1984) The Early Greek Poets and Their Times, Vancouver: University of British Columbia Press.

Poisson, G. (1945) L'Atlantide devant la science, Paris.

Pomerance, L. (1970) 'The final collapse of Thera', Studies in Mediterranean Archaeology 26.

Popper, K. R. (1945) The Open Society and its Enemies, London: Routledge.

Poursat, J-C. (1990) 'Craftsmen and traders at Thera: a view from Crete', in Hardy and Renfrew (eds) 1, 124–7.

Presiozi, D. (1983) *Minoan Architectural Design*, The Hague: Mouton.

Puchelt, H. (1980) 'Evolution of the volcanic rocks of Santorini', in Doumas (ed.) 1, 131–46.

Pyle, D. M. (1990) 'New estimates for the volume of the Minoan eruption', in Hardy and Renfrew (eds) 2, 113–21.

Rackham, O. (1980) 'The flora and vegetation of Thera and Crete before and after the great eruption', in Doumas (ed.) 1, 755–64.

Ramage, E. S. (ed.) (1978) *Atlantis: Fact or Fiction?* Bloomington and London: Indiana University Press.

Rapp, G. and Kraft, J. C. (1980) 'Aegean sea level changes in the bronze age', in Doumas (ed.) 1, 183–94.

Rauschning, H. (1939) *Hitler Speaks*, London.

Reiche, H. A. T. (1981) 'The language of archaic astronomy: a clue to the Atlantis myth?' in Brecher, K. and Feirtag, M. (eds) *Astronomy of the Ancients*, Cambridge, Massachusetts: MIT Press.

Renfrew, A. C. (1978a) 'The Mycenaean sanctuary at Phylakopi', *Antiquity* 52, 7–15.

—— (1978b) 'Phylakopi and the Late Bronze I period in the Cyclades', in Doumas (ed.) 1, 403–21.

—— (1980) 'Phylakopi and the LBI period in the Cyclades', in Doumas (ed.), 1, 403–21.

—— (1981) 'The sanctuary at Phylakopi', in Hägg and Marinatos (eds), 1984, 67–79.

Renfrew, A. C. and Cherry, J. F. (eds) (1986) *Power Polity Interaction*, Cambridge: Cambridge University Press.

Reshetov, V. (1961) 'The mythology of the Greeks in relation to the Atlantis legend', *Atlantis* (London) 14, 83–90.

Rexine, J. (1975) 'Atlantis: fact or fantasy', *Classical Bulletin* 51, 49–53.

Romm, J. S. (1992) *The Edges of the Earth in Ancient Thought*, Princeton, New Jersey: Princeton University Press.

Rosenmeyer, T. G. (1949) 'The family of Critias', *American Journal of Philology* 70, 404–10.

—— (1956) 'Plato's Atlantis myth: Timaeus or Critias', *Phoenix* 10, 163–72.

Rousseau-Liesens, A. (1956) *Les colonnes d'Hercule et l'Atlantide*, Brussels.

Rudbeck, O., Von (1675) *Atlantica*, Uppsala.

Russell, B. (1946) *History of Western Philosophy*, London: Allen and Unwin.

Saflund, G. (1987) 'The agoge of the Minoan youth as reflected by palatial iconography', in Hägg and Marinatos (eds) 1987, 227–33.

Sakellarakis, J. A. (1990) 'The fashioning of ostrich-egg rhyta in the Creto-Mycenaean Aegean', in Hardy and Renfrew (eds) 1, 285–308.

Sakellariou, A. (1980) 'The West House miniature frescoes', in Doumas (ed.) 2, 147–53.

Sali-Axioti, T. (1990) 'The lightwell of the House of the Ladies and its structural behaviour', in Hardy and Renfrew (eds) 1, 437–40.

Sanders, L. J. (1987) *Dionysius I of Syracuse and Greek Tyranny*, London: Croom Helm.

Sayre, K. M. (1994) *Plato's Analytic Method*, Aldershot: Gregg Revivals.

Scarre, C. (1988) 'A new date for an old disaster', *Current Archaeology* 111, 134–6.

Schachermeyr, F. (1978) 'Akrotiri – first maritime republic?' in Doumas (ed.) 1, 423–8.

Schofield, E. (1982) 'The western Cyclades and Crete: a "special relationship"', *Oxford Journal of Archaeology* 1, 9–25.

—— (1984) 'Destruction deposits of the earlier Late Bronze Age from Ayia Irini, Kea', in MacGillivray and Barber (eds) 179–83.

Schulten, A. (1927) 'Tartessos und Atlantis', *Pettermanns Geographische Mitteilungen* 73, 284.

Scott-Elliott, W. (1962) *The Story of Atlantis and the Lost Lemuria*, London: Theosophical Publishing House.

Seward, D. and Wagner, G. A. (1980) 'Fission track ages of Santorini volcanoes', in Doumas (ed.), 101–8.

Shaw, J. W. (1977) 'Excavations at Kommos (Crete) during 1976', *Hesperia* 46, 199–240.

—— (1980) 'Akrotiri as a Minoan settlement', in Doumas (ed.) 1, 429–36.

—— (1990) 'Bronze age Aegean harboursides', in Hardy and Renfrew (eds) 1, 420–36.

Sigurdsson, H., Carey, S. and Devine, J. D. (1990) 'Assessment of mass, dynamics and environmental effects of the Minoan eruption of Santorini volcano', in Hardy and Renfrew (eds) 2, 100–12.

Soles, J. S. and Davaras, C. (1990) 'Theran ash in Minoan Crete: new excavations on Mochlos', in Hardy and Renfrew (eds) 3, 89–95.

Sotirakopoulou, C. (1990) 'The earliest history of Akrotiri: the late neolithic and early bronze age phases', in Hardy and Renfrew (eds) 3, 41–7.

Spanuth, J. (1956) *Atlantis: The Mystery Unravelled*, London: Arco.

—— (1979) *Atlantis of the North*, London: Sidgwick and Jackson.

Sparks, R. and Wilson, C. J. (1990) 'The Minoan deposits: a review of their characteristics and interpretation', in Hardy and Renfrew (eds) 2, 89–99.

Spence, L. (1924) *The Problem of Atlantis*, New York: Brentano's.

—— (1995) *History of Atlantis*, London: Rider and Co.

Stacy-Judd, R. (1939) *Atlantis: Mother of Empires*, Santa Monica: DeVorss and Co.

Stahel, H. R. (1982) *Atlantis Illustrated*, New York: Grosset and Dunlap.

Steiger, B. (1973) *Atlantis Rising*, New York: Dell.

Steiner, R. (1928) *Unserer Atlantischen Vorfahren*, Berlin; trans K. Zimmer (1959) as *Cosmic Memory, Atlantis and Lemuria*, Blauvelt, New York: Multimedia Publishing.

Stewart, J. A. (1904) *The Myths of Plato*, London: Macmillan.

Stos-Gale, Z. A. and Gale, N. H. (1984) 'The Minoan thalassocracy and the Aegean metal trade', in Hägg and Marinatos (eds) 59–64.

—— (1990) 'The role of Thera in the bronze age trade in metals', in Hardy and Renfrew (eds) 1, 72–92.

Sullivan, D. G. (1990) 'Minoan tephra in lake sediments in western Turkey', in Hardy and Renfrew (eds) 3, 114–18.

Sullivan, D. and Wilder, J. (undated) *Ancient and Sacred Sites of the Cotswolds*, Cheltenham: Gem Publications.

Sykes, E. (1950) 'Orichalcum', *Atlantean Research* 2: 6, 85.

Tarling, D. H. and Tarling, M. P. (1972) *Continental Drift*, Harmondsworth: Pelican.

Taylor, A. E. (1926) *Plato*, London: Methuen.

—— (1928) *A Commentary on Plato's Timaeus*, Oxford: Clarendon Press.

—— (1929) *Plato: Timaeus and Critias*, London: Methuen.

Taylor, T. (1820) *Proclus: Commentaries on the Timaeus of Plato*, London.

Taylour, Lord W. (1964) *The Mycenaeans*, London: Thames and Hudson.

Televantou, C. (1990) 'New light on the West House wall-paintings', in Hardy and Renfrew (eds) 1, 309–24.

Ternier, P. (1915) 'Atlantis', *Annual Report of the Smithsonian Institution* 219–34.

Thorarinsson, S. (1971) 'Damage caused by tephra fall in some big Icelandic eruptions and its relation to the thickness of tephra layers', in *Acta of the First International*

Scientific Congress on the Volcano of Thera, Athens: Archaeological Services of Greece, 213–36.

Tournier, I. (1950) 'The orichalcum of the Atlanteans', *Atlantean Research* 2: 6, 86–7.

Tzachili, I. (1990) 'All important yet elusive: looking for evidence of cloth-making at Akrotiri', in Hardy and Renfrew (eds) 1, 380–9.

Van Andel, T. H. (1989) 'Late Quaternary sea-level changes and archaeology', *Antiquity* 63, 733–45.

—— (1990) 'Addendum to "Late Quaternary sea level changes and archaeology"', *Antiquity* 64, 151–2.

Vaughan, S. J. (1990) 'Petrographic analysis of the Early Cycladic wares from Akrotiri', in Hardy and Renfrew (eds) 1, 470–87.

Velikovsky, I. (1950) *Worlds in Collision*, London: Gollancz.

Vermeule, E. T. (1975) *The Art of the Shaft Graves of Mycenae*, Norman: University of Oklahoma Press.

Vickery, K. F. (1936) 'Food in early Greece', *Illinois Studies in the Social Sciences* 20, 3.

Vidal-Naquet, P. (1964) 'Athenes et l'Atlantide', *Revue des Etudes Grecques* 77, 420–44.

Vitaliano, D. (1971) 'Atlantis: a review essay', *Journal of the Folklore Institute* 8, 68–76.

—— (1978) 'Atlantis from the geologic point of view', in Ramage (ed.) 1978, 137–60.

—— (1980) 'Tephrochronological evidence for the time of the bronze age eruption of Thera', in Doumas (ed.) 1, 217–20.

Vlastos, G. (1975) *Plato's Universe*, University of Washington Press.

Wagstaff, J. M. and Gamble, C. (1982) 'Island resources and their limitations', in Renfrew C. and Wagstaff M. (eds) *An Island Polity: The Archaeology of Exploitation in Melos*, Cambridge: Cambridge University Press, 95–105.

Walcot, P. (1966) *Hesiod and the Near East*, Cardiff University Press.

Warlow, P. (1982) *The Reversing Earth*, London: Dent.

Warren, P. (1967) 'Minoan stone vases as evidence for Minoan foreign connexions in the Aegean late bronze age', *Proceedings of the Prehistoric Society* 33, 37–55.

—— (1979) 'The miniature fresco from the West House at Akrotiri, Thera, and its Aegean setting', *Journal of Hellenic Studies* 99, 115–29.

—— (1980) 'The unfinished red marble jar at Akrotiri, Thera', in Doumas (ed.), 515–70.

—— (1984) 'Absolute dating of the bronze age eruption of Thera', *Nature* 308, 492–3.

—— (1987) 'Absolute dating of the Aegean Late Bronze Age', *Archaeometry* 29, 205–11.

—— (1988) 'Further arguments against an early date', *Archaeometry* 30, 176–9.

Warren, P. M. and Hankey, V. (1989) *Aegean Bronze Age Chronology*, Bristol: Classical Press.

Warren, P. M. and Puchelt, H. (1990) 'Stratified pumice from bronze age Knossos', in Hardy and Renfrew (eds) 3, 71–81.

Watkins, N. D. *et al.* (1978) 'Volume and extent of the Minoan tephra from the Santorini volcano', *Nature* 271, 122–6.

Welliver, W. (1977) *Character, Plot and Thought in Plato's Timaeus–Critias*, Leiden: Brill.

Weninger, B. (1990) 'Theoretical radiocarbon discrepancies', in Hardy and Renfrew (eds) 3, 220–31.

Whishaw, E. M. (1928) *Atlantis in Andalucia*, London: Rider.

Wiener, M.H. (1990) 'The isles of Crete? The Minoan thalassocracy revisited', in Hardy and Renfrew (eds) 1, 128–60.

Willetts, R. F. (1965) *Ancient Crete: A Social History*, London: Routledge and Kegan Paul.

Williams, D. F. (1978) 'A petrological examination of pottery from Thera', in Doumas (ed.) 507–14.

Wilson, J. T. (ed.) (1976) *Continents Adrift and Continents Aground*, San Francisco: W. H. Freeman.

Wilson, L. (1980) 'Energetics of the Minoan eruption: some revisions', in Doumas (ed.) 2, 31–6.

Wright, H. E. (1978) 'Glacial fluctuations, sea level changes and catastrophic floods', in Ramage (ed.) 161–74.

Woudhuizen, F. (1992) *The Language of the Sea Peoples*, Amsterdam: Najade Press.

Yokoyama, I. (1980) 'The tsunami caused by the prehistoric eruption of Thera', in Doumas (ed.) 1, 277–86.

Yokoyama, I. and Bonasia, V. (1971) 'A preliminary gravity survey on Thera Volcano, Greece', pp. 328–36 in *Acta of the First Scientific Congress on the Volcano of Thera*, Athens: Archaeological Services of Greece.

Zangger, E. (1992) *The Flood from Heaven*, London: Sidgwick and Jackson.

Zangger, E. (1993) 'Plato's Atlantis account – a distorted recollection of the Trojan War', *Oxford Journal of Archaeology* 12: 1, 77–87.

Zhirov, N. (1958) 'The Paul Schliemann mystery', *Atlantis* (London) 11, 23–4.

—— (1970) *Atlantis*, Moscow: Progress Publishers.

Zink, D. (1978) *The Stones of Atlantis*, New York: Prentice-Hall.

INDEX

Achaea 161
Achradina (Syracuse) 156, 158, 179
adyton ('lustral basin') 23, 100, 101, 103, 107, 138
Aegean Sea 6, 8, 25, 134, 154
Aeschylus 28
Africa 4, 5, 6, 70, 182, 183
agon 95, 99
agriculture 66–7
Ahmose 125–6, 192
Akrotiri 8, 11, 15, 16, 17, 41, 42, 43–55, 70, 72, 74, 77, 97, 172, 173; Building 1 (Xeste 3) 19, 44, 45, 64, 74, 99–113, 120; Building 2 (Block Gamma) 44, 48, 51; Building 3 44; Building 4 (West House) 22, 38, 44, 46, 48, 53, 55, 60, 61, 7, 75–9, 90–9, 191, 192, 195; Building 5 44; Building 6 (House of the Ladies) 39, 44, 54, 84–6, 119; Building 7 44; Building 8 44; Building 9 44; Building 10 44; Building 11 (Block Beta) 44, 48, 51, 82, 86–8; Building 12 (Block Delta) 39, 43, 44, 45; Building 13 (Block Delta) 44, 45, 89, 115; Building 14 44; Building 15 (Xeste 4) 44, 52, 106; Building 16 44; Building 17 (Xeste 2) 44, 53, 114, 116; Building 18 44; Building 19 (Xeste 5) 44; Building 20 44; destruction 114–26; East Square 44, 50, 53, 114; North Square 39, 44, 50; South Square 44, 50; Spring Fresco 43; Telchines Street 44, 45, 48, 50, 51, 52, 115; Triangle Square 44, 45, 50, 53, 55, 99, 116
Alcibiades 160
Alcinous, King 157
altar, incurved 109
Amasis 167
Amnisos (Crete) 26, 69, 124, 129, 135

Amorgos 6, 129
Anafi 122, 124
Anatolia 6, 10, 23, 60, 68, 69, 70, 73, 97, 124, 125, 129, 141, 164, 172, 174
Andikythera 6
Andimelos 69
Andros 6
Anemospilia (Crete) 33
Anemospilia temple (Crete) 103
Antarctica 182
antelope 82, 86, 88
Antiparos 19
Apuleius 77
Arcadia 161
architecture 48, 51, 52, 53, 54, 56, 72, 73, 90, 91, 96, 97, 98, 100, 101, 106, 107, 133, 138–40, 142, 173, 174
Argolis 161
Argos 94
Ariston 165
Aristotle 200
Arkhanes (Crete) 135
Arvanitis, Stathis, 37
ashfall 116, 118, 119, 120, 121, 124, 125, 131–2, 168, 175
Asia 3, 5, 137, 138, 178
Aspronisi (Santorini) 8, 9
Astipalaia 69
Athena 3, 179
Athenian Acropolis 28–30, 172
Athens 1, 2, 3, 6, 7, 28–31, 34, 128, 151, 154, 155, 158, 159, 160, 161, 163, 166, 170, 171, 172, 174, 175, 177, 178, 179, 180
Atlantic Ocean (modern sense) 4, 168, 176, 178, 181, 182, 183, 184, 185, 186
Atlantis: age 2, 24, 144, 179, 181; architecture 22, 47, 48, 80, 101, 138–40, 157; army 2, 3; art 2;

destruction and disappearance 4, 9, 128, 135; dress 25; empire 26; fall from grace 159, 179; fortification 29; geared for war 179, 203; geography 3, 4, 8, 94–9, 134, 137, 144, 150, 157, 178, 186; harbours 20, 137, 157; houses 44, 46; invasion 3; kings 80, 163; location 3, 4, 178; metropolis 14, 46; pillar 145; population 26, 97–8; religion 23, 25, 112; size 3, 5, 134, 150, 172; society 98, 99, 106, 112; street plans 18, 21, 44, 48, 50; submergence 6, 8, 128, 150; temples 80, 138–9, 144; wealth 7, 24, 144
Atlantis (Hellanicus) 164, 177
Atlantis Panorama Fresco (Building 4 frieze) 56, 72, 75, 77–9, 90–9
Attica 161
Australis, Terra 182
Ayia Irini (Kea) 17, 20, 22, 23, 30, 32–4, 51, 72, 73, 74, 83, 86, 94, 97, 98, 109, 131, 136, 173
Ayia Triadha (Crete) 61, 62, 103, 104, 131, 135, 157, 162
Azores 187, 190
Azov, Sea of 182

Bacon, Francis 182
Baikie, James 26
Balos 16, 46, 120
Bankos Reef 9
bed 45, 64
Berlitz, Charles 187
Bermuda Triangle 187
Black Sea 69
Blest, Isles of the 164
Blue Monkeys Fresco 82
Bodrum (Anatolia) 69
bog-oak, Irish 191
book 31
Boxing Boys Fresco 82, 86—8
boys 61, 86–8, 90, 98, 103–7, 110, 113, 143, 161
Boys Initiation Fresco 103–7
breasts, exposed 85, 101
Bulgaria 69
bull-leaping ritual 25, 139, 140, 147, 173
bull sacrifice 25, 145, 147
burial 71

cabin 99
caldera, Theran 8, 9, 10, 11, 21, 35, 37, 55, 56, 117, 120, 121–2, 151, 175

calibration of radiocarbon dates 192
Callipus 155
Carthage 154, 158, 159, 179, 180
Carthaginian Wars 154
Caskey, John 32–3, 74.
Catania, Plain of (Sicily) 179
cattle 66
Chadwick, John 74
Charmides 165, 177
Childress, David 189
China 125
chronology, alteration of 169, 170, 176, 179–80
Cleinias 138
Cleisthenes 163
Cleito 112, 138, 164
climate 66, 138, 174
coastline 46, 118, 124, 128, 187, 190
colony, Minoan 33
comet 187
copper 71
Corfu 74
Corinth 160, 161
cornice 52, 53, 54
Cranaus 28
Crantor 167, 168
Crete 5, 6, 7, 10, 14, 17, 19, 21, 22, 26, 32, 42, 58, 60, 61, 66, 67, 70, 73, 80, 84, 94, 98, 99, 103, 121, 124, 129, 134, 136, 137, 150, 154, 162, 168, 172, 175, 176, 181
Critias 1, 2, 164, 165, 176, 177
Critias 2, 4–5, 8, 14, 28, 29, 66, 67, 70, 76, 79, 89 , 101, 112, 127, 128, 130, 134, 136, 137, 140, 144, 145, 150, 152, 154, 157, 159, 171, 177, 190, 201
crocus 67, 78, 86, 109, 110
Crocus Gatherers Fresco 67
crops 67
Cyclades 17, 19–23
Cycladic culture, Early 19, 20–1
Cyprus 69, 125

Danaus 14
Daniel, Glyn 28
Delos 69
Demosthenes 159, 160
demotic 169
Dendra 70
Deucalion 28
Diodorus 112, 156, 158, 164
Dion 155, 159
Dionysius I 154, 155, 156, 157, 179

Dionysius II 155, 159
dolphin 82
Dombrowski, Daniel 148
Donnelly, Ignatius 182–7, 188, 189, 190
double-axe 43, 62, 80, 104, 139, 145, 146, 147, 174
Doumas, Christos 45, 131
drainage system 48, 51
dress 61–4, 67, 76, 79, 85, 87, 92, 96, 101, 102, 104, 105, 109, 140
Dropides 164, 165, 177, 202

Early Cycladic culture 19, 20–1
Early Minoan culture 20
earthquake 3, 8, 9, 22, 29, 40, 52, 103, 114, 115, 116, 123, 130, 175
Egypt 1, 2, 5, 6, 7, 8, 14, 31, 32, 69, 70–1, 73, 77, 78, 84, 87, 95, 120, 125–6, 141, 147, 151, 167, 168, 169, 171, 175, 176, 177, 178, 191, 192
elephant 70, 136
Etna 192
Etruria 75
Euboea
Eunomia 170
Euripides 28, 127
Evans, Arthur 1, 5, 23, 26, 140–1, 143
Exekestides 165, 202

face painting 64, 99
Faure, Paul 141
feet, terracotta 33
Figuier, Louis 16
Fisher Boys Fresco 90–1
Fletcher, Ron 189
floods 3, 130
Flying Fish Fresco 17
Folegandros 69, 71
Fouque, Ferdinand 15, 16, 25, 37, 80, 191
fortifications 18, 20, 22, 29, 30, 32, 47, 71, 72, 154–5, 156, 173
frescoes 15, 17, 22, 23, 25, 27, 43, 46, 48, 54, 55, 56, 67, 80, 82–9, 90–111, 133, 172
Frost, K. T. 26
furniture 43, 64–5, 196

Galanopoulos, Angelos 34, 37, 169
Giali 59
Gibraltar 137, 158, 168, 178, 182
Gilgamesh 81
girls 67, 83, 101–3, 107, 110
glaciation 187

Glaucon 165, 177
goddess 2, 34, 64, 84, 109–12, 133, 139, 142, 173
gold 60, 74, 138
Gorceix 15–16, 25, 37, 38
Gorgias 148, 152
Gournia (Crete) 52, 97
Grandstand Fresco 25
'Great Green' 168, 176
Greece 25, 68, 70, 94, 128
Greenland 191, 192
griffin 23, 84, 95, 108, 109, 110

hairstyle 104, 105, 106
harbour 47, 49, 56, 127, 131
Hatshepsut 70
Hawara (Egypt) 144
Heaven 110, 189
Heligoland 182
Hellanicus 28, 164
Hellespont 69
helmet 75, 79, 99
Heracles, Pillars of 3, 4, 5, 6, 127, 137, 138, 150, 168, 172, 174, 181
Hermocrates 152, 201
Hermocrates 152, 201
Herodotus 14, 73, 167, 170, 202
Hesiod 80, 164, 177
hieratic 169
hieroglyphs 169, 176
Hitler, Adolf 1
Homer 26, 29, 80, 157
Hood, Sinclair 97, 141–3

Iasos 136
Ida, Mount (Crete) 135, 175
initiation ceremony 45, 61, 64, 87, 98, 99–113, 143
Ios 6, 71, 114, 129
Isocrates 148
Isopata Tomb (Crete) 144
Italy 6
ivory 70, 136, 172

James, Peter 167, 168, 169, 170
Juktas, Mount (Crete) 80, 94, 103, 135

Kadmos 14
Kallisti 14
Kalokairinos, Minos 23
Kameini, Nea (Santorini) 9, 10, 11, 12
Kameini, Palea (Santorini) 9, 10
Karpathos 6, 69

Kastri (Kythera) 74, 127, 136
Kea 19, 20, 32–4, 35, 61, 69, 71, 74, 94, 129, 145, 173, 175
Khania (Crete) 69, 129, 136, 173
kings 55, 141, 145, 162, 163, 173, 174, 179, 196
Kircher, Athanasius 182, 183
Knidos 136
Knossos 1, 5, 6, 17, 22, 23, 24, 26, 28, 33, 34, 39, 48, 52, 59, 64, 69, 70, 80, 85, 94, 99, 101, 111, 112, 122, 128, 135, 136, 138, 139, 140, 141, 151, 173, 174, 197; adyta 108; age 144; Bull Court 138, 142, 145, 157, 173; discovery 23; destruction 7, 22, 82, 127, 131, 170; East Wing 48, 138, 143, 174; Grand Staircase Fresco 103, 106, 107; Great Goddess sanctuary 144; House of the Frescoes 86; Late Dove Goddess Sanctuary 33; Monolithic Pillar Basement 143; Pillar Crypt 142, 145, 146, 174; population 97; Procession Corridor 54, 86, 174; Refectory 147; Silver Vessels Sanctuary 5; Snake Goddess Sanctuary 145; as temple 139–43; Temple Workshops 34, 59; Throne Sanctuary 23, 33, 54, 84, 108; Town Mosaic 80; Tripartite Shrine 94, 142, 145, 147, 173, 200; West Court 25, 52, 142; West Wing 23, 145
Kommos 69, 94, 197
Kos 6, 58, 69, 73
Kouloumbos Reef 10
Krakatao 121–2
Kythera 6, 74, 130
Kythnos 71

Laconia 94, 161
Laconia, Gulf of 6, 172
Laurion 60, 69, 71
Laws 1, 138, 151, 163
Lerna (Peloponnese) 73
Lesbos 6, 164
Leychester, Lt 10
Libya 3, 137, 138, 178
life expectancy 109
lightwell 54, 119
Linear A 16, 37, 80, 181
Linear B 28, 29, 80, 169, 170, 181
Lisbon 123
literacy 28, 29
loom 61
Luce, John 121, 167

lyre 80
Lysander 160
Lysis 152

Mackenzie, Duncan 17
Magnusson, Magnus 40
Mari 69, 141
Malea, Cap 138, 174
Mallia 97, 124, 127, 129, 136, 197
Mamet 15–16, 25, 38
Marinatos, Nanno 85, 86
Marinatos, Spyridon 26–7, 32, 35, 37–42, 43–5, 75, 85, 121, 124, 129, 191, 193, 196
Marsa Matru (north Africa) 69, 70
masonry techniques 39, 52, 71, 146
Mavor, James 34–8, 40–2, 169, 193
Mavros Rachidhi (Thera) 46, 47, 49, 89, 94
measurement 51, 58, 60, 74
Medinet Habu 6, 126
Meeting on the Hill Fresco 92, 94
Megara (Greece) 155, 166, 177
Megaris (Greece) 161
Melos 6, 17, 19, 21, 22, 35, 58, 59, 69, 85, 121, 130, 145, 175
Menderes, River (Anatolia) 95
Menes 170
Menexenus 28, 148
Mesa Vouno (Thera) 12, 14, 37, 46, 56
Mesara, Plain of 8, 66, 70, 134, 135, 138, 174, 181
Messenia (Greece) 94, 161
metal-working 60, 71
Michell, John 189
Mid-Atlantic Ridge 184–6
Middle Cycladic culture 19, 21–2
Miletus (Miletos) 95, 98, 127, 129, 130, 136
Millawanda (Anatolia) 129
Minoan civilization 1, 6, 8, 17, 19, 25–6, 27, 63, 74, 81, 82, 132, 133, 157, 167, 172, 173, 177; end of 27, 30, 121, 128, 130, 133, 177; parallels with Plato's Atlantis 173–5, 181; rediscovery of 15, 23, 24, 25–6
Minoan culture, Early 20
Minoan trading empire 6, 7, 17, 21, 34, 68–75, 95, 128, 136–7, 147, 150, 175
Minos, King 25, 69, 138, 172
Mokhlos (Crete) 20, 73, 131, 137
monkey 80, 82, 86, 110
Monolithos (Thera) 12, 128

mortar, stone 36, 38, 59, 70, 71
mud surrounding Atlantis 4, 126–7, 136, 175
music 80, 104
Mycenae 6, 7, 15, 29, 61, 68, 70, 73, 74, 75, 80, 128, 141
Mycenean civilization 17, 23, 25, 28–30, 32, 75, 128, 130, 131, 172, 173, 175, 176

Naucratis (Egypt) 167
Naxos 6, 19, 22, 69, 71, 129
Necho II 176, 178
Nicias 159, 160
Nile, River 95, 126, 165, 167
Nile Scene 95
Nirou Khani (Crete) 124
Nova Atlantis 182
nudity 61, 87, 92, 97, 105, 106

obsidian 19, 21, 59
offering and sacrifice 90–1, 101–4, 144
Oia (Thera) 56
orichalchum 157
Ortygia (Syracuse) 155, 156, 157, 158, 179
ostrich egg 70, 172

Palaikastro (Crete) 20, 69, 70, 73, 94, 97, 98, 112, 127, 173
palanquin 99, 197
Panormos (Naxos) 20
papyrus 84, 95
Parian Marble 14
Paroikia (Paros) 21, 136
Paros 6, 19, 59, 129, 130
Pashley, Robert 23
passage, rite of see initiation ceremony
pastoralism 66–7, 92, 94
peak sanctuary 94, 143
Pègues, Abbé 37
Peloponnese 6, 25, 30, 138, 158, 178
Peloponnesian War 28, 154, 160, 160
perception, shift in geographical 57, 70, 150, 180–1
Perictione 165, 176
Petsofa 94
Phaeacians 157
Phaedo 152
Phaedrus 152
Phaistos 26, 127, 135, 136, 173
Philolaus of Croton 148
Philostratus 10

Phira (Thera) 8
Phira Quarry (Thera) 118, 128, 199
Phylakopi (Melos) 17, 18, 21, 22, 23, 51, 58, 69, 70, 72, 73, 74, 83, 97, 127, 131, 136, 173
pier-and-door partition 51, 54, 101, 138, 198
pillar, sacred 145, 146, 147
pillar crypt 51, 85
Pinatubo 199
Pindar 129–30, 168
Piraeus 160, 166
Plato 1, 5, 7, 14, 26, 28, 29, 30, 32, 48, 51, 52, 55, 56, 66, 89, 101, 115, 128, 130, 138, 139, 144, 145, 147–68, 172, 173, 175, 178, 179, 180, 181, 187, 190, 202
Platon, Nicolas 27, 35
Pleistocene Ice Age 187
Pliny 144
Plutarch 166, 170
poetry 80, 81, 155, 171
Politicus 153
Poseidon 9, 52, 55, 80, 112, 125, 127, 129, 130, 138, 139, 140, 145, 147, 164, 173, 193
Potamos ravine 16, 128
Potnia 139
pottery 58–9, 64, 70, 72, 73, 74, 80, 85
preservation of tradition 29, 30–1
priestesses 25, 63, 91, 139, 141, 143, 174
priests, Egyptian 32, 165, 175, 176, 178, 180, 202
Procession Fresco 86
Proclus 112, 167–8, 169
Profitis Elias (Thera) 12, 13, 56
Protagoras 152
Pseira 97
pumice 19, 27, 40, 114, 116, 124, 125

radiocarbon dates, calibration of 192
Rauschning, Hermann 1
refraction, wave 122
Rekhmire, Tomb of 70
religious ritual 33, 63, 77, 83, 90–1, 99–113
Renfrew, Colin 17, 131
Republic 1, 2, 8, 152, 163
Riva, Cape 11, 12, 36
Rhodes 6, 9, 14, 68, 69, 74, 130, 131, 164
Rhytiassos 129
rhyton 70, 85, 103
robing ceremony 85

sacral horns 102, 104, 139
saffron 67
Saffron Gatherers Fresco 74
saga 81
Sais (Egypt) 2, 148, 151, 165, 167, 168, 170, 175, 176, 178, 181, 202
Salamis (Greece) 158, 166, 171, 175, 177
Salamis 171
Samothrace 136
Santorini 8–13 *see* Thera
Scheria 129, 157
Schliemann, Heinrich 23, 27, 74, 141, 184
sea level change 187, 190
Sea Peoples 6
Serifos 71
sheep 66
shield 79, 93, 157
Ship Fresco 67, 75–9
ships 56, 57, 67, 75–9, 96, 157, 158, 160, 175, 194
shipshed 57, 93, 94, 197
shipwreck 78, 194
Sicily 1, 5, 151, 154–60, 158, 177, 178, 180
Sifnos 71
Sikinos 129
Silanion 149
silver 60, 68, 75
Sion, Priory of 189
Socrates 148, 153, 181
Solon 1, 2, 6, 8, 28, 30, 126, 128, 130, 137, 138, 147, 153, 164, 165, 166, 167, 168, 169 , 170, 171, 175, 176, 177, 180, 181, 202
Sonchis 178
Sophocles 28
Spain 4
Sparta 59, 101, 151, 154, 160–3, 177, 178, 179, 181
Spring Fresco 17, 56, 58, 59, 82, 89
Spring Nautical Festival 77, 81, 95, 99
staircase 54, 56, 115, 119, 131, 138
statues 80, 142, 144
Steiner, Rudolf 189
Stillman, W. J. 23
Stonehenge 120, 189
stone-working 59–60
Strabo 5, 26, 164
Strongyle 14
subsidence 6, 7, 8, 36, 135, 175
submergence 46, 175
Suez Canal 15

swallow 86, 89, 101
sympathetic magic 108
Symposium 1, 152
Syracuse 148, 151, 154, 155, 156, 157, 159, 177, 178, 179, 181
Syria 70, 73, 74
Syrtis, Gulf of 182

Tainaron, Cape 138, 174
Tambora 121, 125, 199
Tel Aviv 122
temple, Cycladic 33, 37, 99–113
temple, Minoan 5, 7, 15, 22, 24, 25, 26, 52, 73, 98,101, 125, 140-4, 174
temple, Syracusan 156, 179
Temple Tomb (Crete) 144
textiles 60–4, 66
Theaetetus 148
Theia 10
Themistocles 158
Theogony 164
Thera 6, 8–13, 14, 15, 19, 26, 35, 66–79, 82–9, 154, 191; bronze age destruction 14, 23, 127, 132; parallels with Plato's Atlantis 173, 175
Therasia (goddess) 111–12, 144, 173
Therasia (island) 8, 9, 11, 12, 15, 36, 56, 128, 132, 191
Therassos 28, 42, 82, 111, 173
Thorikos 69
Thucydides 28
Tigani 136
Timaeus 1–4, 5, 19, 28, 126, 128, 130, 134, 135, 137, 147, 154, 163, 164, 170, 177, 178, 190, 201
timber 53
Tiryns (Peloponnese) 69, 141
town 71, 93, 95, 96, 97
trade 67–75
tree-ring dating 191–2
Triandha (Rhodes) 51, 69, 74, 97, 128, 132, 136
Tribute-Children 25
trident 139, 140
tsunamis 10, 27, 32, 122, 123, 124, 125, 129, 130, 135
Tiryns 29
Troy 69, 184
Tuthmosis (Thutmose) III 81
Tuthmosis IV 70
Tycha 158, 179
Typhon 164

Ugarit 69, 97

Velikovsky, Immanuel 187
Vermeule, Emily 40
Verne, Jules 182
Vesuvius 192
volcanic activity 8, 10–13, 17, 21, 22, 27,
    32, 35, 45, 55, 89, 114–26, 150, 173,
    187, 191–2, 199
wall, town 156, 173
Walls, Long 160, 179
war 3, 4

Warlow, Peter 187
Warren, Peter 70, 84, 192
wind 66, 124, 133, 199
women, status of 25, 108–9, 174
Woodchester Mosaic 189
wool 60, 66
writing 80–2

Zahn, Robert 16, 25, 37, 46
Zakro (Crete) 7, 20, 27, 35, 69, 73, 97,
    127
Zeus 4, 98, 129, 130, 162, 164, 171